D0288569

TCE 33

THE ANCIENT NEAR EAST

THE ANCIENT NEAR EAST

Edited by
WILLIAM H. MC NEILL
and
JEAN W. SEDLAR

NEW YORK
OXFORD UNIVERSITY PRESS
LONDON   1968   TORONTO

Copyright © 1968 by Oxford University Press, Inc.
Library of Congress Catalogue Card Number: 68-8409

This reprint, 1974

Printed in the United States of America

Preface

The readings gathered in this volume all date from before 500 B.C., when the civilization of the Near East was still clearly the most advanced in the world. For more than a millennium, the achievements of peace had alternated with perennial wars and invasions, as the wealth of cities and farmlands continually tempted military conquerors. From the confusion of the age, three long-term trends stand out: (1) the elaboration of imperial government, (2) the standardization of law throughout large areas, and (3) the rise of ethical monotheism.

All three of these developments made it easier for men of varied antecedents and differing customs to live together within a cosmopolitan social framework. This was a great and lasting achievement. Early Mesopotamian and Egyptian civilization had presupposed an almost complete uniformity of viewpoint among the members of the civilized community. But by 500 B.C. people of widely divergent traditions and customs had been folded into the larger framework of empire. They were over-awed by professional standing armies and bureaucracies, linked by published laws, and supported to some degree by mono-theistic religion. The heirs of this Near Eastern civilization never entirely forgot the value of these institutions as ways of channeling human interaction into more peaceful and pre-dictable forms of behavior than could otherwise be possible. Here, we believe, is the central significance of the Near East to human history.

Section I illustrates the succession of empires in the ancient Near East and some facets of their political evolution. The first documents reflect the casual inter-regionalism of the Bronze Age, when Egyptian and Hittite kings fought and negotiated familiarly with one another, while conducting their

diplomatic intercourse in the Babylonian tongue. Unfortu-
nately, no surviving documents cast much light on the disrup-
tions of civilized society caused by the invasions of crudely
organized war bands in the Iron Age. But we can observe
the rise of royal, bureaucratic government among one of these
invading peoples—the Hebrews—by offering excerpts from the
Biblical record of Saul's elevation to kingship, David's victorious reign, and Solomon's imperial splendor. The concluding
documents in this section offer a brief insight into the character of the Assyrian and Persian empires. Here the unre-
strained nature of Assyrian militarism comes out more clearly
than the religious inhibitions which surrounded Assyrian kingship, while the Behistun inscription shows how carefully Darius
I of Persia emphasized the religious sanctions for his power.

Reflection upon the respective roles of officials, armies, com-
munications, religion, law, and commerce in the age of the
later Egyptian and Hittite empires, say about 1275 B.C., or the
Assyrian and Persian empires between 700 and 500 B.C., offers
ample scope for contrast with their counterparts in the age of
Gilgamesh (third millennium B.C.), Sargon of Akkad (ca. 2300
B.C.), or the Egyptian Old Kingdom (ca. 2600-2200 B.C.). Such
a review highlights the gradual but cumulative improvements
that occurred in techniques of administration amid the rise and
fall of states. It also raises the question of the reality of progress in history as against the theory that all civilized societies
must pass through an inevitable cycle of ascent and decline.
Such broad formulations of the historical process should be
tested from time to time against the actual materials of world
history.

In Section II, selections from ancient law codes have been
arranged under a number of more or less arbitrary rubrics.
This makes comparison easy—indeed inescapable. Specific par-
allels, though sometimes astonishingly close, are less important
than the general principles deducible from the texts. For instance, a major thrust of each legal system was to reduce
random violence to a minimum. The devices designed for this
purpose often resemble one another, e.g. the substitution of
money-payment for blood feud and private retaliation. The

laws also testify to the position of social classes, foreigners, women, children, and slaves, and to their authors' notions of property rights and governmental power as against human rights. Clearly, the laws reflect the social and economic conditions of the societies to which they applied; and ultimately they rest upon certain more abstract notions of justice.

Section III reproduces documents from three religions unique in their concept of a single god: Atonism in Egypt, the worship of Yahweh in Palestine, and Zoroastrianism in Persia. Atonism arose in an age when the Egyptian empire extended widely into Asia, and the conquerors had ample opportunity to discover that their own religious presuppositions had little hold outside of the Nile Valley. They could not help knowing that each foreign people had its own gods and religious practices which, being mutually contradictory, could not possibly all be true. In the Aton—the sun-disk—Egyptians could discern a divine force that was truly universal. The reasons both for the high emotional fervor aroused by the Aton-revolution and its no less emphatic repudiation are worth exploring—whether religious ideas themselves were the central issue or merely the vehicle for some political clash of priest versus soldier or Pharaoh versus nobles.

The Biblical texts* have been chosen to illustrate the development of Hebrew ideas about God from the time of the Exodus to that of the great eighth-century prophet Isaiah. The notion that religious ideas are subject to evolution may conflict with more orthodox views of the consistency and infallibility of Scripture; but the ultimate solution to the question can lie only in the documents themselves. Biblical materials, like any others, must be studied in the light of their historical and political context. In this regard one may investigate the interaction between prophecy and specific historical circumstances and the relevance of prophecy at a later date when the context in which it arose, say the Assyrian attack on Jerusalem or the Persian liberation of the Jews, had long since passed away.

---

* Though many translations of the Bible exist, our selections are taken from the King James version because of its unique status as a classic of the English language.

The fundamental prophetic idea was that God requires his people to act justly. Therefore man must try to discover exactly what God wishes in every particular circumstance—that is, to develop an elaborate religious law. The essential character both of Judaism and later of Islam rests upon this logical consequence of prophecy. Whenever legal routine confronts fresh manifestations of prophetic inspiration, or political expediency confronts religious scruple, tensions necessarily arise. The divergencies between laws growing out of prophetic tradition and those decreed by political rulers are well worth examining.

The selections from Zoroaster's prophecies are often unclear in meaning: the history and influence of Zoroastrianism in the Near East is a matter of guesswork. The dates and the meaning of his message are surrounded with obscurities. Still, the Gathas can fruitfully be compared with the ideas of the Hebrew prophets, e.g., the consistency of their monotheism, their conceptions of the end of the world, their ethical imperatives, the use of divine inspiration as a source of religious truth and its relation to tradition and priestcraft.

Finally, one may ask the general question how the political, legal, and religious developments of the ancient Near East fitted together—whether a kind of universal culture emerged, whether this culture restricted men's awareness of the world, and whether alternatives to the Near Eastern polarity between throne and altar were conceivable in that age and place. By 500 B.C., the end of the period considered here, distinct styles of civilization had already arisen in Greece, India, and China—styles utilizing aspects of the human potentiality which were but slightly developed in the ancient Near East.

Chicago, Illinois   W. H. M.
August 1968

The editors wish to extend special thanks to Professor J. A. Brinkman of the Oriental Institute of the University of Chicago for his aid in identifying various Assyrian terms.

Our chronology for Assyria follows J. A. Brinkman, "Mesopotamian Chronology of the Historical Period," in A. Leo Oppenheim's *Ancient Mesopotamia*. For Egyptian dates we are indebted to Professor Klaus Baer of the Oriental Institute. Hittite chronology has been correlated with the Egyptian.

As a general rule, the texts in this volume have been reprinted just as they appear in our sources. The present editors have made no attempt either to standardize spelling as between English and American usage or to adopt a consistent system of transliterating foreign terms into English. Diacritical marks which indicate linguistic distinctions in the original languages have been almost entirely omitted, except for the letter "š," used by some translators for the sound "sh."

The editors have supplied numerous footnotes to render the texts more easily comprehensible to the non-specialist. In many cases, notes or other explanatory material provided by the translator have been adapted for this purpose. Other notes have been included to identify terms or explain unfamiliar allusions, provide supplementary background information, call attention to particular items, or compare the passage at hand with some other passage or source. Technical discussions and scholarly references have been almost completely omitted.

Although the significance of brackets, ellipses, and other punctuation marks varies somewhat with different translators, where both types of marks appear the usual system is as follows: Square brackets indicate restorations made by the translator where the original inscription or manuscript was fragmentary or otherwise undecipherable; parentheses (round brackets) indicate interpolations made to better explain the meaning of the text. Doubtful translations and foreign words sometimes appear in italics or followed by a question mark in parentheses. Three dots mark a place in the text which cannot be restored; a full line of ellipses indicates material omitted by the present editors. For the Biblical selections, a few words have been inserted in brackets to place the passage in context.

Black Sea

CAUCASUS MTS.

Caspian

PHRYGIA

Halys R.

HATTI
•Boghazkoy
(Hattusas)

ARMENIA

LYDIA
•Sardis

CAPPADOCIA

TAURUS MTS.

KIZZUWATNA

AMANUS MTS.

MITANNI

L. Van

L. Urmia

Araxes R.

•Harran
Carchemish•
NAHARIN

ASSYRIA
Nineveh•
•Nimrud (Calah)

Upper Zab R.

MED

Ugarit•

Assur•

Lower Zab R.

Ecbatana•

CYPRUS

Orontes
R.

SYRIA
•Kadesh

•Mari

Euphrates R.

Tigris R.

ZAGROS MTS.

•Behistun

Mediterranean Sea

Sidon•
Tyre•

LEBANON

•Damascus

SYRIAN

AKKAD
Babylon•

ELAM
•Susa

MT. CARMEL

←Jordan R.

DESERT

BABYLONIA
•Nippur

SUSIANA

PALESTINE
Gaza•
Beersheba•

•Jerusalem

Dead Sea

SUMER
Uruk•   •Larsa
Ur•

Memphis• •Heliopolis

Gulf of Suez

Present-day coastline

EGYPT
•Beni-Hasan

Tel-el-Amarna•
(Akhetaton)

Nile R.

•Thebes

ARABIAN

Red

ARABIA

•Elephantine

Sea

DESERT

THE ANCIENT NEAR EAST

0   250   500 Miles

Contents

II LAW

III MONOTHEISM

Map

THE ANCIENT NEAR EAST

I

Empire

THE EGYPTIANS

Empire

THE EGYPTIANS

Introduction to The Inscription of Amenemhet

The Amenemhet of this inscription was a nomarch (provincial ruler) of the Benihasan family, so-called from the place of that name, about 170 miles south of Cairo, where a group of their tombs stand. The rulers of this family flourished during the early years of the Middle Kingdom,* when the powerful Pharaohs of the Twelfth Dynasty were gradually bringing order out of chaos and putting an end to the feudal de-centralization and discord which had prevailed during the preceding several centuries in Egypt. The tombs at Benihasan provide valuable information regarding the relations between the nomarchs and the royal house at this period. The Benihasan princes were clearly supporters of the central power: through at least four generations they were confirmed by successive Pharaohs in their dominion over the Oryx nome. The first king of the Twelfth Dynasty, Amenemhet I (reigned *ca.* 1991-1962 B.C.) had personally visited this region "to cast out evil," i.e., to defeat rebellion against his authority, and appointed the first of the Benihasan princes to rule there. The latter's son, Amenemhet, though calling himself "hereditary prince," was confirmed in the same dominion by the Pharaoh Sesostris I.

---

* Egyptian history is generally periodized into Old Kingdom, Middle Kingdom, and New Kingdom. The dating of these epochs depends upon one's definition of the intermediate periods. One possible scheme is as follows: Old Kingdom, 2640-2170 B.C.; Middle Kingdom, 2050-1650 B.C.; New Kingdom, 1552-1080 B.C., followed by a period of decline until the conquest of Egypt by Alexander the Great in 332 B.C. brought an end to native rule there.

THE INSCRIPTION OF AMENEMHET (AMENI)

Year 43 under the majesty of Sesostris I,[1] living forever and ever; corresponding to year 25 in the Oryx nome with the hereditary prince, count,————Amen[emhet],[2] triumphant. Year 43, second month of the first season, fifteenth day. O ye who love life and hate death, say ye, one thousand loaves and beer, one thousand oxen and geese for the ka[3] of the hereditary prince, count,————, great lord of the Oryx nome,————, attached to Nekhen, lord of Nekhbet,[4] chief of prophets, Ameni, triumphant.

First Expedition

I followed my lord when he sailed southward to overthrow his enemies among the four barbarians. I sailed southward, as the son of a count, wearer of the royal seal, and commander in chief of the troops of the Oryx nome, as a man represents his old father,[5] according to [his] favor in the palace and his love in the court. I passed Kush,[6] sailing southward, I advanced the boundary of the land, I brought all gifts; my praise, it reached heaven. Then his majesty returned in safety, having overthrown his enemies in Kush the vile. I returned, following him, with ready face.[7] There was no loss among my soldiers.

From *Ancient Records of Egypt*, Vol. I, J. H. Breasted, ed., Chicago: University of Chicago Press, 1906, pp. 250-53.

1. Reigned *ca.* 1971-1928 B.C. (jointly with his father for nine years). Also spelled Sen-Usert or Senwosret.

2. Amenemhet ("Amon is in front") is the prince's full name. Another form of the name, Ameni ("Belonging to Amon") is frequently used in the inscriptions.

3. The vital force in a person; the personality.

4. An ancient goddess of Upper Egypt.

5. This shows that Ameni must have succeeded his father as ruler of the Oryx nome.

6. Nubia (now southern Egypt and northern Sudan).

7. Egyptian idiom meaning "prepared for service." Orders were always given "in the face of" an officer.

Second Expedition

I sailed southward, to bring gold ore for the majesty of the King of Upper and Lower Egypt, Kheperkere (Sesostris I), living forever and ever. I sailed southward together with the hereditary prince, count, oldest son of the king, of his body, Ameni.[8] I sailed southward, with a number, four hundred of all the choicest of my troops, who returned in safety, having suffered no loss. I brought the gold exacted of me; I was praised for it in the palace; the king's son praised god for me.

Third Expedition

Then I sailed southward to bring ore to the city of Coptos, together with the hereditary prince, count, governor of the city and vizier, Sesostris. I sailed southward with a number, six hundred of all the bravest of the Oryx nome. I returned in safety, my soldiers uninjured; having done all that had been told me.

Ameni's Able Administration

I was amiable, and greatly loved, a ruler beloved of his city. Now, I passed years as ruler in the Oryx nome. All the imposts of the king's house passed through my hand. The gang-overseers of the crown possessions of the shepherds of the Oryx nome gave to me three thousand bulls in their yokes.[9] I was praised on account of it in the palace each year of the loan-herds. I carried all their dues[10] to the king's house; there were no arrears against me in any office of his. The entire Oryx nome labored for me[11] in [widely extended activity].

8. This second Ameni is the crown prince, afterward King Amenemhet II.
9. This means that Amenemhet received cattle from the royal herds, to be maintained by him on shares. He maintained them so well that he was praised for it each year when his payments fell due.
10. For the herds which he had received.
11. To labor for a king or nobleman is to pay him an impost from the products of one's labor.

Ameni's Impartiality and Benevolence

There was no citizen's daughter whom I misused, there was no widow whom I oppressed, there was no peasant whom I repulsed, there was no shepherd whom I repelled, there was no overseer of serf-laborers whose people I took for (unpaid) imposts, there was none wretched in my community, there was none hungry in my time. When years of famine came I plowed all the fields of the Oryx nome, as far as its southern and northern boundary, preserving its people alive and furnishing its food so that there was none hungry therein. I gave to the widow as (to) her who had a husband; I did not exalt the great above the small in all that I gave. Then came great Niles,[12] possessors of grain and all things,[13] (but) I did not collect the arrears of the field.[14]

12. Inundations.
13. Meaning that the inundations brought these things.
14. Meaning that he did not collect the balance due after the short payments of taxes during the unfruitful years.

Introduction to The Battle of Megiddo

The battle of Megiddo, fought between the Egyptians under King Thutmose III (reigned 1490-1436 B.C.) and a confederacy led by the ruler of Kadesh in Lebanon, is the first military campaign in history of which a detailed record has survived. In the period of the New Kingdom in Egypt it was customary for a scribe to keep a regular campaign diary, copies of which were deposited in the archives of the temple of Amun-Re at Thebes. Thutmose III also caused records of his exploits to be carved upon the stone of the temple walls. The battle of Megiddo, his first victory, is described in more detail than usual.

The following text begins with the army in Yehem, some two hundred miles from the Egyptian frontier. The troops had covered this distance in about seventeen days, showing an average rate of march of about twelve miles a day—a fair speed for infantry on desert roads.

THE BATTLE OF MEGIDDO

Year 23,[1] first month of summer, sixteenth day, at the town of Yehem.[2] [His Majesty] ordered a consultation with his victorious army, saying thus: "Yon [wretched] foe of Kadesh has come and entered into Megiddo, and he is [there] at this moment, for he has gathered to himself the chieftains of [all] the countries [which were] subject to Egypt and (from) as far away as Naharin. . . . Syrians, Kode-folk,[3] their horses, their soldiers, [and their people], for he says—so it is reported— 'I will stand to [fight with His Majesty here] in Megiddo.' Tell ye me [what is in your hearts]."

And they said unto His Majesty: "How can one go [upon] this road which is so narrow? It [is reported] that the enemy are standing yonder [outside, and that they have] become numerous; will not horse have to go behind [horse, and the soldiers] and the people likewise? Shall our vanguard be fighting while the [rearguard] is standing yonder in Aruna unable to fight? Now here are two roads; behold, one road is . . . our [lord], and he will come out at Taanach; and behold, the other is at the north side of Djefti, and we will come out at the north of Megiddo. Let our victorious lord proceed upon whichever of [them] seems best to him; but do not let us go upon yon difficult road."

Then [there were brought in (?)] dispatches [concerning yon wretched foe, and there was further discussion (?)] on the subject of [that] plan of which they had previously spoken. What was said in the royal tent: "[As] I [live], as Re loves me, as my

From "The Battle of Megiddo," R. O. Faulkner, *Journal of Egyptian Archaeology*, XXVIII (1942), 3-4. Reprinted by permission.
  1. Twenty-third regnal year of King Thutmose III, 1468 B.C.
  2. Probably modern Yemma (Palestine).
  3. Naharin: a country on the Upper Euphrates. Kode-folk: inhabitants of the coastal region of southern Asia Minor and northern Syria.

father Amun[4] favours me, as my nostrils are refreshed with life and strength, I will proceed on this Aruna road. Let him of you who so desires go on these roads of which ye speak, and let him of you who so desires come in the train of My Majesty, for behold, they will say, namely the foes whom Re detests, 'Has His Majesty gone upon another road because he is afraid of us?' they will say." And they said unto His Majesty: "May thy father Amun, Lord of the Thrones of the Two Lands, who dwells in Karnak,[5] perform [thy desire]! Lo, we are in the train of Thy Majesty wheresoever [Thy Majesty] goest, for a servant ever follows [his] master."

[And His Majesty caused a proclamation to be made] to the whole army: "[Your victorious lord will lead your marches upon (?)] yon road which is so narrow." [And behold, His Majesty sware] an oath, saying: "I will not [permit my victorious army(?)] to go forth in front of My Majesty [in this place," for His Majesty desired (?)] to go forth in person in front of his army. And [every man] was instructed as to his order of march, horse following after horse, while [His Majesty] was at the head of his army.

Year 23, first month of summer, nineteenth day, One awoke in the royal tent at the town of Aruna. My Majesty proceeded northward under my father Amun-Re, Lord of the Thrones of the Two Lands, [that he might open the ways] before me, Harakhti[6] . . . , my father Amun strengthening [My Majesty's] arm, and . . . over My Majesty.

(His) Majesty went forth [at the head of] his [army], which was org[anized] into many battalions . . . one; [their] southern wing was at Tannach, [while their] northern wing was at the south[ern] bend [of the valley of Kina (?). And] His Majesty called out upon [this road (?)] . . . they fell, while yon

4. Amun, or Amun-Re, was the state god of the New Kingdom. Originally he was the local god of Thebes, but was later identified with the sun-god, Re, to become Amun-Re. When Thebes became the capital of Egypt during the Eighteenth Dynasty, Amun-Re became the most important of all the gods.

5. The main section of Thebes, where the great temple of Amun was located.

6. The name of the sun-god in Heliopolis, the sacred city of that god, near modern Cairo.

[wretched] foe. . . . [Praise (?)] ye [him and extol the might of (?)] His Majesty, because his arm is stronger than (that of) [any king]. . . . His Majesty's army in Aruna. Now while the rear-guard of His Majesty's victorious army was (yet) in the town of Aruna, the vanguard had come out at the valley of Kina, and they filled the mouth of this valley.

Then said they unto His Majesty: "Behold, His Majesty has come forth with his victorious army and they have filled the valley; let our victorious lord hearken unto us this once, and let our lord guard for us the rear of his army and his people. When the rear of the army comes out to us, then will we fight against these foreigners, then shall we not have to worry about the rear of our army." And His Majesty took post outside . . . guarding the rear of his victorious army. Now when the [leading] detachments had finished coming forth upon this road, the shadow turned.

His Majesty arrived at the south of Megiddo on the bank of the brook Kina in seven hours from the turning in the sun. Camp was pitched there for His Majesty, and an order was given to the whole army, sa[ying]: "Prepare ye, make ready your weapons, for One will engage with yon wretched foe in the morning, because One is . . ." One went to rest in the royal camp. The officers were provided for, rations were released (?) to the retainers, and the sentries of the army were posted, having been told: "Be steadfast and vigilant."

One woke in the royal tent, and they came to tell His Majesty: "The coast is clear, and the southern and northern troops (are safe) also."

Year 23, first month of summer, twenty-first day, the exact day of the festival of the New Moon, the King appeared in the morning. The entire army was ordered to deploy (?) . . . and His Majesty set forth in a chariot of fine gold, being adorned with his panoply of war like Horus the Strong-armed,[7] Lord of Action, and like Mont[8] of Thebes, his father Amun strengthening his hands. The southern wing of His Majesty's army was at a

7. The ancient sky- and sun-god, the prototype of the kings.
8. The hawk-headed war-god.

hill south of . . . Kina, and the northern wing was on the northwest of Megiddo. And His Majesty was in the midst of them,
Amun guarding his person (in) the melee and the strength [of
Seth[9] pervading] his members. And His Majesty prevailed indeed at the head of his army. And they saw His Majesty prevail-
ing, and they fled headlong [towards] Megiddo with frightened
faces. They abandoned their horses and their chariots of gold and
silver, that they might be dragged up into this city by their garments, for the people had shut up this city against them, [but
lowered] garments to hoist them up into this city. Would that
His Majesty's soldiers had not devoted themselves to looting the
goods of the foe! They would have [captured] Megiddo then and
there while the wretched foe of Kadesh and the wretched foe of
this city were being dragged up scrambling (?) to get them into
their city, for fear of His Majesty entered [into their bodies] and
their arms were weakened, his uraeus[10] having overpowered
them. And their horses and their chariots of gold and silver were
captured as easy [prey], their ranks lay prostrate like fish in the
bight of a net, and His Majesty's victorious army counted up
their goods, for there was captured the tent of [yon] wretched
[foe], which was wrou[ght with silver]. . . . And the whole
army fell to rejoicing and giving praise to Amun [because of the
victory] which he had vouchsafed to his son [this day. And they
gave praise] to His Majesty, extolling his victory, and they
brought the booty which they had taken, even hands, prisoners,
horses, chariots of gold and silver, and [fine linen].

9. War-god and storm-god.
10. The royal serpent which the king and the sun-god wore as a diadem.

Introduction to The Hymn of Victory

King Thutmose III (reigned *ca.* 1490-1436 B.C.) is generally regarded
as the greatest military leader produced by ancient Egypt. In seventeen seasons of campaigning, he extended his frontiers northward to

Asia Minor and eastward as far as the Euphrates. The annals of his wars, carved on the walls of the great temple of Amon at Karnak, form the longest surviving record of the achievements of any Egyptian king.

The following hymn, though rhetorical in style and extravagant in its praise of the Pharaoh, constitutes a valuable supplement to the annals. It proved so popular that several later Egyptian kings borrowed substantial portions of it in praising their own respective conquests.

THE HYMN OF VICTORY

Utterance of Amon-Re, lord of Thebes:
Thou comest to me,[1] thou exultest, seeing my beauty,
O my son, my avenger, Menkheperre,[2] living forever.
I shine for love of thee,
My heart is glad at thy beautiful comings into my temple;   5
(My) two hands furnish thy limbs with protection and life.
How pleasing is thy pleasantness toward my body.[3]
I have established thee in my dwelling,[4]
I have worked a marvel for thee;
I have given to thee might and victory against all countries,   10
I have set thy fame, (even) the fear of thee, in all lands.
Thy terror as far as the four pillars of heaven;[5]
I have magnified the dread of thee in all bodies,
I have put the roaring of thy majesty among the Nine Bows.[6]
The chiefs of all countries are gathered in thy grasp,   15
I myself have stretched out my two hands,

From *Ancient Records of Egypt*, Vol. II, J. H. Breasted, ed., Chicago: University of Chicago Press, 1906, pp. 263-6.
  1. The king comes victorious to Thebes, and the image of the god carried in procession comes out to meet him.
  2. Thutmose III's official name.
  3. Referring to the king's adornment of the divine image as prescribed by the ritual.
  4. I.e., the god has in return established an image of the king in his temple.
  5. The pillars which were believed to hold up the sky.
  6. Ancient expression for the neighboring peoples, who according to tradition were nine in number. Note that the gods of Egypt were likewise grouped into nines: the Great Ennead and the Lesser Ennead.

I have bound them for thee.[7]
I have bound together the Nubian Troglodytes[8] by tens of
    thousands and thousands,
The Northerners by hundreds of thousands as captives.
I have felled thine enemies beneath thy sandals,   20
Thou hast smitten the hordes of rebels according as I commanded
    thee.
The earth in its length and breadth, Westerners and Easterners
    are subject to thee,
Thou tramplest all countries, thy heart glad;
None presents himself before thy majesty,[9]
While I am thy leader, so that thou mayest reach them.   25
Thou hast crossed the water of the Great Bend of Naharin[10] with
    victory, with might.

I have decreed for thee that they hear thy roarings and enter into
    caves;
I have deprived their nostrils of the breath of life.
I have set the terrors of thy majesty in their hearts,
My serpent-diadem upon thy brow, it consumes them,   30
It makes captive by the hair the Kode-folk,[11]
It devours those who are in their marshes with its flame.
Cut down are the heads of the Asiatics, there is not a remnant of
    them;
Fallen are the children of their mighty ones.
I have caused thy victories to circulate among all lands,   35
My serpent-diadem gives light to thy dominion.
There is no rebel of thine as far as the circuit of heaven;
They come, bearing tribute upon their backs,
Bowing down to thy majesty according to my command.
I have made powerless the invaders who came before thee;   40
Their hearts burned, their limbs trembling.

7. Metaphors from fowling.
8. A predatory tribe.
9. I.e., no one dares to attack the king.
10. The Upper Euphrates.
11. A people occupying the coast of southern Asia Minor and northern Syria.

I have come, causing thee to smite the princes of Zahi;[12]
I have hurled them beneath thy feet among their highlands.
I have caused them to see thy majesty as lord of radiance,[13]
So that thou hast shone in their faces like my image.   45
I have come, causing thee to smite the Asiatics,
Thou hast made captive the heads of the Asiatics of Retenu.[14]
I have caused them to see thy majesty equipped with thy
    adornment,
When thou takest the weapons of war in the chariot.
I have come, causing thee to smite the eastern land,   50
Thou hast trampled those who are in the districts of God's-Land.[15]
I have caused them to see thy majesty like a circling star,
When it scatters its flame in fire, and gives forth its dew.

I have come, causing thee to smite the western land,
Keftyew[16] and Cyprus are in terror.   55
I have caused them to see thy majesty as a young bull,
Firm of heart, ready-horned, irresistible.
I have come, causing thee to smite those who are in their
    marshes,
The lands of Mitanni tremble under fear of thee.
I have caused them to see thy majesty as a crocodile,   60
Lord of fear in the water, unapproachable.

I have come, causing thee to smite those who are in the Isles;
Those who are in the midst of the Great Green (Sea) hear thy
    roarings.
I have caused them to see thy majesty as an avenger
Who rises upon the back of his slain victim.[17]   65
I have come, causing thee to smite the Tehenu (Libyans),

---

12. Syria-Palestine.
13. I.e., the sun.
14. Palestine.
15. The region of Arabia—the land of sunrise.
16. (Keftiu): Crete.
17. Reference to the legendary battle between the gods Horus and Seth.
Horus, the victor, sits as a hawk upon defeated Seth.

The isles of the Utentyew[18] are (subject) to the might of thy
    prowess.
I have caused them to see thy majesty as a fierce-eyed lion,
Thou makest them corpses in their valleys.

I have come, causing thee to smite the uttermost ends of the
    lands,   70
The circuit of the Great Circle (Okeanos)[19] is inclosed in thy
    grasp.
I have caused them to see thy majesty as a lord of the wing,[20]
Who seizeth upon that which he seeth, as much as he desires.
I have come, causing thee to smite those who are in front of
    their land.
Thou hast smitten the Sand-dwellers as living captives.   75
I have caused them to see thy majesty as a southern jackal,
Lord of running, stealthy-going, who roves the Two Lands.
I have come, causing thee to smite the Nubian Troglodytes,
As far as (Nubia) (they) are in thy grasp.
I have caused them to see thy majesty as thy two brothers,[21] 80
I have united their two arms for thee in v[ictory].[22]

Thy two sisters,[23] I have set them as protection behind thee,
The arms of my majesty are above, warding off evil.
I have caused thee to reign, my beloved son,
Horus, Mighty Bull, Shining in Thebes, whom I have begotten,
    in [uprightness of heart].
Thutmose, living forever, who hast done for me all that my *ka*
    desired;
Thou hast erected my dwelling as an everlasting work,
Enlarging and extending (it) more than the past which had
    been.
The great doorway————.

18. Unknown.
19. Reference to the ocean supposed to surround the outer edge of the lands
of the earth.
20. I.e., as a hawk.
21. I.e., as the gods Horus and Seth.
22. Meaning: together they give thee the victory.
23. I.e., the goddesses Isis and Nephthys.

Thou hast fêted the beauty of Amon-Re,   90
Thy monuments are greater than (those of) any king who has
    been.
When I commanded thee to do it, I was satisfied therewith;
I established thee upon the Horus-throne of millions of years;
Thou shalt continue life————.

Introduction to the Official Record of the Battle of Kadesh

The battle of Kadesh (ca. 1286 B.C.) was an incident in the contest
between the Egyptians and the Hittites for control of Syria and
Palestine. Since the time of Thutmose III (reigned ca. 1490-1436
B.C.), these territories had been Egyptian provinces. But the preoccu-
pation of the Pharaoh Amenhotep IV (Akhnaton: reigned ca. 1362-
1345 B.C.) with his religious reforms* led to neglect of the empire,
enabling the Hittites gradually to advance southward from their
base in Asia Minor. Ramses II (reigned ca. 1290-1224 B.C.) took it
upon himself to restore Egypt's old position in Syria. The Hittites
were a powerful adversary; and the struggle between the two empires lasted for twenty years.

The battle of Kadesh occurred during the initial period of this conflict. Ramses, having pushed forward his frontier in Phoenicia,
marched down the Orontes and encountered the Hittite king, Muwatallis, at Kadesh. Caught by surprise, Ramses barely managed to
avoid the destruction of his forces.

Though celebrated in Egypt as a great victory, the battle of Kadesh brought Ramses little more than a reputation for personal courage and adeptness at having extricated himself from a perilous situation with a mere fraction of his army. The political results of the
battle were nil. He did not take Kadesh; and northern Syria remained in Hittite hands, while Ramses returned to Egypt.

Years later, Ramses again confronted the Hittites (now led by
King Hattusilis) in northern Syria. This time his progress was such

* See "Hymn to the Aton," p. 214.

that the Hittites agreed to renounce all further attempts at conquest in Syria and negotiate a permanent peace settlement.*

OFFICIAL RECORD OF THE BATTLE OF KADESH

Date

Year 5, third month of the third season, ninth day[1]; under the majesty of Horus: Mighty Bull, Beloved of Truth; King of Upper and Lower Egypt: Usermare-Setepnere[2]; Son of Re; Ramses-Meriamon, given life forever.

Camp South of Kadesh

Lo, his majesty was in Zahi[3] on his second victorious campaign. The goodly watch in life, prosperity and health, in the tent of his majesty, was on the highland south of Kadesh.

False Message of the Shasu near Shabtuna

When his majesty appeared like the rising of Re, he assumed the adornments of his father, Montu.[4] When the king proceeded northward, and his majesty had arrived at the locality south of the town of Shabtuna,[5] there came two Shasu,[6] to speak to his majesty as follows: "Our brethren, who belong to the greatest of the families with the vanquished chief of Kheta,[7] have made us come to his majesty, to say: 'We will be subjects of Pharaoh, L.P.H.,[8] and we will flee from the vanquished chief of Kheta; for the vanquished chief of Kheta sits in the land of

---

* See "Treaty between Hattušili and Ramesses II," p. 42.

From *Ancient Records of Egypt*, Vol. III, J. H. Breasted, ed., Chicago: University of Chicago Press, 1906, pp. 143-7.

1. This is about the end of May.
2. Official name of Ramses II.
3. Region comprising Palestine, part of Lebanon, and southern Syria.
4. (Month): the god of war.
5. Small town some 7½ miles south of Kadesh.
6. Bedouins.
7. Hatti (land of the Hittites).
8. Abbreviation for the conventional "Life! Prosperity! Health!"

Aleppo, on the north of Tunip. He fears because of Pharaoh, L.P.H., to come southward.' " Now, these Shasu spake these words, which they spake to his majesty, falsely, (for) the vanquished chief of Kheta made them come to spy where his majesty was, in order to cause the army of his majesty not to draw up to fight him,[9] to battle with the vanquished chief of Kheta.

Positions of the Two Armies

Lo, the vanquished chief of Kheta came with every chief of every country, their infantry and their chariotry, which he had brought with him by force, and stood, equipped, drawn up in line of battle behind Kadesh the Deceitful, while his majesty knew it not. Then his majesty proceeded northward and arrived on the northwest of Kadesh; and the army of his majesty [made camp] there.

Examination of Hittite Scouts

Then, as his majesty sat upon a throne of gold, there arrived a scout who was in the following of his majesty, and he brought two scouts of the vanquished chief of Kheta. They were conducted into the presence, and his majesty said to them: "What are ye?" They said: "As for us, the vanquished chief of the Kheta has caused that we should come to spy out where his majesty is." Said his majesty to them: "He! Where is he, the vanquished chief of Kheta? Behold, I have heard, saying: 'He is in the land of Aleppo.' " Said they: "See, the vanquished chief of Kheta is stationed, together with many countries, which he has brought with him by force, being every country which is in the districts of the land of Kheta,[10] the land of Naharin, and all Kode. They are equipped with infantry and chariotry, bearing their weapons; more numerous are they than the sand of the shore. See, they are standing, drawn up for battle, behind Kadesh the Deceitful.

9. I.e., to keep the Egyptians in marching order, so that he might find them unprepared for battle (as he actually did).
10. This indicates the composite nature of the Hittite kingdom.

The Council of War

Then his majesty had the princes called into the presence, and had them hear every word which the two scouts of the vanquished chief of Kheta, who were in the presence, had spoken. Said his majesty to them: "See ye the manner wherewith the chiefs of the peasantry and the officials under whom is the land of Pharaoh,[11] L.P.H., have stood, daily, saying to the Pharaoh: 'The vanquished chief of Kheta is in the land of Aleppo; he has fled before his majesty, since hearing that, behold, he came.' So spake they to his majesty daily. But see, I have held a hearing in this very hour, with the two scouts of the vanquished chief of Kheta, to the effect that the vanquished chief of Kheta is coming, together with the numerous countries [that are with] him, being people and horses, like the multitudes of the sand. They are stationed behind Kadesh the Deceitful. But the governors of the countries and the officials under whose authority is the land of Pharaoh, L.P.H., were not able to tell it to us."

Said the princes who were in the presence of his majesty: "It is a great fault, which the governors of the countries and the officials of Pharaoh, L.P.H., have committed in not informing that the vanquished chief of Kheta was near the king; and (in) that they told his report[12] to his majesty daily."

The Divisions in the South Are Ordered Up

Then the vizier was ordered to hasten the army of his majesty, while they were marching on the south of Shabtuna, in order to bring them to the place where his majesty was.[13]

The Attack of the Asiatics

Lo, while his majesty sat talking with the princes, the vanquished chief of Kheta came,[14] and the numerous countries,

11. I.e., the officers both of Egypt and of his Asiatic provinces.
12. I.e., the false report sent out by the two Shasu.
13. Ramses lay in camp north of Kadesh while the main body of his troops was on the march south of Kadesh in the vicinity of Shabtuna.
14. The messenger announcing the attack on the Egyptian division south of Shabtuna had up to this point not yet arrived. Ramses apparently received no report of the Hittite attack until it was upon him.

which were with him. They crossed over the channel on the south of Kadesh, and charged into the army of his majesty while they were marching, and not expecting it. Then the infantry and chariotry of his majesty retreated before them, northward to the place where his majesty was. Lo, the foes of[15] the vanquished chief of Kheta surrounded the bodyguard of his majesty, who were by his side.[16]

Ramses' Personal Attack

When his majesty saw them, he was enraged against them, like his father, Montu, lord of Thebes. He seized the adornments of battle, and arrayed himself in his coat of mail. He was like Baal[17] in his hour. Then he betook himself to his horses, and led quickly on, being alone by himself. He charged into the foes of the vanquished chief of Kheta, and the numerous countries which were with him. His majesty was like Sutekh,[18] the great in strength, smiting and slaying among them; his majesty hurled them headlong, one upon another into the water of the Orontes.[19]

Ramses' Own Statement

"I charged all countries, while I was alone, my infantry and my chariotry having forsaken me. Not one among them stood to turn about. I swear, as Re loves me, as my father, Atum, favors me, that, as for every matter which his majesty has stated, I did it in truth, in the presence of my infantry and my chariotry."

15. Of: belonging to.
16. The Hittites have isolated Ramses and a portion of his troops, enfolding them between two wings.
17. The god of the Phoenicians.
18. Another form of the name Seth (the war-god and storm-god).
19. Ramses evidently attacked the enemy's right wing before it was sufficiently strong to withstand him. In so doing he forsook his camp, which fell into the hands of the Hittites, diverting them until another body of Egyptian troops could arrive to rescue Ramses from his exposed position.

Introduction to *The Hymn on the Victory over the Libyans*

For a number of years preceding the events recorded in the following hymn, tribes from the Libyan desert had been gradually pushing into Egypt, occupying the western Delta region almost to the gates of Memphis. At the same period, a confederation of maritime peoples from southern Europe was moving southward across the Mediterranean and infiltrating into Africa. During the fifth year of the reign of the Pharaoh Merneptah (*ca.* 1220 B.C.), the Libyan king put himself at the head of these allies and invaded Egypt. Evidently he intended a permanent occupation; for he brought his wives and belongings with him. Merneptah met him in the western Delta. In six hours of slaughter he routed the Libyans and their allies and pushed them westward into the desert.

This "Hymn of Victory," a poetic encomium to Merneptah in a style favored by the Pharaohs of the Nineteenth Dynasty, is one of four extant inscriptions recording the events of the Libyan invasion. Found on a column in the ruins of Merneptah's mortuary temple at Thebes, the hymn has attracted particular attention as the earliest known mention of Israel in any ancient literature, including even the Old Testament. It is likewise the only reference whatsoever to Israel or the Israelites in ancient Egyptian literature.

THE HYMN ON THE VICTORY OVER THE LIBYANS

Date and Introduction

Year 5, third month of the third season (eleventh month), third day, under the majesty of Horus: Mighty Bull, Rejoicing in Truth; King of Upper and Lower Egypt: Binre-Meriamon,

From *Ancient Records of Egypt*, Vol. III, J. H. Breasted, ed., Chicago: University of Chicago Press, 1906, pp. 259-64.

Son of Re: Merneptah-Hotephirma, magnifying might, exalting the victorious sword of Horus, Mighty Bull, smiter of the Nine Bows,[1] whose name is given forever and ever.

The Great Deliverance

His victories are published in all lands, to cause that every land together may see, to cause the glory of his conquests to appear; King Merneptah, the Bull, lord of strength, who slays his foes, beautiful upon the field of victory, when his onset occurs; the Sun, driving away the storm which was over Egypt, allowing Egypt to see the rays of the sun, removing the mountain of copper from the neck of the people so that he might give breath to the people who were smothered.[2] He gratified the heart of Memphis on their foes, making Tatenen[3] rejoice over his enemies. He opened the gates of the walled city[4] which were stopped up, and caused his temples to receive their food (even), King Merneptah, the unique one, who establishes the hearts of hundreds of thousands of myriads, so that breath enters into their nostrils at the sight of him. He has penetrated the land of Temeh[5] in his lifetime, and put eternal fear in the heart of the Meshwesh.[6] He has turned back Libya, who invaded Egypt, and great fear of Egypt is in their hearts.

The Rout of the Libyans

Their advanced columns they left behind them, their feet made no stand, but fled. Their archers threw down their bows, and the heart of their fleet ones was weary with marching. They loosed their water skins and threw them to the ground, their (sacks) were taken and thrown out.[7]

1. The peoples surrounding Egypt.
2. I.e., in captivity.
3. A name for the god Ptah, patron deity of Memphis.
4. I.e., Memphis, which had been threatened by the Libyans.
5. Libya. The Temeh were a Libyan tribe.
6. A Libyan tribe.
7. In order to make flight easier.

The Fall of the Libyan Chief

The wretched, fallen chief of Libya, fled by favor of night alone, with no plume upon his head,[8] his two feet [failed]. His women were taken before his face, the grain of his supplies was plundered, and he had no water in the skin to keep him alive. The face of his brothers was hostile to slay him, one fought another among his leaders. Their camp was burned and made a roast, all his possessions were food for the troops. When he arrived in his country, he was the complaint of every one in his land. [Ashamed], he bowed himself down, an evil fate removed (his) plume. They all spoke against him, among the inhabitants of his city: "He is in the power of the gods, the lords of Memphis; the lord of Egypt has cursed his name, Meryey,[9] the abomination of Memphis, from son to son of his family, forever. Binre-Meriamon[10] is in pursuit of his children, Merneptah-Hotephirma[11] is appointed to be his fate."

Merneptah's Fame in Libya

He has become a proverb for Libya; the youth say to youth, concerning his victories: "It has not been done to us [before] since the time of Re,"[12] say they. Every old man says to his son: "Alas for Libya!" They have ceased to live in the pleasant fashion of walking in the field; their going about is stopped in a single day. The Tehenu[13] are consumed in a single year. Sutekh[14] has turned his back upon their chief; their settlements are desolated with his [consent]. There is no work of carrying [baskets] in these days. Concealment is good; there is safety in the cavern. The great lord of Egypt, possessor of might and victory! Who will fight, knowing his stride? The fool, the witless is he who

8. The plume was the distinguishing mark of the Libyans.
9. Or Muroayu: the Libyan chieftain's name.
10. Title of King Merneptah. "Meriamon" means "Beloved of Amon."
11. "Hotephirma" means "Contented with Truth."
12. These are Libyans speaking, despite the reference to Re.
13. A Libyan tribe.
14. Seth, a war-god.

receives him;[15] he shall not know the morrow, who transgresses his boundary.

Divine Protection of Egypt

Since the time of the gods, say they, Egypt has been the only daughter of Re; his son is he who sits upon the throne of Shu.[16] No one can make a design to invade her people, for the eye of every god is behind him who would violate her; it (the eye) captures the rear of her foes. . . . A great wonder has happened for Egypt, the power of which has made her invader a living prisoner. The divine king [exults] over his enemies, in the presence of Re. Meryey, the evil-doer, whom the god, the lord who is in Memphis, has overthrown, he has been judged with him in Heliopolis,[17] and the divine Ennead[18] declared him guilty of his crimes.[19]

Merneptah Divinely Appointed

The All-Lord has said: "Give the sword to my son,[20] the upright of heart, the good and kindly Merneptah, the [champion] on behalf of Memphis, the advocate of Heliopolis, who opens the towns that were closed up. Let him set free multitudes who are bound in every district, let him give offerings to the temples, let him send in incense before the god, let him cause the princes to [recover] their possessions, let him cause the poor to [re-enter] their cities."

Heliopolis Praises Merneptah

They say among the lords of Heliopolis regarding their son, Merneptah: "Give to him duration like Re, let him be advocate of him who is oppressed in every country. Egypt has been assigned to him as the portion of [him who has gained it] for him-

15. I.e., who receives his onslaught in battle.
16. Son of Re and god of the atmosphere.
17. Sacred city of the sun-god.
18. The Nine Great Gods.
19. This passage plays on the theme of the legendary lawsuit between the gods Horus and Seth, in which Seth was judged guilty.
20. I.e., the god commissioned Merneptah to undertake a campaign.

self forever. His strength is its people. Lo, when one dwells in the time of this hero, the breath of life comes immediately . . . so they say.

The Gods Delivered Meryey to Merneptah

Meryey, the wretched, vanquished chief of Libya, came to invade the "Walls-of-the-Sovereign" (Memphis), [who is its lord,] whose son shines in his throne, the King Merneptah. Ptah[21] said concerning the vanquished (chief) of Libya: "All his crimes shall be gathered and returned upon his (own) head. Deliver him into the hand of Merneptah, that he may make him disgorge what he has swallowed, like a crocodile. Behold, the swift is the captor of the swift; and the king shall snare him, (though) his strength be known; for Amon shall bind him in his hand and shall deliver him to his *ka* in Hermonthis,[22] (to him) the King Merneptah."

Rejoicing of the Egyptians

Great joy has come in Egypt, rejoicing comes forth from the towns of Tomeri.[23] They converse of the victories which Merneptah has achieved among the Tehenu: "How amiable is he, the victorious ruler! How magnified is the king among the gods! How fortunate is he, the commanding lord! Sit happily down and talk, or walk far out upon the way, (for) there is no fear in the heart of the people. The strongholds are left to themselves, the wells are opened (again).[24] The messengers [skirt] the battlements of the walls, shaded from the sun, until their watchmen wake.[25] The soldiers lie sleeping, and the border scouts are in the field at their (own) desire.[26] The herds of the field are left as cattle sent forth, without herdsmen, crossing (at will) the fulness of the stream. There is no uplifting of a shout in the night:

21. The god of Memphis, fashioner of all things.
22. City of the war-god, Month, south of Thebes.
23. Or Timuris: another name for Egypt.
24. Reference to the fortified oasis of the desert.
25. I.e., the watchmen who should receive the messengers' news are asleep, for they feel secure. The messengers do not wake them, since in time of peace the news is not urgent.
26. I.e., the scouts patrol only when they so desire.

'Stop! Behold, one comes, one comes with the speech of strangers!' One comes and goes with singing, and there is no lamentation of mourning people. The towns are settled again anew; as
for the one that ploweth his harvest, he shall eat it. Re has turned
himself to Egypt; he was born, destined to be her protector, the
King Merneptah."

Concluding Strophe

"The kings are overthrown, saying: 'Salam!'[27]
Not one holds up his head among the Nine Bows.
Wasted is Tehenu,
Kheta[28] is pacified,
Plundered is Pekanan[29] with every evil,
Carried off is Askalon,[30]
Seized upon is Gezer,[30]
Yenoam[30] is made as a thing not existing.
Israel[31] is desolated, his seed is not;[32]
Palestine has become a widow[33] for Egypt.
All lands are united, they are pacified;
Everyone that is turbulent is bound by King Merneptah,
    given life like Re, every day.

27. Canaanite word for "hail," "peace."
28. Hatti.
29. Canaan.
30. Towns in Palestine.
31. In contrast to the foregoing names, which indicate places, "Israel" is
written here as the name of a tribe, not a country. The scribe did not regard the Israelites as a settled people.
32. A conventional phrase applied to any defeated and plundered people.
33. I.e., a land without a protector. Palestine is unprotected against the
might of Egypt.

Introduction to Victory over the "Peoples of the Sea"

Like his predecessor Merneptah, Ramses III (reigned 1194-1163 B.C.)
was obliged to repel an invasion by the so-called Peoples of the Sea.

In this case the threat to Egypt came from the north. Various maritime tribes of uncertain origin (but including the Cretan Peleset, some of whom later settled in Palestine to become the Philistines of the Bible) had migrated south-eastward along the coast of Asia Minor and Syria, accompanied by a strong fleet. Ramses advanced to meet them—whether in Syria or in Egypt itself is not clear—and defeated the invaders on both land and sea. His victory appears to have been decisive, for during the remainder of his reign the Sea Peoples are not known to have given Egypt any more trouble.

VICTORY OVER THE "PEOPLES OF THE SEA"

Northern Invasion of Syria

"The countries ————, the [Northerners] in their isles were disturbed, taken away in the [fray] . . . at one time. Not one stood before their hands, from Kheta, Kode, Carchemish, Arvad, Alasa,[1] they were wasted. [The]y [set up] a camp in one place in Amor.[2] They desolated his people and his land like that which is not. They came with fire prepared before them, forward to Egypt. Their main support was Peleset, Thekel, Shekelesh, Denyen, and Weshesh.[3] (These) lands were united, and they laid their hands upon the land as far as the Circle of the Earth. Their hearts were confident, full of their plans."

Ramses' Preparations

"Now, it happened through this god, the lord of gods, that I was prepared and armed to [trap] them like wild fowl. He furnished my strength and caused my plans to prosper. I went forth, directing these marvelous things. I equipped my frontier in Zahi,[4] prepared before them. The chiefs, the captains of in-

From *Ancient Records of Egypt*, Vol. IV, J. H. Breasted, ed., Chicago: University of Chicago Press, 1906, pp. 37-9.

1. Kheta was the Hittite empire, Kode the coast of southern Asia Minor and Syria, Carchemish a city on the Euphrates, Arvad somewhere in the coastal region of Asia Minor, and Alasa probably Cyprus.
2. Perhaps in the north Syrian plain.
3. The Peleset were a Cretan tribe; the Shekelesh might be the Siculi of Sicily. The others are unknown.
4. (Djahi): the coastlands of Palestine-Syria.

fantry, the nobles, I caused to equip the harbor-mouths,[5] like a strong wall, with warships, galleys, and barges. . . . They were manned [completely] from bow to stern with valiant warriors bearing their arms, soldiers of all the choicest of Egypt, being like lions roaring upon the mountain-tops. The charioteers were warriors . . . , and all good officers, ready of hand. Their horses were quivering in their every limb, ready to crush the countries under their feet. I was the valiant Montu,[6] stationed before them, that they might behold the hand-to-hand fighting of my arms. I, King Ramses III, was made a far-striding hero, conscious of his might, valiant to lead his army in the day of battle."

Defeat of the Enemy

"Those who reached my boundary, their seed is not;[7] their heart and their soul are finished forever and ever. As for those who had assembled before them on the sea, the full flame[8] was in their front, before the harbor-mouths, and a wall of metal[9] upon the shore surrounded them. They were dragged, overturned, and laid low upon the beach; slain and made heaps from stern to bow of their galleys, while all their things were cast upon the water. (Thus) I turned back the waters to remember Egypt;[10] when they mention my name in their land, may it consume them, while I sit upon the throne of Harakhte,[11] and the serpent-diadem is fixed upon my head, like Re. I permit not the countries to see the boundaries of Egypt to . . . [among] them. As for the Nine Bows,[12] I have taken away their land and their boundaries; they are added to mine. Their chiefs and their people (come) to me with praise. I carried out the plans of the All-Lord, the august, divine father, lord of the gods."

5. This word usually refers to the mouths of the Nile, though in this case it may mean harbors in Syria.
6. The war-god.
7. I.e., they were utterly destroyed.
8. The Egyptian fleet in the harbor.
9. The Egyptian infantry ashore.
10. I.e., that the foe may remember Egypt.
11. The sun-god in Heliopolis.
12. Egypt's neighbors, supposed to be nine in number.

THE HITTITES

THE HITTITES

Introduction to The Apology of Hattusilis

Succession to the throne of the Hittites was governed by a set of laws which had been laid down during the Hittite "Old Kingdom" by King Telepinus (reigned *ca.* 1511-1486 B.C.). Their purpose was to prevent the internal strife and disunity which would likely result from a contested succession; and they seem to have been observed with considerable fidelity down to the end of the Hittite empire. The following document is the personal testimony of King Hattusilis III (reigned *ca.* 1275-1251 B.C.)—his attempt to explain and justify his contravening these laws.

Hattusilis was the son of one Hittite king (Mursilis I) and the younger brother of another (Muwattallis). By his own account, he held a position of considerable power and influence under his brother; and we may suppose that, upon the latter's death, he could easily have made an attempt upon the throne. But according to the laws of Telepinus, the succession belonged by right to the young son of Muwattallis, Urhitesupas (Urhi-Teshub); and Hattusilis permitted him to assume the kingship in peace.

Hattusilis retained his governorship over the land of Hakpissas, in the northeast, which was doubtless a personal power base. It was natural, if perhaps unwise, for Urhitesupas to try to deprive him of it by gradually encroaching on his uncle's prerogatives. For Hattusilis, the alternative eventually became one of either submitting to his nephew or of raising the standard of revolt against him. He chose the latter. The apparent ease of his coup suggests that Urhitesupas had not been a popular or wise ruler. Probably he was also no match in battle for his uncle, a field commander of many years' experience.

Hattusilis III thus came to the throne as a mature man of about fifty years of age. His reign was marked by general peace and prosperity. It was he who concluded, in 1270 B.C., the famous treaty with Egypt which divided Syria into spheres of influence and guaranteed peace throughout the Levant. It is remarkable—and absolutely unique in the annals of the ancient East—that a ruler of Hattusilis'

stature felt the need to justify the means by which he came to power.
The *Apology* is a telling witness to the respect with which the Hittites regarded their laws.

THE APOLOGY OF HATTUSILIS

1

Thus (speaks) King Hattusilis, the great king, king of the
land of Hatti, son of Mursilis,[1] the great king, king of the land
of Hatti, grandson of Suppilulyumas,[2] the great king, king of
the land of Hatti, descendant of Hattusilis,[3] king of the city of
Kussaras.[4]

2

I tell Ishtar's[5] divine power; let mankind hear it. And in the
future among the gods of My Majesty, of his son, of his grandson, of the descendants of My Majesty, let there be reverence to
Ishtar.

3

My father Mursilis begot us four children, Halpasulupis,
Muwattallis,[6] Hattusilis, and Dingirmesiris, a daughter. Now of
them all I was the last child. And while I was still a child (and)
was groom, My Lady Ishtar by means of a dream sent to my
father Mursilis my brother Muwattallis (with this message):
"For Hattusilis the years (are) short; he is not to live. Now give
him to me; and let him be my priest. Then he (shall be) alive."

From *A Hittite Chrestomathy*, Edgar H. Sturtevant and George Bechtel,
Philadelphia: Linguistic Society of America, 1935, pp. 65-83. Reprinted by
permission of The Linguistic Society and George Bechtel.
  1. Mursilis II, reigned *ca.* 1331-1301 B.C.
  2. Suppilulyumas I, reigned *ca.* 1366-1332 B.C.
  3. Hattusilis I, reigned *ca.* 1636-1606 B.C.
  4. Early capital of the Hittite monarchy. The site of Kussaras has not been
discovered, but presumably lies somewhat south of the great bend of the River
Halys.
  5. The goddess of love.
  6. Reigned *ca.* 1301-1282 B.C.

And my father took me, (still) a child, and gave me to the goddess for service. And, serving as priest to the goddess, I poured libations. And so at the hand of My Lady Ishtar I saw prosperity. And My Lady Ishtar took me by the hand; and she guided me.

4

But when my father Mursilis became a god, and my brother Muwattallis sat upon the throne of his father, I became a general in the presence of my brother, and then my brother appointed me to the office of chief of the *Mešedi*,[7] and gave me the Upper Country[8] to rule. Then I governed the Upper Country. Before me, however, Armadattas, son of Zidas, had been ruling it. Now because My Lady Ishtar had favored me and my brother Muwattallis was well disposed toward me, when people saw My Lady Ishtar's favor toward me and my brother's kindness, they envied me. And Armadattas, son of Zidas, and other men too began to stir up ill will against me. They brought malice against me, and I had bad luck; and my brother Muwattallis named me for the wheel (?).[9] My Lady Ishtar, however, appeared to me in a dream, and by means of the dream said this to me: "Shall I abandon you to a (hostile) deity?[10] Fear not." And I was cleared from the (hostile) deity. And since the goddess, My Lady, held me by the hand, she did not ever abandon me to the hostile deity, the hostile court; and the weapon of (my) enemy never over-threw me. My Lady Ishtar always rescued me. If ever ill-health befell me, even (while) ill I observed the goddess's divine power. The goddess, My Lady, always held me by the hand. Because I, for my part, was an obedient man, (and) because I walked be-fore the gods in obedience, I never pursued the evil course of mankind. Thou, goddess, My Lady, dost always rescue me. Has it not been (so)? In fact, the goddess, My Lady, did not ever in time of danger (?) pass me by; to an enemy she did not ever

7. An Akkadian word, designating some high court official.
8. The mountainous region to the east of the plain on which Hattusas stood.
9. A legal phrase, perhaps meaning "indict, bring action," or the like.
10. A god inevitably determines the action of a court.

abandon me, and no more to my opponents in courts, my enviers, did she abandon me. If it was a plot of an enemy, if it was
a plot of an opponent at law, if it was a plot of the palace, My
Lady Ishtar always held over me protection. She always rescued
me. Envious enemies My Lady Ishtar put into my hand; and I
destroyed them utterly.

5

When, however, my brother Muwattallis came to understand
the matter, and there remained no ill repute against me, he took
me back; and he put the infantry (and) charioteers of the land
of Hatti into my hand, and I commanded all the infantry (and)
charioteers of the land of Hatti. And my brother Muwattallis
used to send me on expeditions. And as My Lady Ishtar had
granted me her favor, wherever among the countries of the enemy I turned my eyes, not an enemy turned back his eyes upon
me. And I kept conquering the countries of the enemy. The
favor of My Lady Ishtar, as ever, was mine. And whatever
enemy there was within the lands of Hatti, I drove clear out of
the lands of Hatti. However, what countries of the enemy I conquered while I was a minor, that I shall make (into) a tablet
separately; and I shall set it up before the goddess.

6

When, however, my brother Muwattallis at the command of
his (patron) deity went down to the Lower Country[11] and left
Hattusas, my brother took the gods of Hatti and the Manes and
carried them down into the Lower Country. During (his) absence all the land of Gasga,[12] the land of Pishurus, the land of
Ishupitta, (and) the land of Daistipassa revolted.[13] And they took
away the land of Landas (?) and the land of Maristas[13] and the
fortified cities. And the enemy crossed the Halys and he began
to attack the land of . . . and he began to attack the land of

---

11. Region to the south of Hattusas.
12. The Gasga country lay to the northeast of Hattusas, and its people frequently raided the Hittite border regions.
13. These places evidently lay near the Gasga country.

Kanes.[14] . . . However H . . . , Kurustamas, and Gaziuras[15] immediately made war, and they began to attack the ruined cities of Hatti.[16] The enemy from the land of Durmittas, however, began to attack the land of Tuhuppiya. And since the land of Ippassanama was deserted, he kept making incursions into the country of Suwatara. And only the cities of . . . and Istaharas escaped. But in the districts that had been cut off they did not plant seed for ten years. Thenceforth, moreover, during the years while my brother Muwattallis was in the land of Hatti, all the Gasga countries made war; and they devastated the land of Sadduppa and the land of Dankuwa. Now my brother Muwattallis sent me (into the field), and established (my headquarters) in Pattiyarigas. However, he gave me troops (and) charioteers in small numbers. Now I took with me auxiliary troops of the country in small numbers; and I marched and cut the enemy off in Hahhas, and I gave him battle. Then My Lady Ishtar marched before me, and I defeated him. And I set up a trophy (?). And every Hittite he had brought with him I took away and established again (in his former dwelling place). Moreover, I took (his) allies and delivered them to my brother. And this was my first manly deed; My Lady Ishtar in this campaign for the first time proclaimed my name.

7

The Pishuruwian enemy, however, came (and) made an incursion, and Karahnas (and) Maristas were in the midst of the enemy; and on that side Takkastas was his boundary, and on this side Talmaliyas was his boundary. (His) horses were 800 teams, while it was impossible to count the infantry. My brother Muwattallis, however, sent me (to meet him), and he gave me 120 teams of horses, but as to infantry not even a single man

14. This city was the seat of an important Assyrian merchant colony about 1900 B.C. It has been identified with the mound Kul Tepe, about a hundred miles southeast of Boghazkoy (the former Hattusas).
15. Perhaps the Gaziura mentioned by the Greek geographer Strabo (63 B.C.–A.D. 24), some fifty miles northeast of Hattusas.
16. It is not clear why the enemy should attack ruined cities. Perhaps this was the current designation of a district that had lain in ruin for many years, but had been occupied again.

was with me. And then also My Lady Ishtar marched before me; and then also with my own resources I conquered the enemy. But when I slew every man who was an ally, the enemy fled. The cities of the land of Hatti, however, which had been cut off were now taking up arms, and they began to attack the enemy. But I set up a trophy (?) in Wistawanda. And then also the favor of My Lady Ishtar was mine. The weapon, moreover, which I carried on that occasion I enclosed (in a case?), and I set it before the goddess, My Lady.

8

And after me my brother Muwattallis came and fortified (?) Anziliyas and Tapikkas; and he went right back; he did not come near me at all.[17] And he caused the troops (and) charioteers of the land of Hatti to march before him for a while, and he took them back. Then he gathered in (one) spot the gods of Hatti and the Manes, and carried them down to Dattassas; and he took Dattassas (for his residence). But he did not go to Durmittas (and) Kurustamas. At that time he left me in these countries. And he gave me these depopulated countries to govern. I ruled over the country of Ishupitta, the country of Maristas, the country of Hissashapa, the country of Katapas, the country of Hanhana, the country of Darahna, the country of Hattena, the country of Durmittas, the country of Pala, the country of Tumanna, the country of Gassiya, the country of Sappa, the country of the Yellow River, the charioteers and all the golden grooms. The land of Hakpissas, moreover, and the land of Istaharas he gave me to be my subjects; and he made me king in the land of Hakpissas. Now (in) the above mentioned depopulated countries which my brother had put into my hands, since My Lady Ishtar held me by the hand, I conquered some enemies and others made peace with me. And these depopulated countries I myself caused to be inhabited again. And I made them Hittite again.

17. Probable meaning: While I was waging a successful war with my own resources, Muwattallis took the field with the main body of the Hittite army; but he did not give me any real assistance, and presently retired with his army.

9

When once my brother came (and) marched against the land of Egypt, these countries which I had caused to be inhabited again—the army (and) charioteers of this country I led for my brother's campaign against the land of Egypt.[18] Now because, in the presence of my brother, infantry and charioteers of the land of Hatti were in my hands, I commanded them. Now when Armadattas, son of Zidas, saw the kindness to me of My Lady Ishtar and of my brother, he (nevertheless) did not in any respect show them any reverence; and thereupon he with his wife and his sons tried to bewitch me. And he filled Samuhas, the city of the goddess, with witchcraft. When, however, I was on my way back from the land of Egypt, I journeyed to Lawazantiyas to pour libations to the goddess; and I worshipped the goddess. And at the command of the goddess I took in marriage Puduhepas, the daughter of Pentipsarris, the priest.[19] And we founded a family, and the goddess gave us the love of husband and wife. And we got us sons (and) daughters. Furthermore the goddess, My Lady, said to me: "Do you with (your) house be subject to me." And with my house I was true to the goddess. And for us the goddess dwelt within the house that we were making us. . . . Hakpissas, however, revolted; and I drove out the men of the Gasga countries, and I subjected it. And I became king of the land of Hakpissas and you became queen of the land of Hakpissas.

10

When, however, an indictment was brought again from the palace, My Lady Ishtar at that time also showed her divine power. And she brought a new indictment out of the indictment. Now they found witchcraft in Armadattas along with his wife and his sons, and they established it against him; and he had

18. This refers to Muwattallis' campaign against Ramses II of Egypt, which culminated in Hattusilis' encounter with Ramses at the Battle of Kadesh. See "The Battle of Kadesh," above, p. 15.

19. Puduhepas was a princess of the Hittite protectorate state of Kizzuwadna and a political personality in her own right.

filled even Samuhas, the city of the goddess, with witchcraft.
Now the goddess, My Lady, made him lose the case to me; and
my brother delivered him to me with his wife, his sons, (and)
his house. Then my brother said to me "Sippaluis (is) not in
(it)." And because my brother made me, the innocent (? party),
victorious in the trial, I did not thereafter repay him in malice.
Now because Armadattas was a man related (?) to me, (and)
besides he was an aged man, and he was ill, I let him off. And I
let Sippaluis off. When, however, I had let them off and had
done nothing to them, I actually sent Armadattas and his son to
Alasiya, and I took half of his estate and gave it back to Armadattas.

[This break in the text seems to have contained a summary of Hattusilis' relations with his brother Muwattallis during the latter's
reign.]

And my brother died. I, however, firm in (my) respect for my
brother, did not act selfishly; but, as at this time my brother did
not yet have a legitimate son, I took Urhitesupas, the son of a
secondary wife, and set him in authority in the land of Hatti.[20]
And I put all the army in his hands. And in the lands of Hatti
he was the great king. I, however, was king in Hakpissas. And
with army and charioteers I took the field. And, since Nerikkas
had been in ruins from the day of Hantilis,[21] I took it and rebuilt
it. And the countries which were near Nerikkas and had made
Neras (and) Hassuras (their) boundary, all these I subjected
and made tributaries.

. . . .

11

Now when Urhitesupas thus observed the kindness of the goddess to me, he envied me, and he brought ill will upon me. He
took away from me all (my) subjects; Samuhas also he took

20. According to Hittite law, a son by a king's secondary wife (who in this
case may even have been a captive woman) must succeed him in default of
a prince of the first rank.
21. Ruler of the Hittites *ca.* 1576-1546 B.C. Nerikkas thus had been in ruins
for three centuries.

away from me; the depopulated lands also that I had settled again, all those too he took away from me, and he made me weak. Hakpissas, however, according to the command of a god he did not take away from me. Because I was priest of the storm god of Nerikkas, for that reason he did not take it away from me. And, firm in (my) respect for my brother, I did not act selfishly. And for seven years I submitted. But he (Urhitesupas) at the command of a god and the suggestion of man tried to destroy me. And he took Hakpissas and Nerikkas away from me. And I did not submit any longer. And I made war upon him. But when I made war upon him, I did not do it (as) a crime. Did I rebel against him in the chariot or rebel against him within the palace? I sent him a declaration (of war) as an (open) enemy: "You started hostilities with me. Now you (are) a great king; but as for me, the one fortress that you have left me—of (that) one (I) am king. Come! Ishtar of Samuhas and the storm god of Nerikkas shall decide the case for us." Now whereas I wrote Urhitesupas thus, if any one speaks as follows: "Why did you formerly establish him on the throne? And why are you now declaring war upon him?" (I answer, "Very well), if he had never started hostilities with me." Would (the gods) have subjected a great king (who was) upright to a small king? Now because he started hostilities with me, they subjected him to me in the trial. Now when I communicated these words to him (saying) "Come on" to him, he marched out from Marassantiyas, and came to the Upper Country. And Sippaluis, the son of Armadattas, was with him. And he appointed him to gather the troops of the Upper Country. But because Sippaluis was hostile to me, he did not succeed against me.[22]

12

Now, while My Lady Ishtar had even before this been promising me the kingship, at that time My Lady Ishtar appeared to my wife in a dream: "I shall march before your husband. And all Hattusas shall be led with your husband. Since I thought

22. Apparently this means that Hattusilis got more recruits in the Upper Country than Sippaluis did.

highly of him, I did not—no, not ever—abandon him to the hostile trial, the hostile deity. Now also I will exalt him, and make him priest of the sun goddess of Arinnas.[23] Do you also make me, Ishtar, (your) patron deity."[24] And My Lady Ishtar stood behind (i.e., supported) me; and whatever she promised me occurred. And My Lady Ishtar then also showed me her divine power abundantly. To whatever nobles Urhitesupas had ever banished, My Lady Ishtar appeared in a dream: "You (are) summoned to your strength; but I, Ishtar, have turned all the lands of Hatti to the side of Hattusilis." And then also I saw the divine power of Ishtar abundantly. Whereas she did not ever at another time abandon Urhitesupas, she shut him up in Samuhas like a pig in a sty. As for me, however, the Gasga men who had been hostile supported me; and all Hattusas supported me. But, firm in (my) respect for my brother, I did not act selfishly. And I marched back to Samuhas (to be) with Urhitesupas and I brought him down like a captive. And I gave him fortified towns in the land of Nuhasse, and he dwelt there. He would have planned another plan, (and) would have proceeded into the land of Karaduniya; but when I heard of the matter, I arrested him and banished him across the sea. And they sent Sippaluis across the border; but I took (his) house from him, and gave it to My Lady Ishtar. Now I gave that to My Lady Ishtar, and My Lady Ishtar thereafter granted me desire after desire.

13

Now I was a prince, and became chief of the *Mešedi*. Again I, chief of the *Mešedi*, became king of Hakpissas. Again I, king of Hakpissas, later became great king. Thereupon My Lady Ishtar put into my hands (my) enviers, enemies, and opponents at law. And some (of them) died by the weapon, but others died on the (appointed) day; and I completely got rid of them all. And My Lady Ishtar gave me the kingship of the land of Hatti also, and I became a great king. My Lady Ishtar took me (as a) prince

23. Great religious center, whose goddess was regarded as the supreme patroness of the Hittite state and monarchy.
24. Hattusilis' wife, the servant of Ishtar of Lawazantiyas, is now to take Ishtar of Samuhas as her patron deity.

and placed me on the throne. And (those) who had been well disposed toward the kings, my predecessors, became well disposed toward me. And they began to send me messengers, and they began to send me gifts as well. But such gifts as they kept sending me, they had not sent to any of my fathers and forefathers. On the other hand, whatever king owed me homage paid me homage. But (the lands) that were hostile to me I conquered; I annexed district after district to the lands of Hatti. And (those) who had been hostile in the time of my fathers and of my forefathers made peace with me. And since the goddess, My Lady, had thus favored me, (being) firm in (my) loyalty to my brother, I did not act selfishly. And I took my brother's son Kalas, and set him upon a throne in the very spot, (namely) Dattasas, which my brother Muwattallis used for (his) palace. Insignificant as I was when thou, My Lady Ishtar, didst take me, thou didst set me in the high place in the land of Hatti, upon the throne. For my part I gave My Lady Ishtar the house of Armadattas. I consecrated (?) and gave it (to her). What was (there) previously, I gave her; and what I had, that also I gave. I consecrated it and gave it to the goddess. Furthermore, as to the house of Armadattas that I gave her, and the cities that belonged to Armadattas, behind every one they are again setting up her statue (?), and distributing libation cups (?). Ishtar is my goddess, and for themselves (men) pour libations to Ishtar, the Highest(?). Whatever mausoleum I have built, that I have given to the goddess. And my son Duthaliyas[25] I gave for thy service; may my son Duthaliyas rule the house of Ishtar. I (am) the servant of the goddess; let him also be the servant of the goddess. And whatever (birth-)house I have dedicated to the goddess, let every (child?) celebrate (?) the *seyanan marnan*[26] for the goddess.

14

Now, whoever in the future takes a descendant of Hattusilis (and) Puduhepas away from the service of Ishtar (or) covets the food (?) of the *garupahis*[26] house, the possessions, (or) the granary of Ishtar of Samuhas, let him be an opponent at law of

25. Or Tudhaliyas IV, reigned 1251-1221 B.C.
26. Meaning uncertain.

Ishtar of Samuhas. Let no one assess feudal services (or) taxes   85
upon them.

15

In the future whatever son, grandson, (or) future descendant
of Hattusilis (and) Puduhepas ascends the throne, let him be
reverent toward Ishtar of Samuhas among the gods.

Introduction to the Treaty Between Hattušili and Ramesses II

The following treaty, concluded in about 1270 B.C., brought to an
end the twenty-year rivalry between the kings of Egypt and Hatti
for control of the territories lying between them. Thutmose III
(reigned 1490-1436) had carried the Egyptian frontier into northern
Syria; but his weak successors neglected to defend it, allowing the
Hittites to expand southward. Under King Subbiluliuma I (reigned
1366-1332), the Hittite empire in Syria extended from the Euphrates
to the sea and southward into Lebanon.

But the Pharaohs of the Nineteenth Dynasty, Seti (Sethos) I
(reigned 1303-1290) and his son Ramesses II (reigned 1290-1224),
were eager to recover the lost empire. Seti I restored effective Egyptian control in Palestine and advanced into Syria. Ramesses II
fought the Hittites intermittently in Syria for some fifteen years,
most notably at the battle of Kadesh (ca. 1286 B.C.).* It seems that
the two empires fought each other to a draw. In any event, by the
year 1270 both were ready to make a lasting peace. The resultant
treaty embodied an offensive-defensive alliance by which each re-
nounced further aggression against the other, though no mention
was made of a boundary between them. Probably the Egyptians retained hegemony in Palestine and southern Syria, the Hittites in
northern Syria.

The treaty is extant in two versions, discovered by archaeologists
at sites a thousand miles apart. One was excavated at Boghazkoy
among the ruins of the former Hittite capital of Hattusas. It is writ-

* See above, "Official Record of the Battle of Kadesh," p. 15.

ten upon two clay tablets in the Babylonian cuneiform script which was then the international language of diplomacy in the Near East. The latter part of the treaty is broken away. The Egyptian version is carved upon the walls of the temple of Amon and of Ramesses' mortuary temple at Thebes. In many paragraphs, at least, it is evidently a translation of the Babylonian original, for it employs modes of expression foreign to the Egyptian idiom. In accordance with contemporary practice, even the names of the gods are translated: Shamash becomes Re; Teshub becomes Seth. The introductory explanation (here omitted) and heading to the Egyptian version were composed by an Egyptian scribe, and are lacking in the Hittite text.

This treaty differs from modern ones in that it is not a single document, of which both parties hold an identical copy. Each treaty was drawn up separately and sent to the other signatory for ratification. Numerous discrepancies exist between the two versions. In the Hittite text Ramesses, as the principal contracting party, speaks in the first person; in the Egyptian version it is Hattušili who does so. In this respect, and in its occasional personal allusions, it resembles the letters by which the diplomacy of the time was ordinarily conducted, rather than a treaty in the modern sense. The Hittite version also omits all reference to previous hostilities with Egypt. Perhaps such references were regarded as an admission, humiliating to Hittite pride, that they were the aggressors against Egypt.

This treaty was celebrated by Ramesses as a victory; and in numerous inscriptions he refers to himself as the conqueror of the Hittites. Thirteen years later he cemented his relations with Hatti by marrying Hattušili's daughter. The peace with the Hittites was maintained throughout the remainder of Ramesses' long reign and into that of his successor.

TREATY BETWEEN HATTUŠILI AND RAMESSES II

Heading to the Egyptian Translation of the Treaty

Copy[1] of the tablet of silver which the great chief of Hatti, Hattušili, caused to be brought to Pharaoh by the hand of his

From "Treaty between Hattušili and Ramesses II" (Egyptian and Hittite versions), S. Langdon and Alan H. Gardiner, *Journal of Egyptian Archaeology*, VI (1920), 185-94. Reprinted by permission.
1. "Copy" here means "translation."

messenger Tartešub and his messenger Ramose,[2] in order to beg
peace from the Majesty [of Usimare-setpenre], son of Re, Ramesse-mi-Amun, bull of rulers, who makes his boundary where
he will in every land.

1   Preamble of the Actual Treaty

HITTITE-BABYLONIAN TEXT:

[And so be it. Riamasesa-mai-]
Amana,[3] the great king, king [of
Egypt, the strong], [with Hattušili, the great king], king of the
land Hatti, his brother, in order
to give good peace, [good brotherhood and to obtain] a mighty
[king]dom (?) between them as
long as we [live] (and) [for-
ever] [a treaty] has made.

EGYPTIAN TEXT:

The treaty which the great
prince of Hatti, Hattušili, the
strong, the son of Muršili,[4] the
great chief of Hatti, the strong,
the son of the son[5] of Šubbi [lu-
liuma,[6] the great chief of Hatti,
the str]ong, made upon a tablet
of silver for Usimare-setpenre,[7]
the great ruler of Egypt, the
strong, the son of Menmare,[8] the
great ruler of Egypt, the strong,
the son of the son of Menpeh-
tire,[9] the great ruler of Egypt,
the strong: the good treaty of
peace and brotherhood, giving
peace [and brotherhood(?) . . .
between us by means of a treaty
(?) of Hatti with Egypt] forever.

HITTITE-BABYLONIAN TEXT:

Riamašeša-mai-Amana,   the
great king, king of Egypt, the
strong in all lands, son [of]

2. Note that the messenger Tartešub has a Hittite name, while Ramose is
an Egyptian name.
3. Babylonian translation of "Ramesses-Beloved-of-Amon."
4. Muršili (Mursilis) II, who ruled in Hatti ca. 1331-1301 B.C.
5. The Egyptian language has no word for "grandson."
6. (Suppiluliumas): king of the Hittites ca. 1366-1332 B.C.
7. (User-maat-Re Setep-en-Re): official name of Ramesses II (reigned 1290-
1224 B.C.).
8. (Men-maat-Re): official name of Seti I (reigned 1303-1290 B.C.).
9. (Men-pehti-Re): official name of Ramesses I (reigned 1304-1303 B.C.).

Minmuaria,[10] the great king, king of Egypt, the strong, son of the son of Minpahiritaria,[11] the great king, [king of Egy]pt, the strong, unto Hattušili, the great king, king of the land Hatti, the strong, the son of Muršili, the great king, king of the land Hatti, the strong, son of the son of Šubbiluliuma, the great king, king of the land Hatti, the strong, behold now I give [good] brotherhood, good peace between us forever, in order to give good peace, good brotherhood, by means of [a treaty (?)] of Egypt with Hatti forever. So it is.

2   The Treaty Is the Resumption of Old Peaceful Relations

HITTITE-BABYLONIAN TEXT:

Behold, the policy of the great king, king of Egypt, [and of the great king], king of Hatti since eternity—god did not permit the making of hostility between them, [by means of a treaty] forever.[12]

Behold,   Riamašeša-mai-Ama-

EGYPTIAN TEXT:

Now aforetime, since eternity, as regards the policy of the great ruler of Egypt and the great chief of Hatti—the god did not permit hostility to be made between them, by means of a treaty.[12]

But in the time of Muwattalli,[13] the great chief of Hatti, my brother, he fought with [Ramesse-mi-Amun],[14] the great ruler of Egypt.

But hereafter, beginning from

10. Official name of Seti I in Babylonian translation.
11. Official name of Ramesses I in Babylonian translation.
12. Possible reference to a previous treaty?
13. (Muwatallis): king of the Hittites *ca.* 1301-1282 B.C.
14. Their best-known encounter was at the battle of Kadesh (*ca.* 1286 B.C.).

na, the great king, king of Egypt, in order to make the policy [which Samaš[15] and] Tešub[16] made for Egypt with the land of Hatti because of his policy which is from eternity, wickedly (?) [will not become host]ile to make hostility between them unto everlasting and unto all (time).

this day, behold Hattušili, the great chief of Hatti, is [in?] a treaty for making permanent the policy which Pre[17] made and Setekh[18] made for the land of Egypt with the land of Hatti, so as not to permit hostilities to be made between them forever.

3   *Declaration of the New Treaty*

HITTITE-BABYLONIAN TEXT:

Riamašeša-mai-Amana, the great king, king of Egypt, has made himself in a treaty upon a silver tablet with Hattušili, the great king, king of the land Hatti, his brother, from this day to give good peace and good brotherhood between us forever; and he is a brother to me and at peace with me, and I am a brother to him and at peace with him forever.

EGYPTIAN TEXT:

Behold, Hattušili, the great chief of Hatti, has made himself in a treaty with Usimare-setpenre, the great ruler of Egypt, beginning with this day, to cause to be made good peace and good brotherhood between us forever; and he is in brotherhood with me and at peace with me, and I am in brotherhood with him and at peace with him forever.

And since Muwattalli, the great chief of Hatti, my brother, hastened after his fate,[19] and Hattušili took his seat as great chief of Hatti on the throne of his father; behold I have become with Ramesse-mi-Amun, the great ruler of Egypt, we (?) being [together in?] our peace and

And we have made brotherhood, peace and goodwill more

15. (Shamash): Hittite (and Babylonian) sun-god.
16. (Teshub): Hittite storm-god.
17. (Re): the sun-god of Egypt.
18. (Seth): Egyptian storm-god.
19. I.e., died: an example of a non-Egyptian idiom showing that the Egyptian text of the treaty is a translation.

than the brotherhood and peace of former times, which was between [Egypt and] Hatti.

Behold, Riamašeša-mai-Amana, the great king, king of Egypt, is in good peace and good brotherhood with Hattušili, the great king, king of the land Hatti.

Behold, the sons of Riamašeša-mai-Amana, the king of Egypt, are at peace (and) are bro[thers with] the sons of Hattušili, the great king, king of the land Hatti, forever; and they are according to our policy of [our] brotherhood [and] our peace.

And Egypt with the land Hatti —they are at peace, they are brothers like us forever.

our brotherhood; and it is better than the peace and the brotherhood of formerly, which was in the land.

Behold, I, being the great chief of Hatti, am with [Ramesse-mi-Amun], the great ruler of Egypt, in good peace and good brotherhood.

And the children of the children [of] the great chief of Hatti shall be (?) in brotherhood and at peace with the children of the children of Ramesse-mi-Amun, the great ruler of Egypt; they being in our policy of brotherhood and our policy [of peace].

[And the land of Egypt?] with the land Hatti [shall be ?] at peace and in brotherhood like us forever; and hostilities shall not be made between them forever.

4   Mutual Assurances with Regard to Invasion

HITTITE-BABYLONIAN TEXT:

And Riamašeša-mai-Amana, the great king, king of Egypt, shall not trespass into the land Hatti to take aught from therein [forever]; and Hattušili, the great king, king of the land Hatti, shall not trespass into Egypt to take aught from therein [forever].

EGYPTIAN TEXT:

And the great chief of Hatti shall not trespass into the land of Egypt forever to take aught from it; and Usimare-setpenre, the great ruler of Egypt, shall not trespass into the land [of Hatti to take] (aught) from it forever.

5   Formal Renewal of the Former Treaty

HITTITE-BABYLONIAN TEXT:

Behold, the decree of eternity which Šamaš and Tešub have

EGYPTIAN TEXT:

made for Egypt and the land Hatti [to make peace] and brotherhood in order not to give hostility between them.

As to the regular treaty[20] which there was in the time of Šubbiluliuma, the great chief of Hatti, and likewise the regular treaty which was in the time of Muwattalli[21] (sic), the great chief of Hatti, my father, I take hold of it. Behold, Ramesse-mi-Amun, the great ruler of Egypt, takes hold [of the peace (?) which it (?)] makes together with us from this day; and we will act according to this regular policy.

And behold, Riamašeša-mai-A[mana, the great king], king of Egypt, takes hold of it to make peace from this day.

Behold, Egypt and Hatti [are at peace, and] they are brothers forever.

6   Undertaking of a Defensive Alliance

HITTITE-BABYLONIAN TEXT:

And if another enemy come [against] the land Hatti, and Hattušili, [the great king of the land Hat]ti, send to me saying, 'Come unto me for [my] help against him'; then Ri[amašeša-mai-Ama]na, the great king, king of Egypt shall send his troops (and) his chariots and shall slay [his enemy and] he shall restore

EGYPTIAN TEXT:

And if another enemy come to the lands of Usimare-setpenre, the great ruler of Egypt, and he send to the great chief of Hatti saying, 'Come with me as help against him'; the great chief of Hatti shall [come to him], the great chief of Hatti [shall] slay his enemy.

20. Perhaps meaning the traditional or normal relations between the two powers.
21. The father of Hattušili was Muršili, not Muwattalli. The term "father" may be a conventional designation for any predecessor on the throne. Hattušili is referring to the time before the Egyptian-Hittite wars.

[con]fidence (?) to the land Hatti.

But if it be not the desire of the great chief of Hatti to come, he shall send his troops and his chariotry and shall slay his enemy.

7   Common Action To Be Taken Against Rebellious Subjects

HITTITE-BABYLONIAN TEXT:

And if Hattušili, the great king, king of the land Hatti, [become incensed] against servants of his [and they] sin against him, and thou send to Riamašeša, the great king, king of [Egypt] concerning it; straight[way] Riamašeša-mai-Amana his troops (and) his chariots shall send, and they shall destroy all [of them] against whom [thou art become incensed].

EGYPTIAN TEXT:

Or if Ramesse-mi-Amun, [the great ruler of Egypt], become incensed against servants of his, and they do another offence against him, and he go to slay his enemy;
the great chief of Hatti shall act with him [to destroy] everyone [against whom] they shall be incensed.

8   Reciprocal Clause Corresponding to No. 6

HITTITE-BABYLONIAN TEXT:

[And if] another enemy come against Egypt, and Riamašeša-mai-Amana, the king of Egypt, thy brother, [send] to Hattušili, king of the land Hatti, his brother, saying, '[Co]me for my help against him'; straightway then shall Ha[ttušili] king of the land Hatti, send his troops (and) his [chariots]; he [shall slay] my enemy.

EGYPTIAN TEXT:

But [if] another enemy [come] against the great chief [of Hatti];

[then shall Usi]ma[re]-setpenre [the great ruler of Egypt] come to him as help to slay his enemy.

(But) if it be (not) the desire of Ramesse-mi-Amun, the great

ruler of Egypt, to come, he . . .
Hatti, [and he shall send his
troops and his] chariotry, besides
returning answer to the land of
Hatti.

9   Reciprocal Clause Corresponding to No. 7

HITTITE-BABYLONIAN TEXT:

And if Riamašeša, [the great
king, king] of Egypt, become incensed against servants of his,
and they commit sin against
[him, and I send] to Hattušili,
king of the land Hatti, my
brother, concerning [it]; then
Hattušili, the great king, king of
Egypt, shall send his troops
(and) his chariots and they shall
destroy all [of them]; and I
will . . .

EGYPTIAN TEXT:

But if servants of the great
chief of Hatti trespass against
him,

and Rames[se]-mi-Amun, [the
great ruler of Egypt,] . . .

10   A Clause Relating to Succession (?)[22]

[Text so fragmentary that it is incomprehensible]

11   Extradition of Important Fugitives[23]

[From this point onward, the Hittite text is missing.]

EGYPTIAN TEXT

[If any great man flee from the land of Egypt and he come to the
lands of (?)] the great chief of Hatti; or a town (or a district . . .)
[belong]ing to the lands of Ramesse-mi-Amun, the great ruler of
Egypt, and they come to the great chief of Hatti: the great chief of
Hatti shall not receive them. The great chief of Hatti shall cause

22. Possibly the missing portions obligate Ramesses, in the event of Hattušili's death, to recognize the lawful successor to the Hittite throne. If so, the
Egyptian text has no corresponding clause relating to the Egyptian succession.

them to be brought to Usimare-setpenre, the great ruler of Egypt, their lord, [on accou]nt of it.[23]

12   Extradition of Fugitives of Humble Birth

EGYPTIAN TEXT

Or if one man or two men who are unknown flee . . . , and they come to the land of Hatti[24] to be servants of another, they shall not be left in the land of Hatti, they shall be brought to Ramesse-mi-Amun, the great ruler of Egypt.

13   Reciprocal Clause Corresponding to No. 11

EGYPTIAN TEXT

Or if a great man flee from the land of Hatti, and [he come to the lands of (?) Usi]ma[re]-setpenre, the [great] ruler of Egypt; or a town or a district or . . . belonging to the land of Hatti, and they come to Ramesse-mi-Amun, the great ruler of Egypt: Usimare-setpenre, the great ruler of Egypt, shall not receive them. Ramesse-mi-Amun, the great ruler of Egypt, shall cause them to be brought to the chief . . . they shall not be left.

14   Reciprocal Clause Corresponding to No. 12

EGYPTIAN TEXT

Likewise, if one man or two men who are [not] known flee to the land of Egypt to be subjects of others, Usimare-setpenre, the great ruler of Egypt, shall not leave them; he shall cause them to be brought to the great chief of Hatti.

15   The Gods of Hatti and Egypt Are Witnesses to the Treaty

EGYPTIAN TEXT

As for these words of the treaty [made by (?)] the great chief of Hatti with Rames[se-mi-Amun], the great ruler [of Egypt, in] writ-

23. This section refers to the Asiatic subjects of Egypt and Hatti who rebel or refuse to pay tribute or flee to the territories of the other power. Egypt and Hatti bind themselves not to take advantage of any such revolt or flight for self-aggrandizement.
24. Note that unknown men (men without rank) come only "to the land of Hatti," whereas the great men go personally to the king.

ing upon this tablet of silver; as for these words, a thousand gods, male gods and female gods of those of the land of Hatti, together with a thousand gods, male gods and female gods of those of the land of Egypt—they are with me as witnesses [hearing (?)] these words.

[A long list of gods and goddesses follows.]

16   Curses or Blessings on Those Who Violate or Keep the Treaty

EGYPTIAN TEXT

As to these words which are upon this tablet of silver of the land of Hatti and of the land of Egypt, as to him who shall not keep them, a thousand gods of the land of Hatti and a thousand gods of the land of Egypt shall destroy his house, his land and his servants. But he who shall keep these words which are on this tablet of silver, be they Hatti, or be they Egyptians, and who do not neglect them (?), a thousand gods of the land of Hatti and a thousand gods of the land of Egypt will cause him to be healthy and to live, together with his houses and his (land) and his servants.

17   Amnesty for Extradited Persons

EGYPTIAN TEXT

If one man flee from the land of Egypt, or two, or three, and they come to the great chief of Hatti, the great chief of Hatti shall seize them and shall cause them to be brought back to Usimare-setpenre, the great ruler of Egypt. But as for the man who shall be brought to Ramesse-mi-Amun, the great ruler of Egypt, let not his crime be charged against him, let not his house, his wives or his children be destroyed, [let him not] be [killed], let no injury be done to his eyes, to his ears, to his mouth or to his legs, let not any [crime be charged] against him.

18   Reciprocal Clause Corresponding to No. 17

EGYPTIAN TEXT

Likewise, if a man flee from the land of Hatti, be he one, be he two, or be he three, and they come to Usimare-setpenre, the great ruler of Egypt, let Ramesse-mi-Amun, the [great] ruler [of Egypt, cause] them to be brought to the great chief of Hatti, and the great chief of Hatti shall not charge their crime against them, and they shall not destroy his house, his wives or his children, and they shall not kill him, and they shall not do injury to his ears, to his eyes, to his mouth or to his legs, and they shall not charge any crime against him.

19   Description of the Silver Tablet

EGYPTIAN TEXT

What is in the middle of the tablet of silver? On its front side: a relief (?) consisting of an image of Setekh embracing an image of the great prince of Hatti, surrounded by a legend (?) saying: the seal of Setekh, the ruler of the sky, the seal of the treaty made by Hattušili, the great chief of Hatti, the strong, the son of Muršili, the great chief of Hatti, the strong. What is within the surrounding (frame) of the relief: the seal [of Setekh, the ruler of the sky]. [What is on] its other side: a relief (?) consisting of a female image of [the] goddess of Hatti embracing a female image of the chieftainess of Hatti, surrounded by a legend saying: the seal of Pre of the town of Arinna,[25] the lord of the land, the seal of Puduhepa,[26] the chieftainess of the land of Hatti, the daughter of the land of Kizuwadna,[27] the [priestess?] of [the town (?) of] Arinna, the lady of the land, the servant of the goddess. What is within the surrounding (frame) of the relief: the seal of Pre of Arinna, the lord of every land.

25. A great Hittite religious center. Its principal deity, the sun-goddess, was regarded as the supreme patroness of the Hittite state and monarchy. According to the laws of the sun-goddess of Arinna, fugitives were supposed to be returned to their native land.
26. Hattušili's queen, who played a prominent part in state affairs and is regularly associated with her husband in official documents.
27. A kingdom in southeastern Asia Minor which in Hattušili's day was a Hittite protectorate.

THE HEBREWS

THE HEBREWS

Introduction to I and II Samuel

The two Books of Samuel recount about one hundred years of the history of the Israelite nation, from the birth of the prophet Samuel to the last days of King David (died *ca.* 973 B.C.). At the beginning of this period, Israel was a loose confederation of semi-nomadic tribes scattered across Palestine and Transjordan, held together by their common faith but politically weak and difficult to arouse to united action. In time, the Israelites acquired more settled habits, chose a king (Saul), and under Saul's successor, David, became a united nation of considerable wealth and power.

First and Second Samuel originally formed a single work. The compiler utilized a variety of sources, as is shown by the fact that at a number of points two accounts of the same incident have been preserved side by side. The books probably acquired their present form sometime between 650 and 550 B.C. The author evidently belonged to the so-called prophetic school of historians, who taught that the history of Israel was not a series of unrelated events, but evidence of the working of God's will on earth. The lesson is clear: obedience to God is rewarded, while disobedience to Him brings punishment. All power belongs to God. Kingship is merely an accommodation to the people's weakness: the king rules in God's name and is constantly answerable to Him for his actions.

FROM THE FIRST BOOK OF SAMUEL

Chapter 7

15   And Samuel judged Israel all the days of his life.

16   And he went from year to year in circuit to Bethel, and

I Samuel 7:15—11:15; 14:47-8, 52; 15:1-35. King James Bible.

Gilgal, and Mizpeh,[1] and judged Israel in all those places.

17 And his return was to Ramah;[2] for there was his house; and there he judged Israel; and there he built an altar unto the Lord.

Chapter 8

1 ¶And it came to pass, when Samuel was old, that he made his sons judges over Israel.

2 Now the name of his firstborn was Joel; and the name of his second, Abiah: they were judges in Beersheba.[3]

3 And his sons walked not in his ways, but turned aside after lucre, and took bribes, and perverted judgment.

4 Then all the elders of Israel gathered themselves together, and came to Samuel unto Ramah.

5 And said unto him, Behold, thou art old, and thy sons walk not in thy ways: now make us a king to judge us like all the nations.[4]

6 ¶But the thing displeased Samuel, when they said, Give us a king to judge us. And Samuel prayed unto the Lord.

7 And the Lord said unto Samuel, Hearken unto the voice of the people in all that they say unto thee: for they have not rejected thee, but they have rejected me, that I should not reign over them.

8 According to all the works which they have done since the

1. All of these towns were evidently ancient sacred places in the hill country north of Jerusalem. Bethel is, after Jerusalem, the most mentioned town in the Bible. Gilgal was the name of several places: it means "circle of stones," i.e., a place designated by a sacred circle of stones.

2. I.e., to his old home, not to Shiloh, which had ceased to be the central sanctuary of the Israelites. Ramah means "the height," and was the name of several towns in Palestine.

3. This town marked the southern limits of Old Testament Palestine, and lay a considerable distance from Samuel's area of activity, which was north of Jerusalem. The expression "from Dan to Beersheba" was used in the sense of "from one end of the land to the other."

4. Surrounding peoples, such as the Philistines, had reached a higher level of civilization than the Hebrews. Perhaps kingship appeared to the Israelites as the mark of a civilized nation; or perhaps they regarded their neighbors as more successful under the rule of kings than they themselves with their theocratic federation.

day that I brought them up out of Egypt even unto this day, wherewith they have forsaken me, and served other gods, so do they also unto thee.

9 Now therefore hearken unto their voice: howbeit yet protest solemnly unto them, and shew them the manner of the king that shall reign over them.

10 ¶And Samuel told all the words of the Lord unto the people that asked of him a king.

11 And he said, This will be the manner of the king that shall reign over you:[5] He will take your sons, and appoint them for himself, for his chariots, and to be his horsemen; and some shall run before his chariots.

12 And he will appoint him captains over thousands, and captains over fifties; and will set them to ear his ground,[6] and to reap his harvest, and to make his instruments of war, and instruments of his chariots.

13 And he will take your daughters to be confectionaries, and to be cooks, and to be bakers.

14 And he will take your fields, and your vineyards, and your olive-yards, even the best of them, and give them to his servants.

15 And he will take the tenth of your seed, and of your vineyards, and give to his officers, and to his servants.

16 And he will take your menservants, and your maidservants, and your goodliest[7] young men, and your asses, and put them to his work.

17 He will take the tenth of your sheep: and ye shall be his servants.

18 And ye shall cry out in that day because of your king which ye shall have chosen you; and the Lord will not hear you in that day.

19 ¶Nevertheless the people refused to obey the voice of Samuel; and they said, Nay; but we will have a king over us;

5. The following critique of monarchy expresses the resistance to change of those who wished to preserve the old patriarchal institutions.
6. I.e., to plow his ground.
7. Best, most handsome.

20   That we also may be like all the nations; and that our king
     may judge us, and go out before us, and fight our
     battles.
21   And Samuel heard all the words of the people, and he re-
     hearsed them in the ears of the Lord.
22   And the Lord said to Samuel, Hearken unto their voice,
     and make them a king. And Samuel said unto the men
     of Israel, Go ye every man unto his city.

Chapter 9

1   ¶Now there was a man of Benjamin,[8] whose name was
     Kish, the son of Abiel, the son of Zeror, the son of
     Bechorath, the son of Aphiah, a Benjamite, a mighty
     man of power.
2   And he had a son, whose name was Saul, a choice young
     man, and a goodly: and there was not among the chil-
     dren of Israel a goodlier person than he: from his
     shoulders and upward he was higher than any of the
     people.
3   And the asses of Kish Saul's father were lost. And Kish said
     to Saul his son, Take now one of the servants with
     thee, and arise, go seek the asses.
4   And he passed through mount Ephraim,[9] and passed
     through the land of Shalisha,[10] but they found them
     not: then they passed through the land of Shalim,[10]
     and there they were not: and he passed through the
     land of the Benjamites, but they found them not.
5   And when they were come to the land of Zuph,[11] Saul said
     to his servant that was with him, Come, and let us re-
     turn; lest my father leave caring for the asses, and take
     thought for us.
6   And he said unto him, Behold now, there is in this city a

8. One of the twelve tribes of Israel. See v. 21 below.
9. Part of the central range of western Palestine. The region is hilly; there
is no one Mount Ephraim. For this reason, modern translations use the expression: "the hill country of Ephraim."
10. Districts of the Ephraim hill country, east of the Jordan River.
11. Location uncertain.

man of God, and he is an honourable man; all that he saith cometh surely to pass: now let us go thither; peradventure he can shew us our way that we should go.

7 Then said Saul to his servant, But, behold, if we go, what shall we bring the man? for the bread is spent in our vessels, and there is not a present to bring to the man of God: what have we?

8 And the servant answered Saul again, and said, Behold, I have here at hand the fourth part of a shekel of silver: that will I give to the man of God, to tell us our way.

9 (Beforetime in Israel, when a man went to enquire of God, thus he spake, Come, and let us go to the seer: for he that is now called a Prophet was beforetime called a Seer.)

10 Then said Saul to his servant, Well said; come, let us go. So they went unto the city where the man of God was.

11 ¶And as they went up the hill to the city, they found young maidens going out to draw water, and said unto them, Is the seer here?

12 And they answered them, and said, He is; behold, he is before you: make haste now, for he came to day to the city; for there is a sacrifice of the people to day in the high place:[12]

13 As soon as ye be come into the city, ye shall straightway find him, before he go up to the high place to eat: for the people will not eat until he come, because he doth bless the sacrifice;[13] and afterwards they eat that be bidden. Now therefore get you up; for about this time ye shall find him.

14 And they went up into the city: and when they were come into the city, behold, Samuel came out against them, for to go up to the high place.

15 ¶Now the Lord had told Samuel in his ear a day before Saul came, saying,

16 To morrow about this time I will send thee a man out of

12. Altars and places of worship were often located on hilltops.
13. Samuel also exercised priestly functions.

the land of Benjamin, and thou shalt anoint him to be captain over my people Israel, that he may save my people out of the hand of the Philistines: for I have looked upon my people, because their cry is come unto me.

17 And when Samuel saw Saul, the Lord said unto him, Behold the man whom I spake to thee of! this same shall reign over my people.

18 Then Saul drew near to Samuel in the gate, and said, Tell me, I pray thee, where the seer's house is.

19 And Samuel answered Saul, and said, I am the seer: go up before me unto the high place; for ye shall eat with me to day, and to morrow I will let thee go, and will tell thee all that is in thine heart.

20 And as for thine asses that were lost three days ago, set not thy mind on them; for they are found. And on whom is all the desire of Israel? Is it not on thee, and on all thy father's house?

21 And Saul answered and said, Am not I a Benjamite, of the smallest of the tribes of Israel? and my family the least of all the families of the tribe of Benjamin?[14] wherefore then speakest thou so to me?

22 And Samuel took Saul and his servant, and brought them into the parlour, and made them sit in the chiefest place among them that were bidden, which were about thirty persons.

23 And Samuel said unto the cook, Bring the portion which I gave thee, of which I said unto thee, Set it by thee.

24 And the cook took up the shoulder, and that which was upon it, and set it before Saul. And Samuel said, Behold that which is left! set it before thee, and eat: for unto this time hath it been kept for thee since I said, I have invited the people. So Saul did eat with Samuel that day.

25 ¶And when they were come down from the high place into the city, Samuel communed with Saul upon the top of the house.

14. I.e., Saul was unsupported by a powerful tribe or influential family.

26   And they arose early: and it came to pass about the spring of the day,[15] that Samuel called Saul to the top of the house, saying, Up, that I may send thee away. And Saul arose, and they went out both of them, he and Samuel, abroad.

27   And as they were going down to the end of the city, Samuel said to Saul, Bid the servant pass on before us (and he passed on)[16] but stand thou still a while, that I may shew thee the word of God.

Chapter 10

1   ¶Then Samuel took a vial of oil, and poured it upon his head, and kissed him, and said, Is it not because the Lord hath anointed thee to be captain over his inheritance?[17]

2   When thou art departed from me to day, then thou shalt find two men by Rachel's sepulchre in the border of Benjamin at Zelzah; and they will say unto thee, The asses which thou wentest to seek are found: and, lo, thy father hath left the care of the asses, and sorroweth for you, saying, What shall I do for my son?

3   Then shalt thou go on forward from thence, and thou shalt come to the plain of Tabor, and there shall meet thee three men going up to God to Bethel, one carrying three kids, and another carrying three loaves of bread, and another carrying a bottle of wine:

4   And they will salute thee, and give thee two loaves of bread: which thou shalt receive of their hands.

5   After that thou shalt come to the hill of God, where is the garrison of the Philistines: and it shall come to pass, when thou art come thither to the city, that thou shalt meet a company of prophets coming down from the high place with a psaltery, and a tabret, and a pipe, and a harp, before them; and they shall prophesy:

6   And the Spirit of the Lord will come upon thee, and thou

15. Break of dawn.
16. The anointing of Saul as king was to remain secret for a while.
17. The ceremony of anointing was the sign and seal of divine choice.

shalt prophesy with them, and shalt be turned into another man.[18]

7   And let it be, when these signs are come unto thee, that thou do as occasion serve thee; for God is with thee.

8   And thou shalt go down before me to Gilgal;[19] and, behold, I will come down unto thee, to offer burnt offerings, and to sacrifice sacrifices of peace offerings: seven days shalt thou tarry, till I come to thee, and shew thee what thou shalt do.

9   ¶And it was so, that when he had turned his back to go from Samuel, God gave him another heart: and all those signs came to pass that day.

10 And when they came thither to the hill, behold, a company of prophets met him; and the Spirit of God came upon him, and he prophesied among them.

11 And it came to pass, when all that knew him beforetime saw that, behold, he prophesied among the prophets, then the people said one to another, What is this that is come unto the son of Kish? Is Saul also among the prophets?

12 And one of the same place answered and said, But who is their father? Therefore it became a proverb, Is Saul also among the prophets?

13 And when he had made an end of prophesying, he came to the high place.

14 ¶And Saul's uncle said unto him and to his servant, Whither went ye? And he said, To seek the asses: and when we saw that they were no where, we came to Samuel.

15 And Saul's uncle said, Tell me, I pray thee, what Samuel said unto you.

16 And Saul said unto his uncle, He told us plainly that the asses were found. But of the matter of the kingdom, whereof Samuel spake, he told him not.

---

18. The bread (v. 4) and the gift of prophesy (v. 6) were to be the proof that Saul was God's choice. "Another man" refers to the conversion which was to prepare Saul for the kingship.

19. Here the central shrine of the twelve-tribe confederacy of Israel, and later the rallying point for resistance in Saul's wars with the Philistines.

17 ¶And Samuel called the people together unto the Lord to Mizpeh;

18 And said unto the children of Israel, Thus saith the Lord God of Israel, I brought up Israel out of Egypt, and delivered you out of the hand of the Egyptians, and out of the hand of all kingdoms, and of them that oppressed you:

19 And ye have this day rejected your God, who himself saved you out of all your adversities and your tribulations; and ye have said unto him, Nay, but set a king over us. Now therefore present yourselves before the Lord by your tribes, and by your thousands.

20 And when Samuel had caused all the tribes of Israel to come near, the tribe of Benjamin was taken.[20]

21 When he had caused the tribe of Benjamin to come near by their families, the family of Matri was taken, and Saul the son of Kish was taken: and when they sought him, he could not be found.

22 Therefore they enquired of the Lord further, if the man should yet come thither. And the Lord answered, Behold, he hath hid himself among the stuff.[21]

23 And they ran and fetched him thence: and when he stood among the people, he was higher than any of the people from his shoulders and upward.[22]

24 And Samuel said to all the people, See ye him whom the Lord hath chosen, that there is none like him among all the people? And all the people shouted, and said, God save the king.

25 Then Samuel told the people the manner of the kingdom,[23] and wrote it in a book, and laid it up before the Lord. And Samuel sent all the people away, every man to his house.

26 ¶And Saul also went home to Gibeah[24]; and there went with

20. Chosen by casting lots.
21. The baggage. This hiding was a sign of Saul's humility.
22. I.e., Saul was the strongest man in Israel, and thus a natural leader in war.
23. The rights and duties of the kingship.
24. A place just north of Jerusalem.

him a band of men, whose hearts God had touched.

27 But the children of Belial[25] said, How shall this man save
us? And they despised him, and brought him no presents. But he held his peace.

Chapter 11

1 ¶Then Nahash the Ammonite[26] came up, and encamped
against Jabesh-gilead[27]: and all the men of Jabesh said
unto Nahash, Make a covenant with us, and we will
serve thee.

2 And Nahash the Ammonite answered them, On this condition will I make a covenant with you, that I may
thrust out all your right eyes, and lay it for a reproach
upon all Israel.

3 And the elders of Jabesh said unto him, Give us seven days'
respite, that we may send messengers unto all the
coasts of Israel: and then, if there be no man to save
us, we will come out to thee.[28]

4 ¶Then came the messengers to Gibeah of Saul, and told
the tidings in the ears of the people: and all the people
lifted up their voices, and wept.

5 And, behold, Saul came after the herd out of the field; and
Saul said, What aileth the people that they weep? And
they told him the tidings of the men of Jabesh.

6 And the Spirit of God came upon Saul when he heard
those tidings, and his anger was kindled greatly.

7 And he took a yoke of oxen, and hewed them in pieces, and
sent them throughout all the coasts of Israel by the
hands of messengers, saying, Whosoever cometh not
forth after Saul and after Samuel, so shall it be done
unto his oxen. And the fear of the Lord fell on the
people, and they came out with one consent.

25. I.e., wicked or worthless people. "Belial" probably means "land without
return," or "perdition."
26. Ammon was the region around the site of present-day Amman (Transjordan).
27. A place east of the Jordan River, just north of the hills of Ephraim.
28. I.e., the men of Jabesh were uncertain what help would come from the
loosely organized and scattered Israelite tribes.

8   And when he numbered them in Bezek, the children of
      Israel were three hundred thousand, and the men of
      Judah thirty thousand.

9   And they said unto the messengers that came, Thus shall
      ye say unto the men of Jabesh-gilead, To morrow, by
      that time the sun be hot, ye shall have help. And the
      messengers came and shewed it to the men of Jabesh;
      and they were glad.

10   Therefore the men of Jabesh said, To morrow we will come
      out unto you, and ye shall do with us all that seemeth
      good unto you.

11   And it was so on the morrow, that Saul put the people in
      three companies; and they came into the midst of the
      host in the morning watch, and slew the Ammonites
      until the heat of the day: and it came to pass, that they
      which remained were scattered, so that two of them
      were not left together.

12   ¶And the people said unto Samuel, Who is he that said,
      Shall Saul reign over us? bring the men, that we may
      put them to death.

13   And Saul said, There shall not a man be put to death this
      day: for to day the Lord hath wrought salvation in
      Israel.

14   Then said Samuel to the people, Come, and let us go to
      Gilgal, and renew the kingdom there.

15   And all the people went to Gilgal; and there they made
      Saul king before the Lord in Gilgal;[29] and there they
      sacrificed sacrifices of peace offerings before the Lord;
      and there Saul and all the men of Israel rejoiced
      greatly.

· · · · · · · · · · · · · · · · ·

Chapter 14

47   ¶So Saul took the kingdom over Israel, and fought against
      all his enemies on every side, against Moab,[30] and

29. I.e., Saul's success in battle secured the acceptance of his kingship by all
Israel.
30. A region southeast of the Dead Sea.

against the children of Ammon, and against Edom,[31] and against the kings of Zobah,[32] and against the Philistines:[33] and whithersoever he turned himself, he vexed them.

48   And he gathered an host, and smote the Amalekites,[34] and delivered Israel out of the hands of them that spoiled them.

. . . .

52   And there was sore war against the Philistines all the days of Saul: and when Saul saw any strong man, or any valiant man, he took him unto him.

Chapter 15

1   ¶Samuel also said unto Saul, The Lord sent me to anoint thee to be king over his people, over Israel: now therefore hearken thou unto the voice of the words of the Lord.

2   Thus saith the Lord of hosts, I remember that which Amalek did to Israel, how he laid wait for him in the way, when he came up from Egypt.

3   Now go and smite Amalek, and utterly destroy all that they have, and spare them not; but slay both man and woman, infant and suckling, ox and sheep, camel and ass.[35]

4   And Saul gathered the people together, and numbered them in Telaim, two hundred thousand footmen, and ten thousand men of Judah.

5   And Saul came to a city of Amalek, and laid wait in the valley.

6   ¶And Saul said unto the Kenites,[36] Go, depart, get you down

31. The region of southern Palestine around Beersheba.
32. An Aramaean state in Syria.
33. A people occupying the coastal region of Palestine.
34. Or Amalek: a tribe that roamed over the region between southern Palestine and Egypt.
35. The entire Amalekite nation and all its property were to be a sacrifice to God—a primitive custom later explained as a means of keeping the Israelites from intermixture with pagans.
36. A nomadic people closely associated with the Amalekites.

from among the Amalekites, lest I destroy you with them: for ye shewed kindness to all the children of Israel, when they came up out of Egypt. So the Kenites departed from among the Amalekites.

7   And Saul smote the Amalekites from Havilah until thou comest to Shur,[37] that is over against Egypt.

8   And he took Agag the king of the Amalekites alive, and utterly destroyed all the people with the edge of the sword.[38]

9   But Saul and the people spared Agag, and the best of the sheep, and of the oxen, and of the fatlings, and the lambs, and all that was good, and would not utterly destroy them: but every thing that was vile and refuse, that they destroyed utterly.

10   ¶Then came the word of the Lord unto Samuel, saying,

11   It repenteth me that I have set up Saul to be king: for he is turned back from following me, and hath not performed my commandments. And it grieved Samuel; and he cried unto the Lord all night.

12   And when Samuel rose early to meet Saul in the morning, it was told Samuel, saying, Saul came to Carmel,[39] and, behold, he set him up a place, and is gone about, and passed on, and gone to Gilgal.

13   And Samuel came to Saul: and Saul said unto him, Blessed be thou of the Lord: I have performed the commandment of the Lord.

14   And Samuel said, What meaneth then this bleating of the sheep in mine ears, and the lowing of the oxen which I hear?

15   And Saul said, They have brought them from the Amal-

---

37. Havilah: a region of Arabia somewhat difficult to locate, probably not the name of a well-defined territory, but of a tribe or people. Shur: a place or district on the northeast border of Egypt.

38. There is no historical evidence that the Amalekite nation was destroyed in Saul's time. They were still a strong and independent people a few years later in the reign of King David, according to I Sam. 27:8, 30:1, and 30:18, and II Sam. 1:1.

39. The hilly region to the south of the Bay of Acre (now Bay of Haifa), proverbial for its beauty and fruitfulness.

ekites: for the people spared the best of the sheep and
of the oxen, to sacrifice unto the Lord thy God; and
the rest we have utterly destroyed.

16   Then Samuel said unto Saul, Stay, and I will tell thee what
the Lord hath said to me this night. And he said unto
him, Say on.

17   And Samuel said, When thou wast little in thine own sight,
wast thou not made the head of the tribes of Israel, and
the Lord anointed thee king over Israel?

18   And the Lord sent thee on a journey, and said, Go and
utterly destroy the sinners the Amalekites, and fight
against them until they be consumed.

19   Wherefore then didst thou not obey the voice of the Lord,
but didst fly upon the spoil, and didst evil in the sight
of the Lord?

20   And Saul said unto Samuel, Yea, I have obeyed the voice
of the Lord, and have gone the way which the Lord
sent me, and have brought Agag the king of Amalek,
and have utterly destroyed the Amalekites.

21   But the people took of the spoil, sheep and oxen, the chief
of the things which should have been utterly destroyed, to sacrifice unto the Lord thy God in Gilgal.

22   And Samuel said,
          Hath the Lord as great delight in burnt offerings and
                sacrifices,
          as in obeying the voice of the Lord?
          Behold, to obey is better than sacrifice,
          and to hearken than the fat of rams.

23   For rebellion is as the sin of witchcraft,
          and stubbornness is as iniquity and idolatry.
      Because thou hast rejected the word of the Lord, he hath also
          rejected thee from being king.

24   ¶And Saul said unto Samuel, I have sinned: for I have
transgressed the commandment of the Lord, and thy
words: because I feared the people, and obeyed their
voice.

25   Now therefore, I pray thee, pardon my sin, and turn again
with me, that I may worship the Lord.

26 And Samuel said unto Saul, I will not return with thee: for
        thou hast rejected the word of the Lord, and the Lord
        hath rejected thee from being king over Israel.

27 And as Samuel turned about to go away, he laid hold upon
        the skirt of his mantle, and it rent.

28 And Samuel said unto him, The Lord hath rent the king-
        dom of Israel from thee this day, and hath given it to
        a neighbour of thine, that is better than thou.

29 And also the Strength of Israel will not lie nor repent:[40]
        for he is not a man, that he should repent.

30 Then he said, I have sinned: yet honour me now, I pray
        thee, before the elders of my people, and before Israel,
        and turn again with me, that I may worship the Lord
        thy God.[41]

31 So Samuel turned again after Saul; and Saul worshipped
        the Lord.

32 ¶Then said Samuel, Bring ye hither to me Agag the king
        of the Amalekites. And Agag came unto him deli-
        cately. And Agag said, Surely the bitterness of death
        is past.

33 And Samuel said, As thy sword hath made women child-
        less, so shall thy mother be childless among women.
        And Samuel hewed Agag in pieces before the Lord in
        Gilgal.

34 ¶Then Samuel went to Ramah; and Saul went up to his
        house to Gibeah of Saul.

35 And Samuel came no more to see Saul until the day of his
        death; nevertheless Samuel mourned for Saul: and the
        Lord repented that he had made Saul king over Israel.

40. I.e., God will not change his mind.
41. Saul accepts responsibility for his disobedience, but asks permission to
continue in the kingship and share in the worship.

FROM THE SECOND BOOK OF SAMUEL

The intervening passages relate that the Lord now chose a king for Israel from among the sons of Jesse. This was the future King David, who became first the servant and then the rival of Saul. After Saul's death, "there was a long war between the house of Saul and the house of David: but David waxed stronger and stronger, and the house of Saul waxed weaker and weaker" (II Sam. 3:1). Subsequently David was recognized as king by all the tribes of Israel.

No king of Israel was more fortunate than David, or has so captured the imagination of the Hebrew people. Yet, as the following selection shows, even he possessed human frailties and was not exempt from the punishment of the Lord.

Chapter 11

1   ¶And it came to pass, after the year was expired, at the time when kings go forth to battle, that David sent Joab, and his servants with him, and all Israel; and they destroyed the children of Ammon,[1] and besieged Rabbah.[2] But David tarried still at Jerusalem.

2   ¶And it came to pass in an eveningtide, that David arose from off his bed, and walked upon the roof of the king's house: and from the roof he saw a woman washing herself; and the woman was very beautiful to look upon.

3   And David sent and enquired after the woman. And one said, Is not this Bathsheba, the daughter of Eliam, the wife of Uriah the Hittite?

4   And David sent messengers, and took her; and she came in unto him, and he lay with her; for she was purified from her uncleanness:[3] and she returned unto her house.

5   And the woman conceived, and sent and told David, and said, I am with child.

II Samuel 11:1—12:25, King James Bible.
  1. Inhabitants of the region around present-day Amman in Transjordan.
  2. The capital city of the Ammonites.
  3. In the sense of (ceremonial) defilement or pollution.

6   ¶And David sent to Joab, saying, Send me Uriah the Hit-
     tite. And Joab sent Uriah to David.

7   And when Uriah was come unto him, David demanded of
     him how Joab did, and how the people did, and how
     the war prospered.

8   And David said to Uriah, Go down to thy house, and wash
     thy feet. And Uriah departed out of the king's house,
     and there followed him a mess of meat from the king.

9   But Uriah slept at the door of the king's house with all the
     servants of his lord, and went not down to his house.

10   And when they had told David, saying, Uriah went not
     down unto his house, David said unto Uriah, Camest
     thou not from thy journey? why then didst thou not
     go down unto thine house?

11   And Uriah said unto David, The ark, and Israel, and Ju-
     dah, abide in tents; and my lord Joab, and the servants
     of my lord, are encamped in the open fields; shall I
     then go into mine house, to eat and to drink, and to lie
     with my wife? as thou livest, and as thy soul liveth, I
     will not do this thing.

12   And David said to Uriah, Tarry here to day also, and to
     morrow I will let thee depart. So Uriah abode in Jeru-
     salem that day, and the morrow.

13   And when David had called him, he did eat and drink be-
     fore him; and he made him drunk; and at even he
     went out to lie on his bed with the servants of his lord,
     but went not down to his house.

14   ¶And it came to pass in the morning, that David wrote a
     letter to Joab, and sent it by the hand of Uriah.

15   And he wrote in the letter, saying, Set ye Uriah in the fore-
     front of the hottest battle, and retire ye from him, that
     he may be smitten, and die.

16   And it came to pass, when Joab observed the city, that he
     assigned Uriah unto a place where he knew that vali-
     ant men were.

17   And the men of the city went out, and fought with Joab,
     and there fell some of the people of the servants of
     David; and Uriah the Hittite died also.

18   ¶Then Joab sent and told David all the things concerning
      the war;

19   And charged the messenger, saying, When thou hast made
      an end of telling the matters of the war unto the king,

20   And if so be that the king's wrath arise, and he say unto
      thee, Wherefore approached ye so nigh unto the city
      when ye did fight? knew ye not that they would shoot
      from the wall?

21   Who smote Abimelech the son of Jerubbesheth? did not a
      woman cast a piece of a millstone upon him from the
      wall, that he died in Thebez?[4] why went ye nigh the
      wall? then say thou, Thy servant Uriah the Hittite is
      dead also.

22   ¶So the messenger went, and came and shewed David all
      that Joab had sent him for.

23   And the messenger said unto David, Surely the men pre-
      vailed against us, and came out unto us into the field,
      and we were upon them even unto the entering of the
      gate.

24   And the shooters shot from off the wall upon thy servants;
      and some of the king's servants be dead, and thy serv-
      ant Uriah the Hittite is dead also.

25   Then David said unto the messenger, Thus shalt thou say
      unto Joab, Let not this thing displease thee, for the
      sword devoureth one as well as another: make thy
      battle more strong against the city, and overthrow it:
      and encourage thou him.

26   ¶And when the wife of Uriah heard that Uriah her hus-
      band was dead, she mourned for her husband.

27   And when the mourning was past, David sent and fetched
      her to his house, and she became his wife, and bare
      him a son. But the thing that David had done dis-
      pleased the Lord.

4. This incident is recounted in Judges 9:50-56. Thebez was a town of
northern Samaria.

Chapter 12

1   ¶And the Lord sent Nathan[5] unto David. And he came unto
    him, and said unto him, There were two men in one
    city; the one rich, and the other poor.

2   The rich man had exceeding many flocks and herds:

3   But the poor man had nothing, save one little ewe lamb,
    which he had bought and nourished up: and it grew
    up together with him, and with his children; it did eat
    of his own meat, and drank of his own cup, and lay in
    his bosom, and was unto him as a daughter.

4   And there came a traveller unto the rich man, and he
    spared to take of his own flock and of his own herd, to
    dress for the wayfaring man that was come unto him;
    but took the poor man's lamb, and dressed it for the
    man that was come to him.

5   And David's anger was greatly kindled against the man;
    and he said to Nathan, As the Lord liveth, the man
    that hath done this thing shall surely die:

6   And he shall restore the lamb fourfold, because he did this
    thing, and because he had no pity.

7   ¶And Nathan said to David, Thou art the man. Thus saith
    the Lord God of Israel, I anointed thee king over Is-
    rael, and I delivered thee out of the hand of Saul;

8   And I gave thee thy master's house, and thy master's wives
    into thy bosom, and gave thee the house of Israel and
    of Judah; and if that had been too little, I would more-
    over have given unto thee such and such things.

9   Wherefore hast thou despised the commandment of the
    Lord, to do evil in his sight? thou hast killed Uriah
    the Hittite with the sword, and hast taken his wife to
    be thy wife, and hast slain him with the sword of the
    children of Ammon.

10 Now therefore the sword shall never depart from thine
    house; because thou hast despised me, and hast taken
    the wife of Uriah the Hittite to be thy wife.

5. One of the prophets.

11 Thus saith the Lord, Behold, I will raise up evil against thee out of thine own house, and I will take thy wives before thine eyes, and give them unto thy neighbour, and he shall lie with thy wives in the sight of this sun.

12 For thou didst it secretly: but I will do this thing before all Israel, and before the sun.

13 And David said unto Nathan, I have sinned against the Lord. And Nathan said unto David, The Lord also hath put away thy sin; thou shalt not die.[6]

14 Howbeit, because by this deed thou hast given great occasion to the enemies of the Lord to blaspheme, the child also that is born unto thee shall surely die.

15 ¶And Nathan departed unto his house. And the Lord struck the child that Uriah's wife bare unto David, and it was very sick.

16 David therefore besought God for the child; and David fasted, and went in, and lay all night upon the earth.

17 And the elders of his house arose, and went to him, to raise him up from the earth: but he would not, neither did he eat bread with them.

18 And it came to pass on the seventh day, that the child died. And the servants of David feared to tell him that the child was dead; for they said, Behold, while the child was yet alive, we spake unto him, and he would not hearken unto our voice: how will he then vex himself, if we tell him that the child is dead?

19 But when David saw that his servants whispered, David perceived that the child was dead: therefore David said unto his servants, Is the child dead? And they said, He is dead.

20 Then David arose from the earth, and washed, and anointed himself, and changed his apparel, and came into the house of the Lord, and worshipped: then he came to his own house; and when he required, they set bread before him, and he did eat.

21 Then said his servants unto him, What thing is this that

---

6. I.e., the Lord has pardoned David, but has not freed him of all penalty.

thou hast done? thou didst fast and weep for the child, while it was alive; but when the child was dead, thou didst rise and eat bread.

22 And he said, While the child was yet alive, I fasted and wept: for I said, Who can tell whether God will be gracious to me, that the child may live?

23 But now he is dead, wherefore should I fast? can I bring him back again? I shall go to him,[7] but he shall not return to me.

24 ¶And David comforted Bathsheba his wife, and went in unto her, and lay with her: and she bare a son, and he called his name Solomon: and the Lord loved him.

25 And he sent by the hand of Nathan the prophet; and he called his name Jedidiah,[8] because of the Lord.

7. I.e., join him in the world of the dead.
8. "Beloved of Yahweh." "Solomon" may have been a throne name.

Introduction to I Kings

The First Book of Kings (which originally formed a unit with II Kings) recounts the history of the Hebrew people during the four-hundred-year period following the death of King David (*ca.* 970 B.C.). It was first compiled around 600 B.C. by an unknown author; but additional material was probably added after 561 B.C., the last date referred to in the book. The compiler drew upon various official archives, which he mentions: "the book of the chronicles of the kings of Israel" (I Kings 14:19), "the book of the chronicles of the kings of Judah" (I Kings 14:29), and "the book of the acts of Solomon" (I Kings 11:41). In addition, he undoubtedly utilized the oral traditions of his people and the records of Temple services kept since the time of King Solomon.

The following selections deal with various aspects of the reign of Solomon, who presided over the Hebrew kingdom at the period of its greatest glory. They show him as a ruler not only renowned for his wisdom, but also anxious to eliminate rivals to his throne. The wealth of Solomon was famous far and wide. He concluded an alliance with Hiram, king of Tyre; and his commercial contacts extended throughout the Near East. Indeed, scholars have speculated that the ivory, apes, and peacocks mentioned in 10:22 may have come from distant India. Solomon's kingdom, though small when measured against the great empires of the ancient East, was greater in extent than any Jewish state would be again.

FROM THE FIRST BOOK OF KINGS

Chapter 2

12 ¶Then sat Solomon upon the throne of David his father; and his kingdom was established greatly.

13 ¶And Adonijah the son of Haggith came to Bathsheba the mother of Solomon. And she said, Comest thou peaceably? And he said, Peaceably.

14 He said moreover, I have somewhat to say unto thee. And she said, Say on.

15 And he said, Thou knowest that the kingdom was mine, and that all Israel set their faces on me, that I should reign: howbeit the kingdom is turned about, and is become my brother's: for it was his from the Lord.

16 And now I ask one petition of thee, deny me not. And she said unto him, Say on.

17 And he said, Speak, I pray thee, unto Solomon the king, (for he will not say thee nay), that he give me Abishag the Shunammite to wife.

18 And Bathsheba said, Well; I will speak for thee unto the king.

19 ¶Bathsheba therefore went unto king Solomon, to speak unto him for Adonijah. And the king rose up to meet her, and bowed himself unto her, and sat down on his throne, and caused a seat to be set for the king's mother; and she sat on his right hand.

20 Then she said, I desire one small petition of thee; I pray thee, say me not nay. And the king said unto her, Ask on, my mother: for I will not say thee nay.

I Kings 2:12-35; 4:20-25; 5:1-18; 10:14-29, King James Bible.

21 And she said, Let Abishag the Shunammite be given to Adonijah thy brother to wife.

22 And king Solomon answered and said unto his mother, And why dost thou ask Abishag the Shunammite for Adonijah? ask for him the kingdom also; for he is mine elder brother; even for him, and for Abiathar the priest, and for Joab the son of Zeruiah.[1]

23 Then king Solomon sware by the Lord, saying, God do so to me, and more also, if Adonijah have not spoken this word against his own life.

24 Now therefore, as the Lord liveth, which hath established me, and set me on the throne of David my father, and who hath made me an house, as he promised, Adonijah shall be put to death this day.

25 And king Solomon sent by the hand of Benaiah the son of Jehoiada; and he fell upon him that he died.

26 ¶And unto Abiathar the priest said the king, Get thee to Anathoth, unto thine own fields; for thou art worthy of death: but I will not at this time put thee to death, because thou barest the ark of the Lord God before David my father, and because thou hast been afflicted in all wherein my father was afflicted.

27 So Solomon thrust out Abiathar from being priest unto the Lord; that he might fulfil the word of the Lord, which he spake concerning the house of Eli in Shiloh.

28 ¶Then tidings came to Joab, for Joab had turned after Adonijah, though he turned not after Absalom.[2] And Joab fled unto the tabernacle of the Lord, and caught hold on the horns of the altar.[3]

29 And it was told king Solomon that Joab was fled unto the tabernacle of the Lord; and, behold, he is by the altar. Then Solomon sent Benaiah the son of Jehoiada, saying, Go, fall upon him.

1. This request aroused Solomon's suspicion of his brother; for the proposed marriage would strengthen the latter's claim to the throne. Joab was the commander-in-chief of the army under Solomon's father, David.

2. The son of King David, who had rebelled against his father.

3. According to Hebrew law, the right of sanctuary must be respected except in cases of intentional homicide.

30   And Benaiah came to the tabernacle of the Lord, and said
          unto him, Thus saith the king, Come forth. And he
          said, Nay; but I will die here. And Benaiah brought
          the king word again, saying, Thus said Joab, and thus
          he answered me.

31   And the king said unto him, Do as he hath said, and fall
          upon him, and bury him; that thou mayest take away
          the innocent blood, which Joab shed, from me, and
          from the house of my father.

32   And the Lord shall return his blood upon his own head,
          who fell upon two men more righteous and better
          than he, and slew them with the sword, my father
          David not knowing thereof, to wit, Abner the son of
          Ner, captain of the host of Israel, and Amasa the son
          of Jether, captain of the host of Judah.[4]

33   Their blood shall therefore return upon the head of Joab,
          and upon the head of his seed for ever: but upon
          David, and upon his seed, and upon his house, and
          upon his throne, shall there be peace for ever from the
          Lord.

34   So Benaiah the son of Jehoiada went up, and fell upon him,
          and slew him: and he was buried in his own house in
          the wilderness.

35   ¶And the king put Benaiah the son of Jehoiada in his room
          over the host:[5] and Zadok the priest did the king put
          in the room of Abiathar.

.   .   .   .

Chapter 4

20   ¶Judah and Israel were many, as the sand which is by the
          sea in multitude, eating and drinking, and making
          merry.

21   And Solomon reigned over all kingdoms from the river[6]
          unto the land of the Philistines, and unto the border of

4. This incident is related in II. Sam. 3:22-30. In the war of succession between David and the son of Saul, Abner was the captain of the latter's forces.
5. I.e., Benaiah succeeded Joab as commander of the army.
6. The river Euphrates.

Egypt: they brought presents, and served Solomon all the days of his life.

22 ¶And Solomon's provision for one day was thirty measures of fine flour, and threescore measures of meal.

23 Ten fat oxen, and twenty oxen out of the pastures, and an hundred sheep, beside harts, and roebucks, and fallow-deer, and fatted fowl.

24 For he had dominion over all the region on this side the river, from Tiphsah[7] even to Azzah,[8] over all the kings on this side the river: and he had peace on all sides round about him.

25 And Judah and Israel dwelt safely, every man under his vine and under his fig tree, from Dan even to Beer-sheba,[9] all the days of Solomon.

· · · · · · · · · · · · · · · · · · ·

Chapter 5

1 ¶And Hiram king of Tyre sent his servants unto Solomon; for he had heard that they had anointed him king in the room of his father: for Hiram was ever a lover of David.

2 And Solomon sent to Hiram, saying,

3 Thou knowest how that David my father could not build an house unto the name of the Lord his God for the wars which were about him on every side, until the Lord put them under the soles of his feet.

4 But now the Lord my God hath given me rest on every side, so that there is neither adversary nor evil occurrent.

5 And, behold, I purpose to build an house unto the name of the Lord my God, as the Lord spake unto David my father, saying, Thy son, whom I will set upon thy throne in thy room, he shall build an house unto my name.

6 Now therefore command thou that they hew me cedar trees

7. A town on the Euphrates.
8. Gaza (southwestern Palestine).
9. Dan was a city at the northern tip of Palestine; Beersheba the southern boundary of the settled land.

out of Lebanon; and my servants shall be with thy
servants: and unto thee will I give hire for thy servants according to all that thou shalt appoint: for thou
knowest that there is not among us any that can skill
to hew timber like unto the Sidonians.[10]

7   ¶And it came to pass, when Hiram heard the words of Solomon, that he rejoiced greatly, and said, Blessed be the
Lord this day, which hath given unto David a wise son
over this great people.

8   And Hiram sent to Solomon, saying, I have considered the
things which thou sentest to me for: and I will do all
thy desire concerning timber of cedar, and concerning
timber of fir.

9   My servants shall bring them down from Lebanon unto the
sea: and I will convey them by sea in floats unto the
place that thou shalt appoint me, and will cause them
to be discharged there, and thou shalt receive them:
and thou shalt accomplish my desire, in giving food
for my household.

10   So Hiram gave Solomon cedar trees and fir trees according
to all his desire.

11   And Solomon gave Hiram twenty thousand measures of
wheat for food to his household, and twenty measures
of pure oil: thus gave Solomon to Hiram year by year.

12   And the Lord gave Solomon wisdom, as he promised him:
and there was peace between Hiram and Solomon; and
they two made a league together.

13   ¶And king Solomon raised a levy[11] out of all Israel; and the
levy was thirty thousand men.

14   And he sent them to Lebanon, ten thousand a month by
courses: a month they were in Lebanon, and two
months at home: and Adoniram was over the levy.

15   And Solomon had threescore and ten thousand that bare
burdens, and fourscore thousand hewers in the mountains;

16   Beside the chief of Solomon's officers which were over the

10. Sidon was a city of ancient Phoenicia subject to Hiram.
11. I.e., forced labor.

work, three thousand and three hundred, which ruled over the people that wrought in the work.

17 And the king commanded, and they brought great stones, costly stones, and hewed stones, to lay the foundation of the house.

18 And Solomon's builders and Hiram's builders did hew them, and the stonesquarers: so they prepared timber and stones to build the house.

. . . .

Chapter 10

14 ¶Now the weight of gold that came to Solomon in one year was six hundred threescore and six talents of gold.

15 Beside that he had of the merchantmen, and of the traffick of the spice merchants, and of all the kings of Arabia, and of the governors of the country.

16 ¶And king Solomon made two hundred targets of beaten gold: six hundred shekels of gold went to one target.

17 And he made three hundred shields of beaten gold; three pound of gold went to one shield: and the king put them in the house of the forest of Lebanon.

18 ¶Moreover the king made a great throne of ivory, and overlaid it with the best gold.

19 The throne had six steps, and the top of the throne was round behind: and there were stays on either side on the place of the seat, and two lions stood beside the stays.

20 And twelve lions stood there on the one side and on the other upon the six steps; there was not the like made in any kingdom.

21 ¶And all king Solomon's drinking vessels were of gold, and all the vessels of the house of the forest of Lebanon were of pure gold; none were of silver: it was nothing accounted of in the days of Solomon.

22 For the king had at sea a navy of Tharshish[12] with the navy

12. (Tarshish): probably a Phoenician colony in southern Spain. Large commercial ships which made long journeys were frequently called "ships of Tarshish."

of Hiram: once in three years came the navy of
Tharshish, bringing gold, and silver, ivory, and apes,
and peacocks.

23 So king Solomon exceeded all the kings of the earth for
riches and for wisdom.

24 ¶And all the earth sought to Solomon, to hear his wisdom,
which God had put in his heart.

25 And they brought every man his present, vessels of silver,
and vessels of gold, and garments, and armour, and
spices, horses, and mules, a rate year by year.

26 ¶And Solomon gathered together chariots and horsemen:
and he had a thousand and four hundred chariots, and
twelve thousand horsemen, whom he bestowed in the
cities for chariots, and with the king at Jerusalem.

27 And the king made silver to be in Jerusalem as stones,
and cedars made he to be as the sycamore trees that are in
the vale, for abundance.

28 ¶And Solomon had horses brought out of Egypt, and linen
yarn: the king's merchants received the linen yarn at
a price.

29 And a chariot came up and went out of Egypt for six hundred shekels of silver, and an horse for an hundred
and fifty: and so for all the kings of the Hittites, and
for the kings of Syria, did they bring them out by their
means.

Introduction to Isaiah

The prophet Isaiah must have been at least three persons. The Isaiah
of chapters 1-39 began his career in 740 B.C., the year of King Uz-
ziah's death; and we hear of him at intervals afterward, down to
the siege of Jerusalem in 701 B.C. The prophet of chapters 40-55
(sometimes known as Second Isaiah) flourished in a different setting, probably Babylonia shortly before its conquest by Cyrus the

Persian in 539 B.C. His message is one of hope to a people exiled from their native land. The Isaiah of chapters 56-66 seems to have flourished in Jerusalem in the middle of the fifth century B.C., after the return of the Jews from their Babylonian exile.

In the time of the First Isaiah, from whom the following selection is taken, the chief threat to Hebrew independence was Assyria. Beginning with Tiglath-pileser III (reigned 744-727 B.C.), Assyria had made giant strides southwestward from its base in northern Mesopotamia. In 734 B.C. the Assyrians extinguished the northern Hebrew kingdom of Israel and deported part of its population. To the south, little Judah attempted to maintain an independence of sorts by allying itself with Egypt (Isaiah 36:6).

In 701 B.C. Sennacherib, king of Assyria, led a campaign into Phoenicia and Palestine. He devastated the Judean countryside, laid siege to the capital, Jerusalem, and exacted a heavy tribute from the helpless King Hezekiah. Amid this series of disasters, Jerusalem withstood the Assyrian attack—an event so unexpected that it was attributed to the special intervention of the Lord.

The kingdom of Judah survived for over a century more. Indeed, it outlasted once-mighty Assyria. But in 586 B.C. Judah fell victim to another Mesopotamian invader: Nebuchadnezzar II, the Chaldean ruler of a new Babylonian empire, who destroyed Jerusalem and its Temple and inaugurated the Babylonian capitivity of the Jews.

An almost parallel account of Sennacherib's siege of Jerusalem may be found in II Kings 18:13—20:39.

FROM THE BOOK OF ISAIAH

Chapter 36

1 ¶Now it came to pass in the fourteenth year of king Hezekiah, that Sennacherib king of Assyria came up against all the defenced cities of Judah, and took them.

2 And the king of Assyria sent Rabshakeh from Lachish to Jerusalem unto king Hezekiah with a great army. And he stood by the conduit of the upper pool in the highway of the fuller's field.

3 Then came forth unto him Eliakim, Hilkiah's son, which

Isaiah 36:1—37:4, 37:21-2, 28-9, 33-8, King James Bible.

was over the house, and Shebna the scribe, and Joah, Asaph's son, the recorder.

4 ¶And Rabshakeh said unto them, Say ye now to Hezekiah, Thus saith the great king, the king of Assyria, What confidence is this wherein thou trustest?

5 I say, sayest thou, (but they are but vain words) I have counsel and strength for war: now on whom dost thou trust, that thou rebellest against me?

6 Lo, thou trustest in the staff of this broken reed, on Egypt; whereon if a man lean, it will go into his hand, and pierce it: so is Pharaoh king of Egypt to all that trust in him.

7 But if thou say to me, We trust in the Lord our God: is it not he, whose high places and whose altars Hezekiah hath taken away, and said to Judah and to Jerusalem, Ye shall worship before this altar?[1]

8 Now therefore give pledges, I pray thee, to my master the king of Assyria, and I will give thee two thousand horses, if thou be able on thy part to set riders upon them.

9 How then wilt thou turn away the face of one captain of the least of my master's servants, and put thy trust on Egypt for chariots and for horsemen?

10 And am I now come up without the Lord against this land to destroy it? the Lord said unto me, Go up against this land, and destroy it.[2]

11 ¶Then said Eliakim and Shebna and Joah unto Rabshakeh, Speak, I pray thee, unto thy servants in the Syrian language; for we understand it: and speak not to us in the Jews' language, in the ears of the people that are on the wall.

12 ¶But Rabshakeh said, Hath my master sent me to thy mas-

1. This refers to the movement, begun in Hezekiah's time but completed only under King Josiah, to abolish the local shrines which had become centers of idolatry and centralize the worship of Yahweh at the Temple in Jerusalem, where it could be better controlled.

2. The prophets regarded Assyria as the instrument of God's anger: thus they represented the Assyrian leader as asserting that the God of the Hebrews had commanded him to destroy the land of Judah.

ter and to thee to speak these words? hath he not sent me to the men that sit upon the wall, that they may eat their own dung, and drink their own piss with you?

13 Then Rabshakeh stood, and cried with a loud voice in the Jews' language, and said, Hear ye the words of the great king, the king of Assyria.

14 Thus saith the king, Let not Hezekiah deceive you: for he shall not be able to deliver you.

15 Neither let Hezekiah make you trust in the Lord, saying, The Lord will surely deliver us: this city shall not be delivered into the hand of the king of Assyria.

16 Hearken not to Hezekiah: for thus saith the king of Assyria, Make an agreement with me by a present, and come out to me: and eat ye every one of his vine, and every one of his fig tree, and drink ye every one the waters of his own cistern;

17 Until I come and take you away to a land like your own land, a land of corn and wine, a land of bread and vineyards.

18 Beware lest Hezekiah persuade you, saying, The Lord will deliver us. Hath any of the gods of the nations delivered his land out of the hand of the king of Assyria?

19 Where are the gods of Hamath and Arphad? where are the gods of Sepharvaim? and have they delivered Samaria out of my hand?[3]

20 Who are they among all the gods of these lands, that have delivered their land out of my hand, that the Lord should deliver Jerusalem out of my hand?

21 ¶But they held their peace, and answered him not a word: for the king's commandment was, saying, Answer him not.

22 ¶Then came Eliakim, the son of Hilkiah, that was over the household, and Shebna the scribe, and Joah, the son of Asaph, the recorder, to Hezekiah with their clothes rent, and told him the words of Rabshakeh.

3. Because Samaria had refused to pay tribute to Assyria, it was conquered by the Assyrian king Sargon II in 722 B.C. and its people were deported.

Chapter 37

1　¶And it came to pass, when king Hezekiah heard it, that
　　he rent his clothes, and covered himself with sackcloth,
　　and went into the house of the Lord.

2　And he sent Eliakim, who was over the household, and
　　Shebna the scribe, and the elders of the priests cov-
　　ered with sackcloth, unto Isaiah the prophet the son of
　　Amoz.

3　And they said unto him, Thus saith Hezekiah, This day is
　　a day of trouble, and of rebuke, and of blasphemy: for
　　the children are come to the birth, and there is not
　　strength to bring forth.

4　It may be the Lord thy God will hear the words of Rabsha-
　　keh, whom the king of Assyria his master hath sent to
　　reproach the living God, and will reprove the words
　　which the Lord thy God hath heard: wherefore lift up
　　thy prayer for the remnant that is left.

.　.　.　.　.　.　.　.　.　.　.　.　.　.　.　.　.

21　¶Then Isaiah the son of Amoz sent unto Hezekiah, saying,
　　Thus saith the Lord God of Israel, Whereas thou hast
　　prayed to me against Sennacherib king of Assyria:

22　This is the word which the Lord hath spoken concerning
　　him;
　　The virgin, the daughter of Zion,
　　hath despised thee, and laughed thee to scorn;
　　the daughter of Jerusalem
　　hath shaken her head at thee.[4]

.　.　.　.　.　.　.　.　.　.　.　.　.　.　.　.　.

28　But I know thy abode, and thy going out, and thy com-
　　ing in,
　　and thy rage against me.

29　Because thy rage against me,
　　and thy tumult, is come up into mine ears,

4. This is Isaiah's prophecy against Assyria, asserting that the Assyrian king
does not realize that all his powers come from God.

therefore will I put my hook in thy nose,
and my bridle in thy lips,
and I will turn thee back by the way
by which thou camest.

. . . .

33   Therefore thus saith the Lord concerning the king of
           Assyria,
      He shall not come into this city,
      Nor shoot an arrow there,
      nor come before it with shields,
      nor cast a bank against it.
34   By the way that he came,
      by the same shall he return,
      and shall not come into this city,
      saith the Lord.
35   For I will defend this city to save it
      for mine own sake, and for my servant David's sake.
36   Then the angel of the Lord went forth, and smote in the
      camp of the Assyrians a hundred and fourscore and
      five thousand: and when they arose early in the morn-
      ing, behold, they were all dead corpses.
37   ¶So Sennacherib king of Assyria departed, and went and
      returned, and dwelt at Nineveh.
38   And it came to pass, as he was worshipping in the house
      of Nisroch his god, that Adrammelech and Sharezer
      his sons smote him with the sword; and they escaped
      into the land of Armenia: and Esarhaddon his son
      reigned in his stead.[5]

   5. Sennacherib was in fact murdered twenty years after these events, in
681 B.C.

Introduction to I Esdras

The First Book of Esdras belongs among the ancient writings dealing with the history of the Jewish people. It covers events beginning with the passover celebrated by King Josiah in 621 B.C. down to the reforms of the prophet Ezra (*ca.* 398 B.C.). In content it reproduces the Old Testament narrative appearing in II Chronicles (35:1-36—36:23), Ezra, and Nehemiah (7:38—8:12), though certain discrepancies exist between the two versions. I Esdras was probably written sometime late in the second century B.C. The Jewish historian Josephus used it rather than the Old Testament books as his authority for the period.

The term "Apocrypha" in present day usage means different things to Protestants and to Roman Catholics. Catholics apply the term to certain books (called pseudoepigraphical by Protestants) which, though originating in Jewish or Christian circles between about 200 B.C. and A.D. 200, are excluded from any version of the Bible. Protestants regard as apocryphal that group of fifteen books written in the same period which, with one exception, do appear in the Greek edition of the Old Testament (the Septuagint) but which are omitted from the Hebrew canon.

The status of these fifteen books has been much disputed throughout the history of the Christian Church. Most of the early Church Fathers, who knew no Hebrew, accepted without question the entire Greek Septuagint. By the fourth century A.D. leading Christian scholars had become aware of the special status of the fifteen books. No less an authority than St. Jerome, translator of the Latin Vulgate, had strong reservations about including them in the authorized version of Scripture. But during the Middle Ages Jerome's doubts were generally ignored, and Latin churchmen treated all the disputed books as inspired.

The Protestant Reformation, with its revived interest in textual criticism, re-opened the question of the canonicity of these books. Most Protestant Bibles followed the Hebrew text and omitted them. In response, the Council of Trent in 1546 declared all but three of the fifteen books to be fully canonical and pronounced an anathema upon anyone refusing to accept them as such.

Among these three is I Esdras. In Catholic Bibles it now appears as III Esdras in an appendix to the New Testament. Nonetheless, though regarded by both Catholics and Protestants as apocryphal, it is of all the disputed books the one most closely resembling portions of the canonical Old Testament.

FROM THE FIRST BOOK OF ESDRAS

Chapter 1

25 After all these acts of Josiah, it happened that Pharaoh, king of Egypt, went to make war at Carchemish on the Euphrates, and Josiah went out against him.[1] 26 And the king of Egypt sent word to him saying, "What have we to do with each other, king of Judea? 27 I was not sent against you by the Lord God, for my war is at the Euphrates. And now the Lord is with me! The Lord is with me, urging me on! Stand aside, and do not oppose the Lord."

28 But Josiah did not turn back to his chariot, but tried to fight with him, and did not heed the words of Jeremiah the prophet[2] from the mouth of the Lord. 29 He jointed battle with him in the plain of Megiddo, and the commanders came down against King Josiah. 30 And the king said to his servants, "Take me away from the battle, for I am very weak."[3] And immediately his servants took him out of the line of battle. 31 And he got into his second chariot; and after he was brought back to Jerusalem he died, and was buried in the tomb of his fathers. 32 And in all Judea they mourned for Josiah. Jeremiah the prophet lamented for Josiah, and the principal men, with the

Text from the Revised Standard Version of the Apocrypha, copyrighted 1957, and used by permission of the National Council of the Churches of Christ in the U.S.A. The notes are adapted largely from *The Oxford Annotated Apocrypha*, Bruce Metzger, ed., New York: Oxford University Press, 1965 I Esdras 1:25—2:30. Used by permission.

1. I.e., Josiah attempted to intercept the Egyptians. The account in II Chronicles 35 gives Pharaoh's name as Necho.

2. Though Jeremiah was known for his unheeded exhortations, this use of his name is evidently erroneous. II Chronicles 35:22 states that Josiah "hearkened not unto the words of Necho [Pharaoh] from the mouth of the Lord."

3. According to II Chronicles 35:23, Josiah was fatally wounded by an arrow.

women, have made lamentation for him to this day; it was ordained that this should always be done throughout the whole nation of Israel. 33 These things are written in the book of the histories of the kings of Judea; and every one of the acts of Josiah, and his splendor, and his understanding of the law of the Lord, and the things that he had done before and these that are now told, are recorded in the book of the kings of Israel and Judah.

34 And the men of the nation[4] took Jeconiah[5] the son of Josiah, who was twenty-three years old, and made him king in succession to Josiah his father. 35 And he reigned three months in Judah and Jerusalem. Then the king of Egypt deposed him from reigning in Jerusalem, 36 and fined the nation a hundred talents of silver and a talent of gold. 37 And the king of Egypt made Jehoiakim his brother king of Judea and Jerusalem. 38 Jehoiakim put the nobles in prison, and seized his brother Zarius and brought him up out of Egypt.

39 Jehoiakim was twenty-five years old when he began to reign in Judea and Jerusalem, and he did what was evil in the sight of the Lord. 40 And Nebuchadnezzar king of Babylon[6] came up against him, and bound him with a chain of brass and took him away to Babylon. 41 Nebuchadnezzar also took some of the holy vessels of the Lord, and carried them away, and stored them in his temple in Babylon. 42 But the things that are reported about Jehoiakim and his uncleanness and impiety are written in the chronicles of the kings.

43 Jehoiachin his son became king in his stead; when he was made king he was eighteen years old, 44 and he reigned three months and ten days in Jerusalem. He did what was evil in the sight of the Lord. 45 So after a year Nebuchadnezzar sent and removed him to Babylon, with the holy vessels of the Lord, 46 and made Zedekiah king of Judea and Jerusalem.

Zedekiah was twenty-one years old, and he reigned eleven

4. "Men of the nation" corresponds to "people of the land" in the parallel account of II Chronicles: the conservative landowners.

5. Called Jehoahaz in II Chronicles 36:1.

6. This was Nebuchadnezzar II (reigned 604-562 B.C.), second king of the Chaldean dynasty which ruled Babylonia between the fall of Assyria and the rise of Persia.

years. 47 He also did what was evil in the sight of the Lord, and did not heed the words that were spoken by Jeremiah the prophet from the mouth of the Lord. 48 And though King Nebuchadnezzar had made him swear by the name of the Lord, he broke his oath and rebelled; and he stiffened his neck and hardened his heart and transgressed the laws of the Lord, the God of Israel. 49 Even the leaders of the people and of the priests committed many acts of sacrilege and lawlessness beyond all the unclean deeds of all the nations, and polluted the temple of the Lord which had been hallowed in Jerusalem. 50 So the God of their fathers sent by his messenger to call them back, because he would have spared them and his dwelling place. 51 But they mocked his messengers, and whenever the Lord spoke, they scoffed at his prophets, 52 until in his anger against his people because of their ungodly acts he gave command to bring against them the kings of the Chaldeans. 53 These slew their young men with the sword around their holy temple, and did not spare young man or virgin, old man or child, for he gave them all into their hands. 54 And all the holy vessels of the Lord, great and small, and the treasure chests of the Lord, and the royal stores, they took and carried away to Babylon. 55 And they burned the house of the Lord and broke down the walls of Jerusalem and burned their towers with fire, 56 and utterly destroyed all its glorious things. The survivors he led away to Babylon with the sword,⁷ 57 and they were servants to him and to his sons until the Persians began to reign, in fulfilment of the word of the Lord by the mouth of Jeremiah: 58 "Until the land has enjoyed its sabbaths, it shall keep sabbath⁸ all the time of its desolation until the completion of seventy years."

Chapter 2

1   In the first year of Cyrus as king of the Persians,⁹ that the word of the Lord by the mouth of Jeremiah might be accomplished, 2 the Lord stirred up the spirit of Cyrus king of the

7. The destruction of Jerusalem occurred in 586 B.C.
8. The land shall lie untended (at rest) until the exiles return.
9. The year 538 B.C.

Persians, and he made a proclamation throughout all his kingdom and also put it in writing:

3   "Thus says Cyrus king of the Persians: The Lord of Israel,
the Lord Most High, has made me king of the world, 4 and he
has commanded me to build him a house at Jerusalem, which
is in Judea. 5 If any one of you, therefore, is of his people, may
his Lord be with him, and let him go up to Jerusalem, which
is in Judea, and build the house of the Lord of Israel—he is
the Lord who dwells in Jerusalem, 6 and let each man, wherever he may live, be helped by the men of his place with gold
and silver, 7 with gifts, and with horses and cattle, besides the
other things added as votive offerings for the temple of the Lord
which is in Jerusalem."

8   Then arose the heads of families of the tribes of Judah and
Benjamin, and the priests and the Levites, and all whose spirit
the Lord had stirred to go up to build the house in Jerusalem
for the Lord; 9 and their neighbors helped them with everything, with silver and gold, with horses and cattle, and with a
very great number of votive offerings from many whose hearts
were stirred.

10   Cyrus the king also brought out the holy vessels of the Lord
which Nebuchadnezzar had carried away from Jerusalem and
stored in his temple of idols. 11 When Cyrus king of the Persians brought these out, he gave them to Mithridates his treas-
urer, 12 and by him they were given to Sheshbazzar the governor of Judea. 13 The number of these was: a thousand gold
cups, a thousand silver cups, twenty-nine silver censers, thirty
gold bowls, two thousand four hundred and ten silver bowls,
and a thousand other vessels. 14 All the vessels were handed
over, gold and silver, five thousand four hundred and sixty-
nine, 15 and they were carried back by Sheshbazzar with the
returning exiles from Babylon to Jerusalem.

16   But in the time of Artaxerxes[10] king of the Persians, Bish-
lam, Mithridates, Tabeel, Rehum, Beltethmus, Shimshai the

10. The chronology is in error here. Artaxerxes I (464-423 B.C.) opposed
rebuilding the walls of Jerusalem; but here he is confused with the predecessor of Darius, Cambyses (529-521 B.C.).

scribe, and the rest of their associates,[11] living in Samaria and other places, wrote him the following letter, against those who were living in Judea and Jerusalem:

17 "To King Artaxerxes our lord, Your servants Rehum the recorder and Shimshai the scribe and the other judges of their council in Coelesyria and Phoenicia: 18 Now be it known to our lord the king that the Jews who came up from you to us have gone to Jerusalem and are building that rebellious and wicked city, repairing its market places and walls and laying the foundations for a temple. 19 Now if this city is built and the walls finished, they will not only refuse to pay tribute but will even resist kings. 20 And since the building of the temple is now going on,[12] we think it best not to neglect such a matter, 21 but to speak to our lord the king, in order that, if it seems good to you, search may be made in the records of your fathers. 22 You will find in the chronicles what has been written about them, and will learn that this city was rebellious, troubling both kings and other cities, 23 and that the Jews were rebels and kept setting up blockades in it from of old. That is why this city was laid waste. 24 Therefore we now make known to you, O lord and king, that if this city is built and its walls finished, you will no longer have access to Coelesyria and Phoenicia."

25 Then the king, in reply to Rehum the recorder and Beltethmus and Shimshai the scribe and the others associated with them and living in Samaria and Syria and Phoenicia, wrote as follows:

26 "I have read the letter which you sent me. So I ordered search to be made, and it has been found that this city from of old has fought against kings, 27 and that the men in it were given to rebellion and war, and that mighty and cruel kings ruled in Jerusalem and exacted tribute from Coelesyria and

11. These persons were officials of the Persian province called "Beyond the River," which included Syria, Phoenicia, and Palestine. "Beltethmus" is the title of the office held by Rehum, not a proper name.

12. The comparable account in Ezra 4:14 fails to mention any rebuilding of the Temple at this point. References in Ezra 4:24 and I Esdras 2:30 to the halting of work on the Temple appear to be in error. The Persian king was concerned about the walls of the city, not the Temple.

Phoenicia. 28 Therefore I have now issued orders to prevent these men from building the city and to take care that nothing more be done 29 and that such wicked proceedings go no further to the annoyance of kings."

30   Then, when the letter from King Artaxerxes was read, Rehum and Shimshai the scribe and their associates went in haste to Jerusalem, with horsemen and a multitude in battle array, and began to hinder the builders. And the building of the temple in Jerusalem ceased until the second year of the reign of Darius king of the Persians.

THE ASSYRIANS

THE ASSYRIANS

Introduction to *The Capture of Babylon from the Kassites*

Assyria, once an outpost on the far northern frontiers of Babylonian civilization, sometimes subject to the great conquerors from the south, gained a measure of independence following the Kassite capture of Babylon. The Kassites, a non-Semitic people from somewhere in the Zagros hills, were strong enough to raid the lowlands within a few years of Hammurabi's death (*ca.* 1750 B.C.), and eventually replaced Hammurabi's dynasty on the throne of Babylon. The Babylonian Chronicle records numerous struggles between the Assyrian and the Kassite kings, though until the time of Tukulti-(Nin)urta I (reigned *ca.* 1244-1208 B.C.), the Assyrian annals take virtually no note of the conflict.

Tukulti-(Nin)urta I, by his victory over the Kassite king Kashtiliash IV in about 1235 B.C., became the first of many Assyrian kings to rule Babylon. This time, Assyrian control lasted for only seven years. But Tukulti-(Nin)urta's conquest, though ephemeral, proved to be merely the beginning of that long expansionist effort which eventually carried Assyrian rule in Mesopotamia as far as the Persian Gulf.

We here reproduce parallel accounts of Tukulti-(Nin)urta's capture of Babylon, the first from the Babylonian Chronicle, the second from the Annals of Assyria.

THE CAPTURE OF BABYLON FROM THE KASSITES

From the Babylonian Chronicle

The defeat of Kashtiliash he brought about . . . Before Urta[1] he set him . . . Tukulti-Urta returned to Babylon and . . .

From *Ancient Records of Assyria and Babylonia*, Vol. I, D. D. Luckenbill, ed., Chicago: University of Chicago Press, 1926-27, pp. 49-52. Reprinted by permission.
  1. Or Ninurta: the god of battles.

they drew near to Babylon. The wall of Babylon he destroyed, the Babylonians he put to the sword. The treasure of Esagila[2] and Babylon he profanely brought forth and the great lord Marduk he removed from his abode and carried him off to Assyria. The rule (*lit.*, way) of his governors he established in Karduniash (Babylonia). For seven years Tukulti-Urta ruled. Thereafter the nobles of Akkad and of Karduniash revolted and they set Adad-shum-usur[3] on the throne of his father. As for Tukulti-Urta, who had brought evil upon Babylon, Assur-nasir-pal, his son, and the nobles of Assyria, revolted and they cast him from his throne; in Kar-Tukulti-Urta they besieged him in his palace and slew him with the sword. For . . . -six[4] years, until the time of Tukulti-Assur,[5] Bel (Marduk) dwelt in Assyria; in the reign of Tukulti-Assur, Bel came (back) to Babylon.[6]

From the Inscriptions of Tukulti-Urta I

Tukulti-Urta, king of universe, king of Assyria, king of the four quarters (of the world), the Sun of all peoples, the mighty king, king of Karduniash (Babylonia), king of Sumer and Akkad, king of the upper (and) lower sea,[7] king of the mountains and the wide (desert) plains, king of the Shubari[8] (and) Kuti,[9] and king of all the Nairi-lands;[10] the king whom the gods have caused to attain unto his heart's desire (*lit.*, victory) and who, through the splendor of his might, has made himself ruler of the four regions (of the world), am I; son of Shalmaneser,[11] king

2. The temple of the god Marduk at Babylon.
3. Another Kassite king. Some scholars, assuming this chronicle to be incorrect, have calculated his reign as 1218-1189 B.C. More recent evidence suggests, however, that the chronicle is accurate and that Babylonian chronology will have to be revised accordingly.
4. Note that this is the final digit of a larger number, possibly ninety-six.
5. An Assyrian king, reigned *ca.* 1134 B.C.
6. I.e., the statue of the god was returned to Babylon.
7. The Mediterranean Sea and the Persian Gulf.
8. Peoples from the land of Subartu (northeast of Assyria).
9. Or Guti, Gutians: people from the land of Gutium, east of Assyria in the northern Zagros hills.
10. The general region of Subartu.
11. Shalmaneser I, king of Assyria 1274-1245 B.C.

of the universe, king of Assyria; (grand)son of Adad-nirari,[12] king of the universe, king of Assyria.

At the beginning of my rule, in my first year of reign, the Kuti, Ukumani, the lands of Elhunia and Sharnida, (and) Mehri,[13] my hand conquered. The tribute of their lands, and the abundance of their mountains, yearly I received, in my city Assur.

At that time the Kurti, the lands of Kutmuhi, Bushshi, Mummi, Alzi, Madani, Nihani, Alaia, Teburzi, Burukuzzi, the whole of the wide Shubari-land,[14] I burned with fire. The kings, their rulers, I brought in submission to my feet and imposed taskwork.

Remote(?) mountains, where there were no roads, whose paths no (former) king knew, in the strength of my transcendent might I crossed and forty-three kings of the Nairi-lands boldly took their stand, offering battle. I fought with them, I brought about their overthrow. With their blood I flooded the ravines and gullies of the mountains. All of their lands I brought under my sway. I imposed tribute and gifts (toll) upon them for all time.

Trusting in Assur, Enlil (Bel) and Shamash,[15] the great gods, my lords, (and) with the help of Ishtar, [16] queen of heaven and earth, who went at the head of my army, I forced Kashtilash, king of Karduniash (Babylonia), to give battle; I brought about the defeat of his armies, his warriors I overthrew. In the midst of that battle my own hand captured Kashtilash, the Kassite king. His royal neck I trod on with my feet, like a *galtappi*.[17] Stripped and bound, before Assur my lord, I brought him. Sumer and Akkad to its farthest border, I brought under my sway. On the lower sea of the rising sun, I established the border (*i.e.*, frontier) of my land.

12. Adad-nirari I, king of Assyria 1307-1275 B.C.
13. The Kuti (Guti) and Ukumani are peoples; the lands mentioned are mountainous territories somewhere to the north of Assyria.
14. I.e., all of these are evidently districts within the Shubari-land (Subartu).
15. Assur was the Assyrian chief god; Enlil was the chief executive of the Sumerian pantheon and Bel (Marduk) his Babylonian counterpart; Shamash was the sun-god.
16. The goddess of love.
17. Probably a footstool.

At that time, in the temple area of my city Assur, on the north side, I cleared away great (quantities) of earth from wide areas, twenty *musaru*,[18] by the rod(?). Below I built (*lit.*, brought) up its foundation. [Like] the solid mountain I made strong [its foundation walls]. I built Elugalukurkurra,[19] my royal dwelling, which I love. From its foundation to its top I completed it, and I set up my memorial stele.

In the days to come, let (some) future prince, when that palace becomes old and falls into decay, restore its ruins, anoint my memorial stele with oil, offer sacrifices, and return it to its place. (Then) Assur and Adad[20] will hear his prayers. He who blots out my inscribed name and writes his name (in its stead), who destroys my memorial stele, puts it in some other place, or some hidden place, whoever plans and does any such evil deed or if he prevents the gods who dwell in Assur from entering into my palace at the feasts, or directs them to another palace, causing them to leave that palace and to desert it, may Assur and Adad, the gods of heaven and earth, ruin his kingdom, destroy his name and his seed from the land. May the king, who would harm him, deprive him of his throne (and) give his land to whomever he pleases. May Ishtar, the lady, lover of the years of my rule, bring about the overthrow of his land. Before his foes may he not be able to stand. Into the hand of his foes may she give him.

18. A measure of area, equivalent to 12 ells (arm lengths) on each side, or approximately 80 square yards. Twenty *musaru* would thus be about one-third of an acre.
19. "The house of the king of the land," i.e., the king's palace.
20. The god of storm and rain.

Introduction to Tiglath-pileser I

Tiglath-pileser I* (reigned 1115-1077 B.C.) was the first of the great Assyrian conqueror-kings. He extended Assyrian hegemony in Asia

* Not to be confused with the Tiglath-pileser of Biblical fame (Tiglath-pileser III, reigned 744-727 B.C.).

Minor farther than any of his predecessors had done, subdued the
nomads along the Mediterranean trade routes, marched on Damas-
cus, and forced the cities of Phoenicia to pay tribute. Like his predecessor, Tukulti-(Nin)urta I, he conquered, then lost, Babylon. Tiglath-pileser, however, was not only a conqueror. In addition to
military expeditions, his annals record a variety of other activities,
including great building projects and agricultural improvements.

TIGLATH-PILESER I: FROM THE ANNALS

Beginning: Assur,[1] the great lord, ruler of all of the gods,
bestower of scepter and crown, who established sovereignty;
Enlil,[2] the lord, the king of all the Anunnaki,[3] the father of the
gods, the Lord of lands; Sin,[4] the wise, the lord of the lunar disk,
exalted in splendor; Shamash,[5] the judge of heaven and earth,
who spies out the evil designs of the enemy, who exposes the
wicked; Adad,[6] the mighty, who overwhelms the regions of the
foe—lands and houses; Urta,[7] the hero, who destroys the wicked
and the enemy, who causes (man) to attain to all that the heart
(desires); Ishtar,[8] first among the gods, the lady of confusion,
who makes battles terrible:—ye great gods, ye rulers of heaven
and earth, whose onward rush is battle and destruction, who
have enlarged the kingdom of Tiglath-pileser, the beloved
prince, the desire of your hearts, the exalted shepherd, whom
in your faithful hearts ye have chosen, and whom ye have
crowned with a lofty diadem, and did solemnly appoint to be
king over the land of Enlil; to him have ye granted majesty,
glory, and power, and ye have decreed that his rule should be

From *Ancient Records of Assyria and Babylonia*, Vol. I, D. D. Luckenbill,
ed., Chicago: University of Chicago Press, 1926-27, pp. 72-4, 80-83, 85-7. Reprinted by permission.
1. The principal god of the Assyrians, who has now become chief of the gods.
2. The god of thunder, still a major deity, though less important than
formerly.
3. The gods of the underworld.
4. The moon-god.
5. The sun-god.
6. The god of storm and rain.
7. (Ninurta): the god of battles.
8. The goddess of love.

mighty, and that his priestly seed should have a place in
Eharsagkurkurra[9] forever.

Tiglath-pileser, the mighty king, king of the universe, who is
without a rival, king of the four quarters (of the world), king
of all princes, lord of lords, shepherd(?), king of kings, the
exalted priest, on whom a shining scepter was bestowed through
the command of Shamash, by which he has come to rule the
nations, the subjects of Enlil, all of them; the rightful ruler
(true shepherd), who (v., whose name) has been proclaimed
over (all) princes; the exalted leader(?), whom Assur has
caused to brandish his weapons, and in order that he should be
the shepherd of the four quarters (of the world) has proclaimed
his name forever; the conqueror of remote territories on the
(his) frontiers, north and south; the fiery tempest, whose
splendor overwhelms the quarters (of the world); the glowing
flame which, like the rush of a storm, overpowers the enemy's
land; who through the command of Enlil has no rival, and has
overthrown the enemies of Assur.

Assur and the great gods, who have made my kingdom great,
and who have bestowed might and power as a (lit., my) gift,
commanded that I should extend the boundary of their land, and
they intrusted to my hand their mighty weapons, the storm of
battle. Lands, mountains, cities, and princes, the enemies of
Assur, I have brought under my sway, and have subdued their
territories. With sixty kings——ly I fought, and established
(my) victorious might over them. I was without an equal in
battle, or a rival in the fight. Unto Assyria I added land, unto
her peoples, peoples. I enlarged the frontier of my land, and
all of their lands I brought under my sway.

.   .   .   .

At that time, in the exalted might of Assur, my lord, through
the sure mercy of Shamash the hero and with the help of the
great gods, I, who have ruled with righteousness in the four
quarters (of the world) and who have not had a conqueror in
battle, nor a rival in the fight, marched over difficult roads and

9. The temple of Ninurta at Ashur.

through steep passes whose interior (heart) no king of former days had ever known, unto the lands of distant kings which are on the shore of the Upper Sea,[10] and which had never known subjection—Assur, the lord, having sent me. By roads that were blocked, by paths that were unopened, I traversed the mountains of Elama, Amadana, Elhish, Sherabeli, Tarhuna, Tirkahuli, Kisra, Tarhanabe, Elula, Hashtarae, Shahishara, Ubera, Miliadruni, Shulianzi, Nubanashe, Sheshe[11]—sixteen mighty mountains, in my chariot where the country was good, and where it was difficult I hewed my way with pickaxes of bronze. *Urumi*-trees, trees of the mountain, I cut down, made strong the bridges for the advance of my troops, and crossed the Euphrates. The king of Tumme, the king of Tunube, the king of Tuali, the king of Kindari, the king of Uzula, the king of Unzamuni, the king of Andiabe, the king of Pilakinni, the king of Aturgini, the king of Kulibarzini, the king of Shinibirni, the king of Himua, the king of Paiteri, the king of Uiram, the king of Shururia, the king of Abaeni, the king of Adaeni, the king of Kirini, the king of Albaia, the king of Ugina, the king of Nazabia, the king of Abarsiuni, and the king of Daiaeni[12]—in all twenty-three kinds of the land of Nairi, gathered their chariots and their hosts from out of their lands and advanced to wage war and combat. With the fury of my terrible weapons I attacked them, and brought about the destruction of their widespreading forces, like a flood of Adad. The dead bodies of their warriors I scattered upon the high places of the mountains and alongside their cities like ———. One hundred and twenty of their armored chariots I captured in the midst of the battle. Sixty kings of the countries of Nairi, together with those who had come to their help, I pursued with the point of my spear even to the Upper Sea. I captured their great cities, their booty, their goods and their possessions I brought out; I burnt their cities with fire, I devastated, I destroyed and into heaps and ruins I turned (them). I led away great herds of horses, mules, grazing cattle(?), and the flocks of their pastures, in countless numbers. My hands cap-

10. The Mediterranean.
11. These are north and west of Assyria.
12. Districts in the land of Nairi (Subartu) to the northeast of Assyria.

tured all the kings of the countries of the Nairi. I had mercy on those kings and I spared their lives. (When they were brought) captive and bound into the presence of Shamash, my lord, I set them free, and I caused them to swear an oath of submission (servitude) to my great gods for future days, and forevermore. Their sons, their royal offspring, I took as hostages; twelve hundred horses, and two thousand (head of) cattle I laid as tribute upon them, and I sent them unto their own lands.

. . . .

Tiglath-pileser, the burning flame, the terrible one, the storm of battle.

With the help of Assur, my lord, I led forth my chariots and warriors and went into the desert. Into the midst of the Ahlami, Arameans,[13] enemies of Assur, my lord, I marched. The country from Suhi[14] to the city of Carchemish[15] in the land of Hatti,[16] I raided in one day. I slew their troops; their spoil, their goods and their possessions in countless numbers, I carried away. The rest of their forces, which had fled from before the terrible weapons of Assur, my lord, and had crossed over the Euphrates —in pursuit of them I crossed the Euphrates in vessels made of skins. Six of their cities, which lay at the foot of the mountain of Beshri,[17] I captured, I burned with fire, I laid (them) waste, I destroyed (them). Their spoil, their goods and their possessions I carried away to my city Assur.

Tiglath-pileser, who tramples down the proud, who subdues the disobedient, who humbles all the mighty.

. . . .

In all, forty-two lands and their princes from beyond the Lower Zab,[18] a region of distant hills, unto the further side of

13. Ahlami, Arameans: probably identical, a people from the region of the Upper and Middle Euphrates.
14. A town on the Middle Euphrates near Mari.
15. A city on the Upper Euphrates.
16. A region of northern Syria west of the Euphrates, formerly part of the Hittite empire. The term "Hatti" sometimes refers to the entire Hittite empire.
17. A high mountain due west of Ashur south of the bend of the Euphrates.
18. A river flowing into the Tigris south of Ashur from the east.

the Euphrates, and the land of Hatti and the Upper Sea of the West, from the beginning of my rule up to the fifth year of my reign, my hand has conquered. I have made them to be under one rule; I have taken hostages from them, and have laid tribute and tax upon them.—This does not include many other wars against enemies who could not oppose my might.—I have pursued them in my chariots where the country was good, and on foot where it was difficult. I have kept back the foot of the enemy from my land.

Tiglath-pileser, the valiant hero, who grasps a bow without equal, who exercises lordship over the field.

The gods Urta and Nergal[19] have given their terrible weapons and their majestic bow into my lordly grasp.

At the bidding of Urta, who loves me, four wild bulls (aurochs), which were mighty and of monstrous size, in the desert, in the country of Mitani,[20] and near to the city of Araziki,[21] which is over against the land of Hatti, with my mighty bow, with my iron spear, and with my sharp darts, I killed. Their hides and their horns I brought unto my city Assur. Ten mighty bull-elephants I slew in the country of Harran,[22] and in the district of the river Habur.[23] Four elephants I caught alive. Their hides and their tusks, together with the live elephants, I brought unto my city Assur.

At the bidding of Urta, who loves me, I have slain one hundred and twenty lions by my bold courage and by my strong attack, on foot; and eight hundred lions I have laid low from my chariot with javelins(?). I have brought down all (kinds of) beasts of the field, and birds of the heavens that fly, among my hunting spoils.

After I had brought all the enemies of Assur under my rule, I completely rebuilt the temple of the Assyrian Ishtar, my lady, the temple of Amurru,[24] the temple of Bel-labiru (the elder Bel),

19. Nergal: a god of the underworld.
20. (Mitanni): a region east of the Upper Euphrates.
21. A city on the east bank of the Upper Euphrates.
22. A city of Syria due east of Carchemish.
23. A tributary of the Euphrates coming from the north.
24. A god of the Amurru (Amorite) people, who were Semites from the Upper and Middle Euphrates region.

the divine temples, the temples of the gods of my city Assur, which had fallen into ruins. The portals of their temples I set up, and caused the great gods, my lords, to dwell therein. I delighted the hearts of the great gods.

The palaces, the royal dwellings, in the great cities of the provinces of my land, which had been deserted from the time of my fathers down through the course of many years, and had decayed and had fallen into ruins, I rebuilt completely.

I strengthened the walls of the cities of my land which were in ruins.

I put the plows to work throughout the whole of Assyria and heaped up grain in greater quantities than my fathers.

Herds of horses, cattle, and asses, which I seized with the help of Assur, my lord, in the lands which I brought under my sway, I have gathered together as the spoil of my hand; and herds of deer, stags, ibex, and wild goats, which Assur and Urta, the gods who love me, have given me for the chase, I have taken in the midst of the lofty hills. Herds of them I gathered and found (*lit.*, counted) their number like unto that of a flock of sheep. Yearly I offered unto Assur, my lord, such of the young wild creatures which were born from them as my heart prompted me (to choose), together with my pure lambs, for sacrifice.

I brought cedars, boxwood, and *allakanish*-trees[25] from the countries which I have subdued, trees the like of which none of the kings, my ancient fathers, had ever planted, and I planted them in the gardens of my land. I took rare garden plants, which were not found in my own land, and caused them to flourish in the gardens of Assyria. I increased the output of chariots, (with their) teams over that of former days, for the strengthening of my land. Unto the land of Assyria I added land, unto her peoples, peoples. I have kept good the condition of my people, and in peaceful habitations I have caused them to dwell.

.   .   .   .

25. A kind of oak.

Introduction to Sennacherib: The Building Inscriptions

Like other Assyrian kings, Sennacherib (reigned 704-681 B.C.) boasts in his inscriptions of great military achievements. But in twenty-four years as king he conducted only eight campaigns; and it is unlikely that he increased Assyrian territory to any significant extent. The Assyrian empire in his day already extended from Asia Minor to the Persian Gulf and southern Syria. Under Sennacherib and his successors, Esarhaddon (r. 680-69 B.C.) and Ashurbanipal (r. 668-27 B.C.), the Near East enjoyed a period of relative peace.

Sennacherib is best known for his attacks upon two great capitals—Babylon and Jerusalem. Once-dominant Babylon, never reconciled to Assyrian hegemony, revolted in 703 B.C. and briefly restored native rule. But Sennacherib destroyed the rebel armies, plundering Babylon with a thoroughness which was not soon forgotten. The Assyrian siege of Jerusalem in 701 B.C. is recorded both in the official annals of Assyria and in the Old Testament books of Isaiah and II Kings.* The Assyrian version claims that Sennacherib won a considerable victory over Hezekiah, king of Judah, depriving him of a number of towns and imposing a heavy tribute. But whereas the Biblical account stresses the Assyrian failure to capture Jerusalem, Sennacherib mentions only that he shut up Hezekiah in his capital "like a bird in a cage," and makes no reference to the plague which, according to the Old Testament, caused the Assyrian army to withdraw.

Like many of his predecessors on the throne of Assyria, Sennacherib was also a great builder. Declining to occupy the splendid palace build by his father, Sargon II, at Khorsabad (Dur-Sharrukin), he constructed a new one for himself at Nineveh. The description of this new palace is the subject of the following inscription.

---

* In Isaiah, chapters 36-37, and II Kings, chapters 18-19. For the Isaiah account, see above pp. 84-9.

SENNACHERIB:
FROM THE BUILDING INSCRIPTIONS

At that time, Nineveh,[1] the noble metropolis, the city beloved of Ishtar,[2] wherein are all the meeting places of gods and goddesses; the everlasting structure, the eternal foundation, whose plan had been designed from of old, along with the writing of the constellations, and whose structure had been made beautiful; the beautiful (artistic) place, the abode of divine law (decision, rule), into which had been brought all kinds of artistic workmanship, every secret and pleasant(?) plan (*or*, command, of god); where from of old, the kings, who went before, my fathers, had exercised the lordship over Assyria before me, and had ruled the subjects of Enlil,[3] and yearly without interruption, had received therein an unceasing income, the tribute of the princes of the four quarters (of the world): not one among them had given his thoughtful attention to, nor had his heart considered, the palace therein, the place of the royal abode, whose site had become too small; (nor) had he turned his thought (*lit.*, ear), nor brought his mind (*lit.*, liver) to lay out the streets of the city, to widen the squares, to dig a canal, to set out trees (plantations).

But I, Sennacherib, king of Assyria, gave my thought and brought my mind to accomplish this work according to the command (will) of the gods. The people of Chaldea, the Arameans, the Manneans, (the people) of the lands of Kue and Hilakku,[4] who had not submitted to my yoke, I deported (from their lands), made them carry the headpad and mold bricks. I cut down the reed marshes which are in Chaldea, and had the

From *Ancient Records of Assyria and Babylonia*, Vol. II, D. D. Luckenbill, ed., Chicago: University of Chicago Press, 1926-27, pp. 160-63. Reprinted by permission.

  1. City on the Tigris which served as the capital of the Assyrian empire under Sennacherib and his successors.

  2. The goddess of love.

  3. Subjects of Enlil: the Babylonians.

  4. The Chaldeans lived immediately to the west of Babylonia, the Arameans in the region of the Upper and Middle Euphrates. The Manneans came from the Zagros Mountains. Hilakku is the area of southeastern Asia Minor called Cilicia by the Romans; Kue also refers to Cilicia, or a part thereof.

men of the foe whom my hands had conquered drag their mighty reeds (to Assyria) for the completion of its work.

The former palace, which was 30 *gar* (360 cubits)[5] on the side and 10 *gar* (120 cubits) on its front, which the kings, who went before, my fathers, had built, whose structure they had not, however, made artistic, up to whose side the Tebiltu River[6] had come from days of old, worked havoc with its foundation and destroyed its platform—that small palace I tore down in its totality. The course (*i.e.*, the channel) of the Tebiltu I improved and directed its outflow.

In a propitious month, on a favorable day, in its (the river's) hidden bed, (for a space of) 60 (*gar*) on the side, and 34 (*gar*) on the front, I covered over great mountain boulders, and made a field rise up from the water, and made it like unto the dry land. Lest in the passing of days its platform should give way before the (floods of) high water, I set up great slabs of limestone around its walls, and strengthened its structure (*lit.*, heaping—of earth); over these (slabs) I filled in the terrace to a height of 170 *tipku*[7]—I added to the site (*lit.*, measurement) of the former palace, and widened its bulwarks(?). Thereon (*lit.*, therein) I had them build a palace of ivory, maple, box-wood, mulberry (*musukannu*), cedar, cypress, spruce and pistachio, the "Palace without a Rival," for my royal abode. Beams of cedar, the product of Mount Amanus,[8] which they dragged with difficulty out of (those) distant mountains, I stretched across their ceilings(?). Great door-leaves of cypress, whose odor is pleasant as they are opened and closed, I bound with a band of shining copper and set them up in their doors. A portico, patterned after a Hittite (Syrian) palace, which they call in the Amorite tongue a *bit-hilani*, I constructed inside them (the doors), for my lordly pleasure.

Eight lions, open at the knee, advancing, constructed out of

5. A *gar* is thus equal to 12 cubits, a cubit being the length of the arm from the elbow to the end of the middle finger. Taking the cubit as measuring 18 inches, the *gar* would be equal to 6 yards.

6. The Tebiltu River flows into the Tigris near Nineveh.

7. A layer (course) of bricks.

8. Probably a mountainous region, rather than a single mountain, in northwest Syria near the Mediterranean coast.

11,400 talents of shining bronze, of the workmanship of the god Nin-a-gal,[9] and full of splendor, together with two colossal pillars whose copper work came to 6,000 talents, and two great cedar pillars, (which) I placed upon the lions (colossi), I set up as posts to support their doors. Four mountain sheep, as protecting deities, of silver and copper, together with mountain sheep, as protecting deities, of great blocks of mountain stone, I fashioned cunningly, and setting them toward the four winds (directions), I adorned their entrances. Great slabs of limestone, the enemy tribes, whom my hands had conquered, dragged through them (the doors), and I had them set up around their walls,—I made them objects of astonishment.

A great park, like unto Mount Amanus, wherein were set out all kinds of herbs and fruit trees,—trees, such as grow on the mountains and in Chaldea, I planted by its (the palace's) side. That (they might) plant orchards, I subdivided some land in the plain above the city, into plots of 3 *pi*[10] each, for the citizens of Nineveh, and gave it to them.

To increase the vegetation, from the border of the town of Kisiri[11] to the plain about Nineveh, through mountain and lowland, with iron pickaxes I cut and directed a canal. For (a distance of) 1½ *beru* ("double-hours")[12] of land, the waters of the Husur (Khosr), which from of old sought too low a level (*lit.*, place), I made to flow through those orchards in irrigation ditches.

After I had brought to an end the work on my royal palace, had widened the squares, made bright the avenues and streets and caused them to shine like the day, I invited Assur, the great lord, the gods and goddesses who dwell in Assyria, into its midst. I offered sacrifices in great numbers and presented my gifts.

In the days to come, whoever among the kings, my sons, whose name Assur calls to rule over land and people, when that

9. The god of bronze-working.
10. The *pi* was a measure of capacity used for grain. A plot of 3 *pi* thus referred to the amount of land required for sowing this quantity of grain, and varied according to the fertility of the land.
11. A town 20 to 30 miles north of Nineveh.
12. *Beru:* the distance which could be covered in two hours of walking. It varied according to the difficulty of the terrain.

palace shall become old and fall to ruins, let him restore its
ruins, look upon the memorial stele with my name inscribed
upon it, anoint it with oil, offer sacrifices, and return it to its
place. Then Assur[13] will hear his prayers.

13. The chief god of the Assyrians.

The Persians

THE PERSIANS

Introduction to The Inscription of Darius on the Rock of Behistun

Darius the Great's famous inscription at Behistun—written in the Persian tongue with Median and Babylonian translations—is probably best known as a landmark in the decipherment of ancient languages. It is also the most important single source for Persian history in the Achaemenian period (555-330 B.C.), recounting the exploits by which Darius became master of the most extensive territories ever to be ruled from one center before the time of Rome.

The Behistun inscription is carved into the precipitous face of a mountain lying on the main route between Baghdad and Teheran, about sixty-five miles from ancient Ecbatana. At the foot of the peak is a pool of clear water, fed by springs, where from time immemorial armies and caravans have paused on their journeys. Probably because of these springs, the rock was regarded as a sacred place. This sacred character and strategic location—and the extreme inaccessibility of the rock—perhaps led Darius to choose it as a fitting spot for his memorial. The inscription stands about five hundred feet above the level of the surrounding plain, in a place beyond the reach of any but the most determined enemy. Indeed, to this day the only defacement of the text has been caused by weathering and the infiltration of water onto the face of the rock.

Although the rock of Behistun was well-known to ancient writers, it was not until 1847 that the inscription was successfully copied and analyzed by Sir Henry Rawlinson, a British officer serving as a military adviser to the Shah of Persia. By identifying and comparing a large number of proper names occurring in all three versions, Rawlinson became the first scholar to make any real advance in the comprehension and translation of the ancient Persian tongue. He was aided by the numerous similarities between the basic cuneiform signs of the Persian and Babylonian alphabets, and by reference to related languages—Sanskrit and the modern Persian dialects.

From a historical as well as a philological point of view, the inscription of Behistun bears a unique significance. It offers a contemporary account of the events it describes, composed by the person most directly involved, probably in 520 B.C. just after Darius had eliminated the last of his nine principal opponents. But like most autobiographies, this one presents the view which the author wished the world to believe, and it cannot be accepted without reservations. Only by reading between the lines would one gather from the Behistun inscription that Darius was a usurper without legitimate claim to the throne.

The founder of the Persian empire was Cyrus (reigned 555-529 B.C.), originally a vassal of the Median king Astyages. The Median empire in those days bordered on the territories of Chaldaea (ancient Babylonia) and Lydia in the west, extending to Armenia on the north and Parthia on the east. In the year 550 Cyrus revolted against his overlord Astyages and captured the Median capital of Ecbatana. He went on to win Lydia and the cities of Greek Ionia, the lands of central Asia to the Jaxartes River and the border of India, and finally, in 539 B.C., the great fortress of Babylon. Cyrus was succeeded by his son Cambyses, who added Egypt to his territories.

Darius' father, Hystaspes, was no more than the satrap of Parthia and Hyrcania under Cyrus. The young Darius served as spear-bearer to Cambyses in Egypt. At the early age of twenty-eight—during the lifetime of his father and grandfather—Darius became king. This fact alone suggests extraordinary circumstances; for had Darius been in the direct line of succession, his father and grandfather would have inherited the throne before him. Instead, we hear of Hystaspes serving as his son's general.

History throws no clear light on the facts surrounding the death of Smerdis, Cambyses' brother. Darius declares that Cambyses killed him. But the possibility remains that the man Darius calls Gaumata was the actual Smerdis, who would naturally be regarded as the legitimate successor to his brother. It is also possible that the Nidintu-Bel of Darius' inscription was the true son of Nabonidus of Babylon. In any event, it is obvious that Darius' succession to the throne of Persia was by no means taken for granted by the subject races of the empire.

Another much-disputed point concerns the religion of Darius and his successors: whether they were followers of the prophet Zoroaster. Some confusion has arisen through the failure to distinguish between the so-called primitive Zoroastrianism, as preached by its founder, and the later religion which bore the same name. Certainly the references in the Behistun inscription to Ahura Mazda as supreme God and to the opposition of righteousness and the Lie indicate the influence of the prophet. But Darius was a king rather than a religious leader; and as such, he recognized the danger of attempting to disturb his subjects' deeply felt convictions. This tolerance—in which Cyrus had led the way—was one of the strengths of the Achaemenian empire.

The following text has been translated from the Persian, though certain missing portions have been supplied by reference to the Median or Babylonian versions.

THE INSCRIPTION OF DARIUS ON THE ROCK OF BEHISTUN

The Persian Text

Column I

1   I am Darius, the great king, the king of kings, the king of Persia, the king of the provinces, the son of Hystaspes, the grandson of Arsames, the Achaemenian.

2   (Thus) saith Darius, the king: My father is Hystaspes; the father of Hystaspes was Arsames; the father of Arsames was Ariyaramnes; the father of Ariyaramnes was [Teispes]: the father of Teispes was Achaemenes.

3   (Thus) saith Darius, the king: On that account are we called Achaemenians; from antiquity are we descended; from antiquity hath our race been kings.

4   (Thus) saith Darius, the king: Eight of my race were kings before (me); I am the ninth. In two lines have we been kings.

5   (Thus) saith Darius, the king: By the grace of Auramazda[1]

From *The Sculptures and Inscription of Behistun*, L. W. King and R. C. Thompson, London: Trustees of the British Museum, 1907, pp. 1-83. Reprinted by permission. The footnotes have been adapted.

1. From Achaemenian times onward, this is spelled in one word, although in Zoroaster's day the two component parts—Ahura ("lord") and Mazda ("wise")—were written separately.

am I king; Auramazda hath granted me the kingdom.

6   (Thus) saith Darius, the king: These are the provinces
     which are subject unto me, and by the grace of Au-
     ramazda became I king of them: Persia, Susiana,
     Babylonia, Assyria, Arabia, Egypt, the (Islands) of
     the Sea, Sparda, Ionia, [Media], Armenia, Cappa-
     docia, Parthia, Drangiana, Aria, Chorasmia, Bactria,
     Sogdiana, Gandara, Scythia, Sattagydia, Arachosia
     and Maka;[2] twenty-three lands in all.

7   (Thus) saith Darius, the king: These are the provinces
     which are subject unto me; by the grace of Auramazda
     they became subject unto me; they brought tribute
     unto me. Whatsoever commands have been laid on
     them by me, by night or by day, have been performed
     by them.

8   (Thus) saith Darius, the king: Within these lands, who-
     soever was a [friend], him have I surely protected;
     whosoever was hostile, him have I utterly destroyed.
     By the grace of Auramazda these lands have con-
     formed to my decrees; even as it was commanded unto
     them by me, so was it done.

9   (Thus) saith Darius, the king: Auramazda hath granted
     unto me this empire. Auramazda brought me help,
     until I gained this empire; by the grace of Auramazda
     do I hold this empire.

10   (Thus) saith Darius, the king: This is what was done by
     me after I became king. He who was named Cambyses,
     the son of Cyrus, one of our race, was king here before
     me. That Cambyses had a brother, Smerdis by name,
     of the same mother and the same father as Cambyses.
     Afterwards Cambyses slew this Smerdis. When Cam-
     byses slew Smerdis, it was not known unto the people

2. "Persia" in this context designates not the entire country, but merely the
region of southwestern Iran now known as Pars or Fars. The Islands of the
Sea may be the Mediterranean coastline. The location of Sparda is uncertain;
probably it is Sardis, the chief city of Lydia in Asia Minor. Parthia, Drangiana,
Aria, Chorasmia, Bactria, Sogdiana, Gandara, Arachosia, and Maka are eastern
provinces of the empire, lying in the general area between the Aral Sea and
India (see map).

that Smerdis was slain. Thereupon Cambyses went into Egypt. When Cambyses had departed into Egypt, the people became hostile, and the lie[3] multiplied in the land, even in Persia, as in Media, and in the other provinces.

11 (Thus) saith Darius, the king: Afterwards there was a certain man, a Magian,[4] Gaumata by name, who raised a rebellion in Paishiyauvada,[5] in a mountain named Arakadrish. On the fourteenth day of the month Viyakhna did he rebel. He lied unto the people, saying: "I am Smerdis, the son of Cyrus, the brother of Cambyses." Then were all the people in revolt, and from Cambyses they went over unto him, both Persia and Media, and the other provinces. He seized on the kingdom; on the ninth day of the month Garmapada he seized on the kingdom. Afterwards Cambyses died by his own hand.

12 (Thus) saith Darius, the king: The kingdom of which Gaumata, the Magian, dispossessed Cambyses, had belonged to our race from olden time. After that Gaumata, the Magian, had dispossessed Cambyses of Persia and of Media, and of the other provinces, he did according to his will, he was (as) king.

13 (Thus) saith Darius, the king: There was no man, either Persian or Median or of our own race, who took the kingdom from Gaumata, the Magian. The people feared him exceedingly, (for) he slew many who had known the former Smerdis. For this reason did he slay them, "That they may not know that I am not Smerdis, the son of Cyrus." There was none who dared say aught against Gaumata, the Magian, until I came.

3. Note the Zoroastrian terminology. The word "Lie," however, meant not only an offense against Truth, but also an attack upon the established order.
4. Though the Magi are sometimes referred to as a Zoroastrian priesthood, they were probably a hereditary caste entrusted with the supervision of the national religion, whatever form this religion might take. They were natives of Media and appear to have held a monopoly on conducting religious ceremonies throughout the western half of the Achaemenian empire.
5. A district in the province of Persia.

Then I prayed to Auramazda; Auramazda brought me help. On the tenth day of the month Bagayadish I, with a few men, slew that Gaumata, the Magian, and the chief men who were his followers. (At) the stronghold named Sikayauvatish, in the district named Nisaya in Media, I slew him; I dispossessed him of the kingdom. By the grace of Auramazda I became king; Auramazda granted me the kingdom.[6]

14 (Thus) saith Darius, the king: The kingdom that had been wrested from our line I brought back (and) I established it in its place as it was of old. The temples which Gaumata, the Magian, had destroyed I restored for the people, and the pasture-lands, and the herds and the dwelling places, and the houses, which Gaumata, the Magian, had taken away. I settled the people in their place, (the people of) Persia, and Media, and the other provinces. I restored that which had been taken away, as it was in the days of old. This did I by the grace of Auramazda, I laboured until I had stablished our house in its place, as in the days of old; I laboured, by the grace of Auramazda, so that Gaumata, the Magian, did not dispossess our house.

15 (Thus) saith Darius, the king: This is what I did after I became king.

16 (Thus) saith Darius, the king: After that I had slain Gaumata, the Magian, a certain man named Atrina, the son of Upadaranma, raised a rebellion in Susiana, (and) he spake thus unto the people of Susiana: "I am king in Susiana." Thereupon the people of Susiana became rebellious, (and) they went over unto that Atrina; he became king in Susiana. And a certain Babylonian named Nidintu-Bel, the son of An[iri], raised a rebellion in Babylon: he lied to the people (saying), "I am Nebuchadnezzar, the son of Nabonidus."[7] Then did all the province of Babylonia go over

6. In the year 521 B.C.
7. The last native king of Babylon (reigned 555-539 B.C.), the last of the Chaldean dynasty.

unto that Nidintu-Bel, (and) Babylonia rose in rebellion. He seized on the kingdom of Babylonia.

17 (Thus) saith Darius, the king: Then sent I (an army) into Susiana; that Atrina was brought unto me in fetters, (and) I killed him.

18 (Thus) saith Darius, the king: Then did I march against Babylon, against that Nidintu-Bel, who was called Nebuchadnezzar. The army of Nidintu-Bel held the Tigris; there they were posted, and they also had ships. Then I divided (?) the army . . . ; some I made riders of camels (?), for the rest I led forward horses. Auramazda brought me help; by the grace of Auramazda we crossed the Tigris. Then did I utterly overthrow that host of Nidintu-Bel. On the twenty-sixth day of the month Atriyadiya we joined battle.

19 (Thus) saith Darius, the king: Then did I march against Babylon; (but) before I reached Babylon, that Nidintu-Bel, who was called Nebuchadnezzar, came with a host and offered battle at the city named Zazana, on the Euphrates. Then we joined battle. Auramazda brought me help; [by the grace] of Auramazda did I utterly overthrow the host of Nidintu-Bel. The enemy fled into the water; the water carried them away. On the second day of the month Anamaka [we joined battle].

Column II

20 (Thus) saith Darius, the king: Then did Nidintu-Bel flee with a few horsemen into Babylon. Thereupon I marched to Babylon. By the grace of Auramazda I took Babylon, and I captured that Nidintu-Bel. Then I slew that Nidintu-Bel in Babylon.

21 (Thus) saith Darius, the king: While I was in Babylon, these provinces revolted from me: Persia, Susiana, Media, Assyria, [Egypt], Parthia, Margiana, Sattagydia, and Scythia.

22 (Thus) saith Darius, the king: A [certain] man named Martiya, the son of Cicikhrish, raised a rebellion [in

a city in Persia] named Kuganaka; this man revolted in Susiana, and [he said] unto the people: "[I am] Ummannish, king in Susiana."

23 (Thus) saith Darius, [the king]: At that time I was friendly with Susiana. Then were the Susians [afraid] of me, and that Martiya, who was their leader, they seized [and] slew.

24 (Thus) saith Darius, the king: A certain [Median named] Phraortes revolted in Media, and he said unto the people: "[I am Khshathrita], of the family of Cyaxares."[8] Then did the Medians who [were in the palace] revolt from me and go over unto that Phraortes; he became [king] in Media.

25 (Thus) saith Darius, the king: The Persian and Median army, which was with me, was small. Then sent I forth the army. A Persian named Hydarnes, my servant, I made their leader, and I said unto him: "Go, smite that Median host which doth not acknowledge me." Then this Hydarnes marched forth with the army. When he was come into Media, at a city in Media named Marush, he gave battle to the Medes. He who was leader of the Medes withstood not (the assault). Auramazda brought me help; by the grace of Auramazda my army utterly defeated that rebel host. On the twenty-seventh day of the month Anamaka the battle was fought by them. Then did my army await me in a district in Media named Kampada, until I came into Media.

26 (Thus) saith Darius, the king: An Armenian named Dadarshish, my servant, I sent into Armenia, and I said unto him: "Go, smite that host which is in revolt, and doth not acknowledge me." Then Dadarshish went forth. When he was come into Armenia, the rebels assembled and advanced against Dadarshish to give him battle. At a place in Armenia named [Zuzza] they

8. A king of Media prior to the foundation of the Persian empire.

fought the battle. Auramazda brought me help; by the grace of Auramazda did my army utterly overthrow that rebel host. On the eighth day of the month Thuravahara the battle was fought by them.

27 (Thus) saith Darius, the king: The rebels assembled for the second time, and they advanced against Dadarshish to give him battle. At a stronghold in Armenia named Tigra they joined battle. Auramazda brought me help; by the grace of Auramazda did my army utterly overthrow that rebel host. On the eighteenth day of the month Thuravahara the battle was fought by them.

28 Thus saith Darius, the king: The rebels assembled for the third time and advanced against Dadarshish to give him battle. At a stronghold in Armenia named U[yam]a they joined battle. Auramazda brought me help; by the grace of Auramazda did my army utterly overthrow that rebel host. On the ninth day of the month Thaigarcish the battle was fought by them. Then Dadarshish waited for me in Armenia, until I came into Media.

29 (Thus) saith Darius, the king: A Persian named Vaumisa, my servant, I sent into Armenia, and I said unto him: "Go, smite the host which is in revolt and doth not acknowledge me." Then Vaumisa went forth. When he was come into Armenia, the rebels assembled and advanced against Vaumisa to give him battle. At a place in Assyria named I[zat]a they joined battle. Auramazda brought me help; by the grace of Auramazda did my army utterly overthrow that rebel host. On the fifteenth day of the month Anamaka the battle was fought by them.

30 (Thus) saith Darius, the king: The rebels assembled a second time against Vaumisa to give him battle. At a place in Armenia named Autiyara they joined battle. Auramazda brought me help; by the grace of Auramazda did my army utterly overthrow that rebel host.

At the end of the month Thuravahara the battle was fought by them. Then Vaumisa waited for me in Armenia, until I came into Media.

31 (Thus) saith Darius, the king: Then I went forth from Babylon and came into Media. When I was come into Media that Phraortes, who called himself king in Media, came against me unto a city in Media named Kundurush to offer battle. Then we joined battle. Auramazda brought me help; by the grace of Auramazda did I utterly overthrow the host of Phraortes. On the twenty-fifth day of the month Adukani we fought the battle.

32 (Thus) saith Darius, the king: Thereupon that Phraortes fled thence with a few horsemen to a district in Media named Raga. Then did I send the army against them. Phraortes was taken and brought unto me. I cut off his nose, and his ears, and his tongue, and I put out his eyes, and he was kept in fetters in my court, and all the people beheld him. Then did I crucify him in Ecbatana, and the men who were his chief followers I imprisoned in the stronghold in Ecbatana.

33 (Thus) saith Darius, the king: A man named Citrantakhma, a Sagartian, revolted from me, and thus he spake unto the people: "I am king in Sagartia, of the family of Cyaxares." Then sent I forth a Persian and a Median army. A Median named Takhmaspada, my servant, I made their leader, and I said unto him: "Go, smite the host which is in revolt and doth not acknowledge me." Thereupon Takhmaspada went forth with the army, and he fought a battle with Citrantakhma. Auramazda brought me help; by the grace of Auramazda my army utterly defeated that rebel host, and they seized Citrantakhma and brought him unto me. Then I cut off his nose and his ears, and I put out his eyes. He was kept in fetters in my court, and all the people beheld him. Afterwards did I crucify him in Arbela.

34 (Thus) saith Darius, the king: This is what was done by me in Media.

35 (Thus) saith Darius, the king: The Parthians and the Hyrcanians revolted from me, and they declared themselves on the side of Phraortes. My father Hystaspes was [in Parthia]; and the people forsook him, they became rebellious. Then Hystaspes [marched forth with the troops which] had remained faithful. At a city [in Parthia] named Vish[pa]uz[a]tish he fought a battle with the Parthians. Auramazda [brought me help]; by the grace of Auramazda Hystaspes [utterly defeated] the rebel host. [On the twenty-second day] of the month Viyakhna the battle was fought by them.

Column III

36 (Thus) saith Darius, the king: Then did I send a Persian army unto Hystaspes from Raga. When that army reached Hystaspes, he marched forth with the host. At a city in Parthia named Patigrabana he gave battle to the rebels. Auramazda brought me help; by the grace of Auramazda Hystaspes utterly overthrew that rebel host. On the first day of the month Garmapada was the battle fought by them.

37 (Thus) saith Darius, the king: Then was the province mine. This is what was done by me in Parthia.

38 (Thus) saith Darius, the king: The province named Margiana revolted against me. A certain Margian named Frada they made their leader. Then sent I against him a Persian named Dadarshish, my servant, who was governor of Bactria, and I said unto him: "Go, smite that host which doth not acknowledge me." Then Dadarshish went forth with the army, and gave battle to the Margians. Auramazda brought me help; by the grace of Auramazda my army utterly overthrew that rebel host. On the twenty-third day of the month Atriyadiya was the battle fought by them.

39 (Thus) saith Darius, the king: Then was the province
     mine. This is what was done by me in Bactria.

40 (Thus) saith Darius, the king: A certain man named
     Vahyazdata dwelt in a city named Tarava in a district
     in Persia named Yautiya. This man rebelled for the
     second time in Persia, and thus he spake unto the
     people: "I am Smerdis, the son of Cyrus." Then the
     Persian people who were in the palace fell away from
     allegiance. They revolted from me and went over to
     that Vahyazdata. He became king in Persia.

41 (Thus) saith Darius, the king: Then did I send out the
     Persian and the Median army which was with me. A
     Persian named Artavardiya, my servant, I made their
     leader. The rest of the Persian army came unto me in
     Media. Then went Artavardiya with the army unto
     Persia. When he came to Persia, at a city in Persia
     named Rakha that Vahyazdata, who called himself
     Smerdis, advanced with the army against Artavardiya
     to give him battle. They then fought the battle. Au-
     ramazda brought me help. By the grace of Auramazda
     my host utterly overthrew the army of Vahyazdata.
     On the twelfth day of the month Thuravahara was the
     battle fought by them.

42 (Thus) saith Darius, the king: Then that Vahyazdata fled
     thence with a few horsemen unto Paishiyauvada. From
     that place he went forth with an army a second time
     against Artavardiya to give him battle. At a mountain
     named Paraga they fought the battle. Auramazda
     brought me help. By the grace of Auramazda my host
     utterly overthrew the army of Vahyazdata. On the
     fifth day of the month Garmapada was the battle
     fought by them. And they seized that Vahyazdata, and
     the men who were his chief followers they also seized.

43 (Thus) saith Darius, the king: Then did I crucify that
     Vahyazdata and the men who were his chief followers
     in a city in Persia named Uvadaicaya.

44 (Thus) saith Darius, the king: This is what was done by
     me in Persia.

45   (Thus) saith Darius, the king: That Vahyazdata, who called himself Smerdis, sent men unto Arachosia against a Persian named Vivana, my servant, the governor in Arachosia. He appointed a certain man to be their leader, and thus he spake unto him, saying: "Go, smite Vivana and the host which acknowledgeth king Darius!" Then that army which Vahyazdata had sent marched against Vivana to give him battle. At a fortress named Kapishakanish they fought the battle. Auramazda brought me help. By the grace of Auramazda my army utterly overthrew that rebel host. On the thirteenth day of the month Anamaka was the battle fought by them.

46   (Thus) saith Darius, the king: The rebels assembled a second time and went out against Vivana to give him battle. At a place named Gandutava they fought a battle. Auramazda brought me help. By the grace of Auramazda my army utterly overthrew that rebel host. On the seventh day of the month Viyakhna the battle was fought by them.

47   (Thus) saith Darius, the king: The man who was commander of that army which Vahyazdata had sent forth against Vivana fled thence with a few horsemen. To a fortress in Arachosia named Arshada he went. Then Vivana with the army marched after them on foot. There he seized him, and he slew the men who were his chief followers.

48   (Thus) saith Darius, the king: Then was the province mine. This is what was done by me in Arachosia.

49   (Thus) saith Darius, the king: While I was in Persia and in Media, the Babylonians revolted from me a second time. A certain man named Arakha, an Armenian, the son of Haldita, rebelled in Babylon. At a place named Dubala he lied unto the people (saying): "I am Nebuchadnezzar, the son of Nabonidus." Then did the Babylonian people revolt from me and went over to that Arakha. He seized Babylon, he became king in Babylon.

50 (Thus) saith Darius, the king: Then did I send an army
    unto Babylon. A Persian named Vindafrana, my serv-
    ant, I appointed as their leader, and thus I spake unto
    them (saying): "Go, smite that Babylonian host which
    doth not acknowledge me!" Then Vindafrana marched
    with the army unto Babylon. Auramazda brought me
    help. By the grace of Auramazda Vindafrana over-
    threw the Babylonians and [brought over (?) the peo-
    ple unto me]. On the twenty-second day of the month
    [Markazanash] that Arakha who called himself Neb-
    uchadnezzar, and the men who [were his chief fol-
    lowers, they seized and fettered. Then I made a decree
    (saying): "Let that Arakha] and the men who were
    his chief followers be crucified in Babylon!"

Column IV

51 (Thus) saith Darius, the king: This is what was done by
    me in Babylon.

52 (Thus) saith Darius, the king: This is what I have done;
    by the grace of Auramazda have I always acted. After
    I became king, I fought nineteen battles, (and) by the
    grace of Auramazda I overthrew nine kings, and I
    made (them) captive. One was named Gaumata, the
    Magian; he lied, saying, "I am Smerdis, the son of
    Cyrus." He made Persia to revolt. Another was named
    Atrina, the Susian; he lied, saying, "I am the king of
    Susiana." He made Susiana to revolt. Another was
    named Nidintu-Bel, the Babylonian; he lied, saying,
    "I am Nebuchadnezzar, the son of Nabonidus." He
    made Babylon to revolt. Another was named Martiya,
    the Persian; he lied, saying, "I am Ummannish, the
    king of Susiana." He made Susiana to revolt. Another
    was named Phraortes, the Mede; he lied, saying, "I am
    Khshathrita, of the race of Cyaxares." He made Media
    to revolt. Another was named Citrantakhma, of Sa-
    gartia; he lied, saying, "I am king of Sagartia, of the
    race of Cyaxares." He made Sagartia to revolt. An-

other was named Frada, of Margiana; he lied, saying, "I am king of Margiana." He made Margiana to revolt. Another was named Vahyazdata, a Persian; he lied, saying, "I am Smerdis, the son of Cyrus." He made Persia to revolt. Another was named Arakha, an Armenian; he lied saying, "I am Nebuchadnezzar, the son of Nabonidus." He made Babylon to revolt.

53 (Thus) said Darius, the king: These nine kings did I capture in these wars.

54 (Thus) saith Darius, the king: As to these provinces which revolted, lies made them revolt, so that they deceived the people. Then Auramazda delivered them into my hand; [I did] unto them according to my will.

55 (Thus) saith Darius, the king: Thou who mayest be king hereafter, beware of lies; the man who is a liar, destroy him utterly if thou thinkest "(thereby) shall my land remain whole."

56 (Thus) saith Darius, the king: This is what I have done, by the grace of Auramazda have I always acted. Whosoever shall read this inscription hereafter, let that which I have done be believed; thou shalt not hold it to be lies.

57 (Thus) saith Darius, the king: I call Auramazda to witness that it is true (and) not lies; all of it have I done.

58 (Thus) saith Darius, the king: By the grace of Auramazda there is also much else that hath been done by me which is not graven in this inscription; on this account it hath not been inscribed lest he who shall read this inscription hereafter should then hold that which hath been done by me to be too much and should not believe it, (but) should take it to be lies.

59 (Thus) saith Darius, the king: It was not done by the former kings during their time, as it hath always been done by me through the favour of Auramazda.

60 (Thus) saith Darius, the king: Now may that appear true unto thee which hath been done by me; so . . . conceal thou not. If thou shalt not conceal this edict (but)

shalt publish it to the world, then may Auramazda be thy friend, may thy house be numerous, and mayest thou thyself be long-lived.

61 (Thus) saith Darius, [the king]: If thou shalt conceal this edict and shalt not publish it to the world, may Auramazda slay thee (and) may thy house cease.

62 (Thus) saith Darius, the king: This is what I have done; by the grace of Auramazda have I always acted. Auramazda brought me help, and the other gods, (all) that there are.

63 (Thus) saith Darius, the king: On this account Auramazda brought me help, and the other gods, (all) that there are, because I was not wicked, nor was I a liar, nor was I a tyrant, neither I nor any of my line. I have ruled according to righteousness, according to . . . Whosoever helped my house, him I favoured; he who was hostile (?), him I destroyed.

64 (Thus) saith Darius, the king: Thou, who mayest be king hereafter, whosoever shall be a liar or a rebel (?), or shall not be friendly, him do thou destroy!

65 (Thus) saith Darius, the king: Thou who shalt hereafter see this tablet, which I have written, or these sculptures, destroy them not, (but) preserve them so long as thou livest!

66 (Thus) saith Darius, the king: If thou shalt behold this tablet or these sculptures, and shalt not destroy them, but shalt preserve them as long as thy line endureth, then may Auramazda be thy friend, (and) may thy house be numerous. Live long, and may Auramazda make [fortunate] whatsoever thou doest.

67 (Thus) saith Darius, the king: If thou shalt behold this tablet or these sculptures, and shalt destroy them and shalt not preserve them so long as thy line endureth, then may Auramazda slay thee, and may thy race come to nought, and whatsoever thou doest may Auramazda destroy!

68 (Thus) saith Darius, the king: These are the men who were there when I slew Gaumata, the Magian, who

was called Smerdis; then these men helped me as my followers. Intaphernes, the son of Vayaspara, a Persian; Otanes, the son of Thukhra, a Persian; Gobryas, the son of Mardonius, a Persian; Hydarnes, the son of Bagabigna, a Persian; Megabyzus, the son of Daduhya, a Persian; Ardumanish, the son of Vahauka, a Persian.

69 (Thus) saith Darius, the king: Thou who mayest be king hereafter, preserve these men [. . .].

70 (Thus) saith Darius, the king: By the grace of Auramazda this inscription [. . .] which I have made [. . .] have I written. This inscription [. . .] and [. . .] me hereafter [. . .] the inscription [. . .] in the provinces [. . .] us altogether.

Column V

71 (Thus) saith Darius, the king: This is what I did [. . .] and [. . .] manner, [after I became] king. The province named Susiana revolted from me. A Susian named [. . .] mamita they made their leader. Then I sent an army unto Susiana. A Persian named Gobryas, my servant, made I their leader. Then Gobryas set forth with the army; he delivered battle against the Susians. Then Gobryas destroyed [many of the host], and that [. . .] mamita, (their) leader, he captured, (and) he brought (him) unto me, and I slew him. Then the province [became mine].

72 (Thus) saith Darius, the king: Then were the Susians [afraid], and Auramazda delivered them into my hand . . . By the grace of Auramazda I did unto them [according to my will].

73 (Thus) saith Darius, the king: He who [respecteth] Auramazda will be . . . so long [as his line en]dureth, and [his] life [will be long].

74 [(Thus) saith] Darius, the king: [With the army (?)] I went to Scythia; against Scythia [I marched . . .] the Tigris . . . [. . .] unto the sea [. . .] I crossed over . . . [. . . many of] the Scythians I

slew, the rest I took prisoners: . . . [was brought]
unto me in fetters and *[I slew] him [. . .] named
[. . .]kha I took prison[er . . .] I then appointed
another as their leader [. . .] was named. Then the
province became mine.

75 (Thus) saith Darius, the king: [. . .] not Auramazda
[. . .] . . . By the grace of Auramazda I did unto
them [according to] my [will].

76 (Thus) saith [Darius], the [king]: Auramazda . . .
[. . .] his life and [. . .].

II
Law

Law

Introduction to the Laws

The Laws of Hammurabi, king of Babylon (reigned 1792-1750 B.C.), form the earliest extensive collection of legal texts to have come down to us from the ancient Near East; but they are not the earliest laws extant. Even before Hammurabi's day, various kings of Babylonian city-states are known to have promulgated laws. Scattered fragments of such laws have survived, e.g., from the reigns of Urukagina of Lagash (*ca.* 2360 B.C.), Sargon of Akkad (*ca.* 2300 B.C.), and Ur-Nammu of Ur (*ca.* 2100 B.C.). Somewhat more extensive are the laws of Lipit-Ishtar, king of Isin (*ca.* 1930 B.C.), of which thirty-eight have come down to us, and the collection from the city of Eshnunna, containing sixty laws, which antedates Hammurabi by only a few decades. It may be supposed that other kings likewise issued laws for their particular states, and that there were written laws in Babylon before the time of Hammurabi.

In view of the very imperfect and probably incomplete copies of these early laws which have so far been discovered, it is impossible to judge the extent to which Hammurabi made use of the work of his predecessors. About three-quarters of the Eshnunna laws are more or less reproduced in various provisions of Hammurabi's collection; but what other sources his jurists may have had available is difficult to say. However, the principles underlying the laws of all the Mesopotamian collections are remarkably similar, e.g., the ubiquitous law of talion, by which the punishment must be exactly like the crime.

The Laws of Hammurabi are not a code in the usual sense of the

The laws in this section have been selected from *The Babylonian Laws*, G. R. Driver and John C. Miles, Oxford: The Clarendon Press, 1952 (reprinted by permission); *The Assyrian Laws*, G. R. Driver and John C. Miles, Oxford: The Clarendon Press, 1935 (reprinted by permission); *The Hittite Laws*, E. Neufeld, London: Luzac and Company, 1951 (reprinted by permission of E. Neufeld); and the Books of Exodus, Deuteronomy, and Numbers from the King James Bible.

word. They do not attempt to cover all possible instances; many of the subjects omitted are of great importance, and there is little attempt at systematization. Hammurabi's work was to reform the existing laws, which he did through a series of amendments and alterations.

To comment on these laws is difficult, since so little is known of pre-existing Babylonian law. On their face, they consist of a heterogeneous series of decisions by judges in a number of isolated cases. There is no reason to suppose that such decisions had any authority as precedents to bind subsequent judgments, as in English law. The laws of Hammurabi are not statutes of the realm, but something resembling English case-law, which lays down a principle to be followed. They set forth what Hammurabi desired to have as the law of the land. The written text of the law was in no sense authoritative, but merely a memorandum which recorded a decision based on Babylonian notions of justice. No record exists of any judgments based on written technicalities or questions of procedure.

The principal and most complete surviving copy of the Laws of Hammurabi was discovered in 1901-02 at Susa, the capital of Elam, in the hill region east of Babylonia. How it got there is unknown, though perhaps it represents a portion of the spoils from some Elamite raid upon the Babylonian lowlands. The laws are inscribed on three large blocks of diorite stone, which fit together to form a cone-shaped monument. Above the actual text stands the figure of Shamash, the sun-god and god of justice, seated on his throne receiving the homage of Hammurabi. No other extant version of Hammurabi's laws is nearly so complete as this Susian stele, though a number of fragments containing portions of the collection have come to light.

The nine clay tablets or parts of tablets containing the so-called Middle Assyrian Laws were excavated between 1903 and 1914 at Ashur, the ancient capital of Assyria. Probably they were inscribed in the time of Tiglath-pileser I (reigned 1115-1077 B.C.), though some of the laws they record may go back to the fifteenth century B.C. Not all of the tablets are by the same hand, and they do not belong to a single collection. Nothing in them shows for certain who composed them or to what territory they were intended to apply, though it is likely that they were in force in the city of Ashur and the surrounding district.

The Assyrian Laws are far less complete than even the Laws of Hammurabi. Tablet A, the longest and best-preserved of the lot, deals exclusively with laws affecting women, and is probably the work of a legislator who wished to grant them either more or fewer rights than they had previously enjoyed. The laws on the other tablets are similarly restricted in scope. Like the Babylonian collection, they appear to be a series of amendments and modifications of existing law. The character of this existing law can only be surmised, though most probably it was based on Babylonian precedents, modified to suit the less commercialized and less civilized state of Assyria. A number of so-called Old Assyrian Laws are also extant, which probably originated around the time of Hammurabi. These, however, are not the law of Ashur, but of an Assyrian trading colony somewhere in Asia Minor, and are in such fragmentary condition that any comment upon them requires considerable guesswork.

The Hittite Laws were discovered between 1906 and 1912 on a number of clay tablets at Boghazkoy, the site of the former Hittite capital. Two of the tablets are nearly complete, and have been largely restored from parallel fragments. Scholars consider them to be part of a continuous series, and have numbered them accordingly. The other fragments give no indication that any other series of laws ever existed among the Hittites. Thus it may be assumed that the subjects omitted in the written laws were covered by the customary law of the people.

The date of the Laws is difficult to determine, since they contain no evidence of authorship or any reference to a king in whose reign they were composed. The tablets in their present form seem to have been inscribed sometime in the thirteenth century B.C., though the original compilation may go back to the seventeenth century. The statutes—as opposed to the court decisions—contained in the collection may perhaps have been the work of King Telepinus* (reigned 1511-1486 B.C.), whose reign was devoted largely to reforming the domestic affairs of his kingdom and resolving internal discords.

Like the Babylonians and Assyrians, the Hittites evidently found it unnecessary to legislate on all subjects. The Laws do not cover every possible case, but aim to settle particular issues. They form a record of various judicial formulae and decisions of the royal court at Hattusas, presumably intended for possible reference in parallel cases in the future. Gradually the collection of decisions was enlarged, and certain ordinances of the king were added. No attempt is made to establish principles of law to be applied to new facts.

* See the Introduction to the "Apology of Hattusilis" in Section I of this volume.

The Hittite Laws make frequent reference to the ordinances in force "hitherto"—presumably the (unwritten) customary law—as contrasted with the laws in force "now." Presumably the laws of "now" represent the introduction of statute law promulgated by a law-giver. The Hittite Laws originated apparently in a period of social and political change, and were perhaps intended to give unity to the various classes and groups which made up the highly heterogeneous Hittite empire.

The Hebrew Laws in several respects form a contrast to the other three collections. Whereas the Hittite and Mesopotamian laws were secular in nature, recording the decisions of jurists or the ordinances of kings, the Hebrew laws were believed to have been dictated by God himself. In conformance with the demands of the Hebrew religion, they show a decided ethical character missing in the legislation of surrounding peoples.

The Hebrew laws here reproduced are taken from the first five books of the Old Testament, known to the Jews as the Torah ("Law") and to the Greeks as the Pentateuch ("Five Rolls"). Scholars believe that these books were compiled from four main sources: the "J" source, in which God is called Jehovah or Yahweh; the "E" source, in which God is called Elohim; the "D" source, or Deuteronomic code; and a "P" source, or priestly code set forth by the priest Ezra in the fifth century B.C. The oldest portion of the laws—including the Ten Commandments—goes back to the time of Moses, when the Hebrews were a group of wandering tribes who had yet to acquire a settled existence or form a state. Over the centuries, new laws were added and the old ones re-interpreted. The Pentateuch in its present form probably dates from around 300 B.C.

The laws here reproduced have been selected from the Babylonian, Middle Assyrian, Hittite, and Hebrew laws and arranged according to subject. Some of these subjects are ignored in one or more of these groups of laws; other major themes which they do cover have had to be omitted for reasons of space. Among the latter are laws dealing with personal injury, sexual offenses, witchcraft, property damage, and land tenure.

ORIGIN OF THE LAWS

Prologue to the Laws of Hammurabi

When the exalted Anum[1] king of the Annunaki[2] (and) Illil[3] lord of heaven and earth, who allots the destinies of the land, allotted the divine lordship of the multitude of the people unto Marduk[4] the first-born son of Ea,[5] magnified him amongst the Igigi,[6] called Babylon by its exalted name (and) so made it pre-eminent in the (four) quarters of the world, and established for him an everlasting kingdom whose foundations are firmly laid like heaven and earth, at that time Anum and Illil for the prosperity of the people called me by name Hammu-rabi, the reverent God-fearing prince, to make justice to appear in the land,[7] to destroy the evil and the wicked that the strong might not oppress the weak, to rise indeed like Shamash[8] over the dark-haired folk[9] to give light to the land.

I, Hammu-rabi the shepherd, called of Illil, who gathers to-gether abundance and plenty, who accomplishes everything for Nippur "bond of heaven and earth,"[10] the reverent (prince) who cares for Ekur,[11] the able king, restorer of Eridu,[12] cleanser of the shrine of Eabzu,[13] who has stormed the four quarters (of

1. (Anu, An): the sky-god, leader of the Sumerian pantheon, worshipped especially at Uruk.
2. The judges of the underworld.
3. Old reading for Enlil, the storm god and chief executive of the gods, wor-shipped especially at Nippur.
4. God of Babylon and in Hammurabi's time the god of the Babylonian em-pire with the functions of Enlil delegated to him.
5. (Enki): lord of the earth and fresh waters, worshipped especially at Eridu.
6. Lesser gods attendant upon Enlil; heavenly deities.
7. I.e., to promote the people's welfare.
8. The sun-god (or here, the sun) and god of justice, worshipped especially at Sippar.
9. Late-Sumerian expression for mankind in general.
10. Sumerian epithet for the city of Nippur, the cult-center of the god Illil (Enlil).
11. The temple of Enlil at Nippur.
12. Southernmost city of Sumer.
13. Temple of Ea (Enki) at Eridu.

the world), who magnifies the fame of Babylon, who gladdens
the heart of Marduk his lord, (who) has borne the charge of
Esagil[14] all his days; the seed royal which Sin[15] has created,
giver of abundant riches to Ur,[16] the humble (prince) deep in
prayer, the bringer of overflowing wealth to Ekishshirgal;[17] the
king endued with authority, obedient to Shamash (and) powerful (?), the establisher of the foundation of Sippar,[18] who
clothes the dark abode of Aya[19] in green foliage, designer of the
house of Ebabbar[20] which is as the habitation of heaven; the
hero who showed grace to Larsa,[21] renewer of Ebabbar for
Shamash his helper: the lord the reviver of Uruk,[22] provider of
abundant waters for his people, raiser up of the top of Eanna,[23]
gathering together rich provision for Anum and Ishtar;[24] the
(protecting) shade of the land, gatherer together of the scattered
people of Isin,[25] giver of plentiful abundance to the house of
Egalmah;[26] the dragon amongst kings, the faithful servant of
Ilbaba,[27] sure founder of the habitation of Kish,[28] who surrounds
Emeteursag[29] with splendours and perfects the grand accoutre-
ments of Ishtar, overseer of the house (of) Harsagkalam;[30] the
net ensnaring the enemy, whose desire Nergal[31] his companion

14. (Esagila): temple of Marduk at Babylon.
15. The moon-god, worshipped especially at Ur.
16. City of southern Sumer, former seat of several dynasties.
17. Temple of Sin at Ur.
18. City of northern Babylonia.
19. A goddess, the wife of the god Shamash.
20. The temple of Shamash at Sippar. Another temple of Shamash at Larsa
bore the same name.
21. City in southern Babylonia, another cult-center of Shamash. It was the
seat of a powerful dynasty until Hammurabi dethroned its last king, Rim-
Sin.
22. (Erech): ancient city of southern Babylonia conquered by Hammurabi,
the cult-center of Anum and Inanna. It is mentioned in the Bible (Gen.
10:10).
23. The temple of Anum and Inanna at Uruk.
24. Ishtar is the Semitic name for Inanna, goddess of Uruk.
25. A city of southern Babylonia conquered by Hammurabi.
26. Temple of Ninkarrak at Isin.
27. (Or Zababa): a form of the god Ninurta, worshipped especially at Kish.
28. A city northeast of Babylon.
29. Temple of the god Ninurta (Ilbaba) at Kish.
30. Temple of Inanna at Kish, where she was the consort of Ilbaba.
31. The god of pestilence and war, worshipped especially at Cuthah (Kutha).

has satisfied, giver of pre-eminence to Cuthah,[32] who grants all increase for Mishlam;[33] the sturdy wild ox who gores the foe, the beloved of Tutu[34] bringing jubilation to Borsippa,[35] the reverent (prince) ceaseless in care for Ezida;[36] a god amongst kings, endued with knowledge and wisdom, who enlarges the tilth of Dilbat,[37] who heaps the garners (full of corn) for the mighty Urash;[38] the lord whose proper ornaments are the sceptre and crown wherewith Mama[39] the wise (goddess) has invested him, who has laid down the ground-plan of Kesh,[40] bountiful provider of holy feasts for Nintu(d);[41] the gracious arbiter(?) who has allotted pasture-land and watering-place to Lagash and Girsu,[42] who maintains great offerings for Eninnu;[43] who takes strong hold of the adversaries, the favourite of the most high (goddess),[44] who fulfils the oracles of Hallab,[45] who rejoices the heart of Ishtar; the prince pure (in heart) whose hands uplifted (in prayer) Adad[46] regards, appeaser of the heart of the heroic Adad in Bit-Karkara,[47] who sets in order the ornaments of Eudgalgal;[48] the king the giver of life to Adab,[49] the watcher over the house of Emakh;[50] the manly (king) amongst kings, the warrior whom none can resist, he who has granted life to Mashkan-shabru,[51] the giver of (the waters of) abundance to Mishlam to

32. City in northern Babylonia.
33. The temple of Nergal at Cuthah.
34. Usually a title of Marduk, but here applied to his son Nabu, the god of Borsippa.
35. A city near Babylon.
36. The temple of Tutu (Nabu) at Borsippa.
37. A city near Babylon.
38. A god worshipped at Borsippa.
39. (Nintu): a goddess worshipped at Kesh.
40. Kesh: a city near Lagash in central Babylonia.
41. See note 39.
42. Twin cities in central Babylonia.
43. The temple of Ningirsu at Lagash-Girsu.
44. Reference to Inanna.
45. A city in Babylonia as yet unidentified, a cult-center of Inanna.
46. The weather-god.
47. Unidentified city.
48. Temple of Adad in Bit-Karkara.
49. A city of central Babylonia.
50. The temple of the goddess Mah at Adab.
51. A city of central Babylonia.

drink; the profoundly wise (ruler) who bears the charge of government, who has attained the source of wisdom, protector of the people of Malgum[52] from annihilation, who has firmly laid (the foundations of) their habitations (and supplies them) with abundance (of good things) for (the pleasure of) Ea and Damgalnunna;[53] the magnifier of his kingdom, (who) has allotted pure sacrifices for ever; the foremost amongst kings, the subduer of (the dwellers in) the towns beside the Euphrates by the oracular command of Dagan[54] his creator, who showed grace to the people of Mari[55] and Hit;[56] the reverent prince who lightens the countenance of Tishpak[57] (and) provides holy feasts for Ninazu;[58] who brings together his people in distress (and) by his friendly act establishes their foundation in the midst of Babylon; the shepherd of the people whose deeds are pleasing to Ishtar, who establishes Ishtar in Eulmash[59] in the midst of the mart of Agade,[60] who makes the truth to appear,[61] guiding the folk aright, restoring its favourable guardian spirit to Asshur,[62] subduer of rebels; the king who has made the titles of Ishtar to appear in Emishmish[63] in Nineveh;[64] the reverent (prince) deep in prayer to the great gods; the scion of Suma-la-el,[65] the powerful heir of Sin-uballit,[66] the everlasting seed royal, the powerful king, the sun-god of Babylon who makes the light to

52. A city apparently on the middle Euphrates, conquered by Hammurabi.
53. (Damkina): the consort of the god Enki.
54. (Biblical Dagon): a west-Semitic grain-god worshipped chiefly along the middle Euphrates.
55. A city on the middle Euphrates conquered by Hammurabi.
56. (Tutul): a city on the middle Euphrates.
57. The chief god of the city of Eshnunna.
58. The god of medicine, worshipped particularly at Eshnunna.
59. Temple of Ishtar at Agade.
60. (Akkad): ancient city of northern Babylonia, the capital of Sargon's empire.
61. Or: law to prevail.
62. Capital city of Assyria, on the upper Tigris; also the name of the national god of Assyria.
63. Temple of Inanna at Nineveh.
64. Later capital of the Assyrian empire, on the upper Tigris.
65. The second king of the First Dynasty of Babylon (Hammurabi's dynasty), reigned ca. 1880-1845 B.C.
66. Hammurabi's immediate predecessor on the throne of Babylon, reigned ca. 1812-1793 B.C.

rise on the land of Shumer and Accad,[67] the king who also brings the four quarters of the world to obedience, the favourite of Ishtar am I.

When Marduk commanded me to give justice to the people of the land and to let (them) have (good) governance, I set forth truth and justice throughout the land (and) prospered the people.

Hebrew Laws ·

12   ¶And the Lord said unto Moses, Come up to me into the mount,[68] and be there: and I will give thee tables of stone,[69] and a law, and commandments which I have written; that thou mayest teach them.

13   And Moses rose up, and his minister Joshua: and Moses went up into the mount of God.

14   And he said unto the elders, Tarry ye here for us, until we come again unto you: and, behold, Aaron and Hur are with you: if any man have any matters to do, let him come unto them.

15   And Moses went up into the mount, and a cloud covered the mount.

16   And the glory of the Lord abode upon mount Sinai, and the cloud covered it six days; and the seventh day he called unto Moses out of the midst of the cloud.

17   And the sight of the glory of the Lord was like devouring fire on the top of the mount in the eyes of the children of Israel.

18   And Moses went into the midst of the cloud, and gat him up into the mount: and Moses was in the mount forty days and forty nights.

Exodus 24

67. Shumer (Sumer) was the ancient name of southern Babylonia and Accad (Akkad) of northern Babylonia.
68. Since in Exodus 24:9-11 Moses is described as being already on the mount, it is likely that 24:12 begins another narrative.
69. Tablets containing the Ten Commandments. From this time onward they were the symbol of Israel's covenant with God.

18   ¶And he [the Lord] gave unto Moses, when he had made
        an end of communing with him upon mount Sinai,
        two tables of testimony, tables of stone, written with
        the finger of God.

                                                    Exodus 31

7   ¶And the Lord said unto Moses, Go, get thee down;[70] for thy
        people, which thou broughtest out of the land of Egypt,
        have corrupted themselves:
8   They have turned aside quickly out of the way which I
        commanded them: they have made them a molten calf,
        and have worshipped it, and have sacrificed thereunto,
        and said, These be thy gods, O Israel, which have
        brought thee up out of the land of Egypt.

.   .   .   .

15   ¶And Moses turned, and went down from the mount, and
        the two tables of the testimony were in his hand: the
        tables were written on both their sides; on the one side
        and on the other were they written.
16   And the tables were the work of God, and the writing was
        the writing of God, graven upon the tables.
17   And when Joshua heard the noise of the people as they
        shouted, he said unto Moses, There is a noise of war
        in the camp.
18   And he said, It is not the voice of them that shout for mas-
        tery, neither is it the voice of them that cry for being
        overcome: but the noise of them that sing do I hear.
19   ¶And it came to pass, as soon as he came nigh unto the camp,
        that he saw the calf, and the dancing[71]: and Moses'
        anger waxed hot, and he cast the tables out of his
        hands, and brake them beneath the mount.

                                                    Exodus 32

70. I.e., down from Mount Sinai.
71. The calf was an idol; the dancing was part of the worship ceremony in its
honor.

1   And the Lord said unto Moses, Hew thee two tables of
     stone like unto the first: and I will write upon these
     tables the words that were in the first tables, which
     thou brakest.

2   And be ready in the morning, and come up in the morning
     unto mount Sinai, and present thyself there to me in
     the top of the mount.

3   And no man shall come up with thee, neither let any man
     be seen throughout all the mount; neither let the flocks
     nor herds feed before that mount.

4   ¶And he hewed two tables of stone like unto the first; and
     Moses rose up early in the morning, and went up unto
     mount Sinai, as the Lord had commanded him, and
     took in his hand the two tables of stone.

5   And the Lord descended in the cloud, and stood with him
     there, and proclaimed the name of the Lord.

. . . .

29   ¶And it came to pass, when Moses came down from mount
     Sinai with the two tables of testimony in Moses' hand,
     when he came down from the mount, that Moses wist
     not that the skin of his face shone[72] while he talked
     with him.

30   And when Aaron and all the children of Israel saw Moses,
     behold, the skin of his face shone; and they were afraid
     to come nigh him.

31   And Moses called unto them; and Aaron and all the rulers
     of the congregation returned unto him; and Moses
     talked with them.

32   And afterward all the children of Israel came nigh: and he
     gave them in commandment all that the Lord had
     spoken with him in mount Sinai.

                                              Exodus 34

72. I.e., shone with a reflection of the divine glory.

JUDICIAL PROCEDURE

SCOPE OF THE LAW

Hebrew Laws

22   Ye shall have one manner of law, as well for the stranger,
as for one of your own country: for I am the Lord
your God.

Leviticus 24

16   And I [Moses] charged your judges at that time,[1] saying,
Hear the causes between your brethren, and judge
righteously between every man and his brother, and
the stranger that is with him.

17   Ye shall not respect persons in judgment; but ye shall hear
the small as well as the great; ye shall not be afraid of
the face of man; for the judgment is God's: and the
cause that is too hard for you, bring it unto me, and I
will hear it.

Deuteronomy 1

JUDGES

Laws of Hammurabi

5   If a judge has tried a suit, given a decision, caused a sealed
tablet to be executed, (and) thereafter[2] varies his
judgement,[3] they shall convict that judge of varying
(his) judgement and he shall pay twelve-fold the
claim in that suit; then they shall remove him from his
place on the bench of judges[4] in the assembly,[5] and he
shall not (again) sit in judgement with the judges.

1. When Moses spoke to the Israelites in the wilderness beyond the River
Jordan.
2. Perhaps in a subsequent suit based on the same claim.
3. The reason for varying judgment would probably be that the judge
had been bribed by one of the litigants.
4. Probably there was a bench of three judges.
5. Apparently this is a larger body than the bench of judges—perhaps the
assembly of freemen of the city, over which the judges presided.

Middle Assyrian Laws

A57   Whether it be beating[6] or . . . [of] a married woman, [which] is prescribed [on] the tablet, [let it be carried out before the judges].

A58   In all penalties [involving either tearing out (the breasts) or] cutting off (the nose or ears) of [a married woman],[7] so let the priest be informed [and let him come];[8] (let it be carried out) according to what [is prescribed on the tablet].

Hebrew Laws

13   ¶And it came to pass on the morrow, that Moses sat to judge the people: and the people stood by Moses from the morning unto the evening.

14   And when Moses' father in law[9] saw all that he did to the people, he said, What is this thing that thou doest to the people? why sittest thou thyself alone, and all the people stand by thee from morning unto even?

15   And Moses said unto his father in law, Because the people come unto me to enquire of God:

16   When they have a matter, they come unto me; and I judge between one and another, and I do make them know the statutes of God, and his laws.

17   And Moses' father in law said unto him, The thing that thou doest is not good.

18   Thou wilt surely wear away, both thou, and this people that is with thee: for this thing is too heavy for thee; thou art not able to perform it thyself alone.

19   Hearken now unto my voice, I will give thee counsel, and God shall be with thee: Be thou for the people to Godward, that thou mayest bring the causes unto God:

20   And thou shalt teach them ordinances and laws, and shalt

6. Presumably a punishment.
7. Certainly a punishment.
8. Whether or not the priest himself performs the mutilation or merely supervises it is not clear.
9. Jethro, a priest of Midian (one of a number of tribes in northwest Arabia)—thus a foreigner.

shew them the way wherein they must walk, and the work that they must do.

21   Moreover thou shalt provide out of all the people able men, such as fear God, men of truth, hating covetousness; and place such over them, to be rulers of thousands, and rulers of hundreds, rulers of fifties, and rulers of tens.

22   And let them judge the people at all seasons: and it shall be, that every great matter they shall bring unto thee, but every small matter they shall judge: so shall it be easier for thyself, and they shall bear the burden with thee.

23   If thou shalt do this thing, and God command thee so, then thou shalt be able to endure, and all this people shall also go to their place in peace.

24   So Moses hearkened to the voice of his father in law, and did all that he had said.

25   And Moses chose able men out of all Israel, and made them heads over the people, rulers of thousands, rulers of hundreds, rulers of fifties, and rulers of tens.

26   And they judged the people at all seasons: the hard causes they brought unto Moses, but every small matter they judged themselves.

27   ¶And Moses let his father in law depart; and he went his way into his own land.

Exodus 18

WITNESSES

Laws of Hammurabi

1   If a man[10] has accused a man and has charged[11] him with manslaughter[12] and then has not proved (it against) him, his accuser shall be put to death.[13]

10. The man who brings the charge is a prosecutor and not a defendant in proceedings for defamation. This is proved by the penalty inflicted upon him if the accused person is innocent, based on the law of talion.
11. Apparently in a court of law.
12. The Laws of Hammurabi appear to recognize some distinction between murder and manslaughter.
13. On the principle of talion, the accuser must pay the same penalty he had sought to bring upon the accused.

3   If a man has come forward in a case to bear witness to a felony and then has not proved the statement that he has made, if that case (is) a capital one,[14] that man shall be put to death.

4   If he has come forward to bear witness to (a claim for) corn or money, he shall remain liable for the penalty[15] for that suit.

127 If a man has caused a finger to be pointed at a high-priestess or a married lady and has then not proved (what he has said), they shall flog that man before the judges and shave half his head.

Middle Assyrian Laws

A18 If a man has spoken to his neighbour either secretly or in a quarrel, saying: "Thy wife has behaved as a (common) whore"[16] (and) saying: "I myself will charge her," (if) he cannot bring a (definite) charge against (her and therefore) has not charged (her), that man shall be beaten forty blows with rods (and) shall do labour for the king for one full month; he shall be cut off[17] (?) and shall pay one talent of lead.

Hebrew Laws

1   Thou shalt not raise a false report: put not thine hand with the wicked to be an unrighteous witness.

7   Keep thee far from a false matter; and the innocent and righteous slay thou not: for I will not justify the wicked.

8   ¶And thou shalt take no gift: for the gift blindeth the wise, and perverteth the words of the righteous.

Exodus 23

15   ¶One witness shall not rise up against a man for any iniq-

14. Capital crimes are punishable by death.
15. The witness who has not proved his case must pay the same penalty that he had tried to bring upon another person.
16. No question of the wife's guilt arises here: she is presumed to be innocent, and the informer is regarded as one who maliciously accuses an innocent woman.
17. Possibly, expelled from the rights and privileges of property or of religion.

uity, or for any sin, in any sin that he sinneth: at the mouth of two witnesses, or at the mouth of three witnesses, shall the matter be established.

16 ¶If a false witness rise up against any man to testify against him that which is wrong;

17 Then both the men, between whom the controversy is, shall stand before the Lord,[18] before the priests and the judges, which shall be in those days;

18 And the judges shall make diligent inquisition: and, behold, if the witness be a false witness, and hath testified falsely against his brother;

19 Then shall ye do unto him, as he had thought to have done unto his brother: so shalt thou put the evil away from among you.

Deuteronomy 19

OATHS[19]

Laws of Hammurabi

20 If the slave escapes from the hand of him who has caught him, that man shall take an oath by the life of a god for (the satisfaction of) the owner of the slave and he then goes free.

23 If the robber is not caught, the man who has been robbed shall formally declare whatever he has lost before a god, and the city and the mayor[20] in whose territory or district[20] the robbery has been committed shall replace whatever he has lost for him.[21]

---

18. I.e., before the supreme tribunal at the sanctuary.

19. The oath is regarded as a means of establishing the facts where there are no witnesses. Extant documents show that this procedure took place in front of a temple or shrine. The oath was accepted as final in any case for which it was prescribed. No doubt the god was thought to punish whoever should swear falsely: the possibility of a false oath was not considered.

20. It is not known how far the jurisdiction of the "city" and the "mayor" extended, nor what was the distinction between their "territory" and "district."

21. The Babylonian rule was that the city or local officers must pay compensation for offenses committed within their jurisdiction, on the theory that they have failed to maintain law and order.

103 If an enemy[22] causes him (a merchant's agent) to jettison anything that he is carrying[23] whilst he is going on the journey (for the merchant), the agent may take an oath by the life of a god and he then goes free.

120 If a man has stored his corn for storage in a bin in a man's house and a loss occurs in the granary, whether the owner of the house has opened the bin and taken the corn or whether he wholly contests (the storage of) the grain which has been stored in his house, the owner of the corn shall formally declare his corn before a god and the owner of the house must double the corn which has disappeared and give (it) to the owner of the corn.

131 If the husband of a married lady has accused her but she is not caught lying with another man, she shall take an oath by the life of a god and return to her house.

266 If the finger of a god touches or a lion kills (a beast) in the fold, the herdsman may purge (himself) before a god and the mischief in the fold shall fall on the owner of the fold.

Hebrew Laws

10 If a man deliver unto his neighbor an ass, or an ox, or a sheep, or any beast, to keep; and it die, or be hurt, or driven away, no man seeing it:

11 Then shall an oath of the Lord be between them both, that he hath not put his hand unto his neighbour's goods; and the owner of it shall accept thereof, and he shall not make it good.

Exodus 22

---

22. Apparently the king's enemies, since an agent suffering loss through the normal perils of the journey must himself repay the amount of the loss.
23. I.e., the property, money, or goods lent to the agent by the merchant.

ORDEALS[24]

Laws of Hammurabi

2   If a man has charged a man with sorcery and then has not
      proved (it against) him, he who is charged with the
      sorcery shall go to the holy river[25]; he shall leap into
      the holy river and, if the holy river overwhelms him,
      his accuser shall take and keep his house[26]; if the holy
      river proves that man clear (of the offence) and he
      comes back safe, he who has charged him with sorcery
      shall be put to death;[27] he who leapt into the holy river
      shall take and keep the house of his accuser.

132 If a finger has been pointed at (a) married lady with re-
      gard to another man and she is not caught lying with
      the other man, she shall leap into the holy river for her
      husband.[28]

Middle Assyrian Laws

A17 If a man has spoken to a man, saying, "Thy wife is behav-
      ing as a (common) whore," (and) there are no wit-
      nesses,[29] they shall make a covenant (and) go to the
      (ordeal by) river.[30]

---

24. The ordeal is not a punishment, but a mode of proof. It is intended to
prove or disprove what cannot be established through the testimony of
witnesses.
25. In this case the river (the Euphrates) was regarded as a god.
26. According to this law, the guilty party sinks and the innocent floats. In
most of the Semitic world, however, the rule was that the innocent man sinks
—i.e. is accepted by the holy river as clean (and is saved from drowning by
the onlookers)—whereas the guilty party is rejected by the river as unclean.
27. This is another example of the law of talion: the punishment for practicing
sorcery was also death.
28. The husband had the power of life and death over his wife. If he
caught her in adultery, he could have her and her partner bound and cast
into the water; but if he chose to let her live, then the man with whom she
committed the offense must also be allowed to live.
29. I.e., she is not caught in the act.
30. Evidently the woman is the one to undergo the ordeal, although both
parties "go to the river." Here the question is not whether the informant
has committed slander, but only whether the wife is guilty of adultery.

Hebrew Laws

24   And he [the priest] shall cause the woman [accused of
     adultery] to drink the bitter water that causeth the
     curse: and the water that causeth the curse shall enter
     into her, and become bitter.

27   And when he hath made her to drink the water, then it
     shall come to pass, that, if she be defiled, and have
     done trespass against her husband, that the water that
     causeth the curse shall enter into her, and become bit-
     ter, and her belly shall swell, and her thigh shall rot:
     and the woman shall be a curse among her people.

28   And if the woman be not defiled, but be clean; then she
     shall be free, and shall conceive seed.[31]

                                                        Numbers 5

31. These three verses are the one clear reference to an ordeal in the Old
Testament.

HOMICIDE

Laws of Hammurabi

153 If a woman has procured the death of her husband on ac-
     count of another man, they shall impale that woman.

206 If a man strikes a (free) man in an affray and inflicts a
     wound on him, that man may swear "Surely I did not
     strike (him) wittingly," and he shall pay the surgeon.

207 If he dies of the striking, he may swear likewise; if (the
     victim is) a (free) man, he shall pay one-half of a
     maneh[1] of silver.

208 If (he is) a villein,[2] he shall pay one-third of a maneh of
     silver.

209 If a man strikes the daughter of a (free)man (and) causes

1. Maneh (or mina): a weight of about 500 grams, divided into 60
shekels. Coinage had not yet been invented; the money was weighed out in
bars.
2. A dependent of some sort, though certainly not a slave.

her to lose the fruit of her womb, he shall pay ten shekels[3] of silver for the fruit of her womb.[4]

210 If that woman dies, they shall put his daughter to death.[5]

211 If he causes the daughter of a villein to lose the fruit of her womb by striking her, he shall pay five shekels of silver.

212 If that woman dies, he shall pay one-half of a maneh of silver.

213 If he has struck the slave-girl of a (free) man and causes her to lose the fruit of her womb, he shall pay two shekels of silver.

214 If that slave-girl dies, he shall pay one-third of a maneh of silver.

218 If the surgeon has made a deep incision in (the body of) a (free) man with a lancet (?) of bronze and causes the man's death or has opened the caruncle (?) in (the eye of) a man and so destroys the man's eye, they shall cut off his fore-hand.

219 If the surgeon has made a deep incision in (the body of) a villein's slave with a lancet (?) of bronze and causes (his) death, he shall replace slave for slave.

220 If he has opened his caruncle (?) with a lancet (?) of bronze and destroys his eye, he shall pay half his price in silver.

229 If a builder has built a house for a man[6] and has not made his work sound, and the house which he has built has fallen down and so caused the death of the householder, that builder shall be put to death.

230 If it causes the death of the householder's son, they shall put that builder's son to death.

3. Shekel: a weight of about 8 grams.

4. It is not stated who is the complainant or who receives the compensation, but presumably it was the husband.

5. This is an instance of the principle of talion. The daughter, rather than the wife, of the offender is put to death, since the daughter will consequently bear no child.

6. Probably a house of sun-baked brick, which remained the most common material for private buildings. Fire-baked bricks were reserved for more important structures.

231 If it causes the death of the householder's slave, he shall give slave for slave to the householder.

250 If an ox as it passes along a street has gored a man and causes his death, that case affords no cause of action.

251 If the man's ox is wont to gore and his district has notified him that (it is) wont to gore and he has not screened its horns (or) has not tied (it) up and that ox has gored the son of a (free) man and so has caused (his) death, he shall give one-half of a maneh of silver.[7]

252 If (the victim is) the slave of a (free) man, he shall give one-third of a maneh of silver.

Middle Assyrian Laws

A10[8] [If] either a man or a woman has entered a man's [house] and has killed [either a man] or a woman, the murderers [shall be given up to the owner of the house]; if he chooses, they shall be put to death, (or), [if he chooses,] he may make a composition (and) take [any of their property].[9] [Or if] the murderers have [no]-thing [to give in (their) house], either a son or [a daughter] . . . in the house . . . who . . .[10]

A21 If a man has struck a lady by birth and has caused her to cast the fruit of her womb (and) charge (and) proof have been brought against him, he shall pay two talents and thirty manehs of lead[11]; he shall be beaten

7. In contrast to the Hebrews, the Babylonians regarded this as a civil offense rather than as murder.

8. This is the only section of Tablet A dealing with murder, as opposed to assault resulting in abortion; and the text is badly mutilated.

9. It is difficult to tell here who executes the sentence, whether the avenger of blood himself or someone else. The idea underlying the compensation for murder by giving another person in exchange is the desire to restore the fighting strength of a tribe which had lost one of its members.

10. Perhaps this refers to vicarious punishment, which was not unknown in Assyria.

11. The essence of this offense is the deprivation of offspring suffered by the husband; thus he gets the compensation. One talent was equal to 60 manehs.

fifty blows with rods (and) shall do labour for the king
for one full month.[12]

A50[13] [If a man] has struck a married [woman] and caused her
to lose [the fruit of her womb, the wife of the man]
who [caused] the (other) married woman [to lose]
the fruit of [her womb] shall be treated as [he has]
treated her; [for the fruit of] her womb he pays (on
the principle of) a life (for a life). But, if that woman
dies, the man shall be put to death; for the fruit of her
womb he pays (on the principle of) a life (for a life).
Or, if that woman's husband has no son (and) his
wife has been struck and has cast the fruit of her
womb, for the fruit of her womb the striker shall be
put to death. If the fruit of the womb is a girl, he none
the less pays (on the principle of) a life (for a life).

A51 If a man has struck a married woman who does not rear her
children[14] and has caused her to cast the fruit of her
womb, this punishment (shall be inflicted): he shall
pay two talents of lead.[15]

A52 If a man has struck a harlot and caused her to cast the fruit
of her womb, blow for blow shall be laid upon him;
(thus) he pays (on the principle of) a life (for a
life).[16]

12. The state is concerned in what happens to a "lady by birth" since she
is a person of higher social standing than the ordinary married woman.
13. In this and the following two laws, the offense is of a private nature,
since the victim is at best an ordinary married woman and at worst a harlot.
There is nothing, however, to indicate whether the assault was intentional or
accidental. Probably Assyrian law drew no such distinctions.
    The principle of talion is difficult to apply here, since the man cannot be
treated in the same way that he treated the woman. Thus talion requires
vicarious punishment.
14. Probably due to ill-health or neglect, though possibly she puts them out
for adoption or sells them.
15. Presumably the husband gets the compensation, since the child is regarded as his property rather than hers.
16. Since the harlot presumably has no husband to support her, the child
represents an economic asset.

Hittite Laws

1   If anyone slays a man or a woman in anger,[17] he shall [bury him] and shall surrender four persons, either man or woman,[18] and his estate shall be liable.[19]

2   If anyone slays a male-slave or a female-slave in anger, he shall bury him and shall surrender two persons, either man or woman, and his estate shall be liable.

3   If anyone smites a free man or a free woman, his hand only transgressing,[20] so that he dies, he shall bury him and shall surrender two persons, and his estate shall be liable.

4   If anyone smites a male-slave or a female-slave, his hand only transgressing, so that he dies, he shall bury him, and shall surrender one person, and his estate shall be liable.

5   If anyone slays a merchant of Hatti, he shall give one and a half manehs of silver, and his estate shall be liable.[21] If it (occurred) in the land of Luiya or in the land of Pala, he shall give one and a half manehs of silver and make restitution for his goods[22]; if in the land of Hatti, he shall bury the merchant.

17   If anyone causes a free woman to miscarry, if in the tenth month, he shall give ten shekels of silver; if in the fifth

17. I.e., intentionally. The expression "in anger" contrasts with "his hand only transgressing" in Laws 3 and 4.

18. Among the Hittites the oldest known sanction for homicide was to hand over a number of "heads"—presumably of slaves or children—from the household of the slayer to that of the slain.

19. His estate shall be liable: This phrase is intended to convey the idea of a joint liability beyond the mere person of the offender. It was quite common for the court to grant the victim of an offense a charge on the property of the offender. In the early stages of legal development the courts did not enforce claims themselves, but left this task to the injured party.

20. I.e., unintentionally. The offense is manslaughter, not murder.

21. The lightness of the penalty (the fact that no persons were handed over) indicates that the trader was regarded as an inferior person.

22. I.e., the merchant was probably on a trading journey with money and goods.

month, he shall give five shekels of silver, and his estate shall be liable.[23]

18   If anyone causes a female-slave to miscarry, if in the tenth month, he shall give five shekels of silver.

37   If anyone elopes with a woman [and] afterwards a rescuer follows them, if two men or three men[24] die, there shall be no compensation. "Thou art a wolf."[25]

38   If men are caught for trial and a rescuer comes to them, and a struggle ensues at the bar and (one of them) smites the rescuer and he dies, there shall be no compensation.[26]

43   If anyone habitually drives his cattle across a river and another pushes him and seizes the tail of the ox and crosses the river, and the river engulfs the owner of the ox, they shall take him.[27]

44A   If anyone pushes a man into the fire and he dies, he shall give him (his) son (in his place).[28]

174   If men fight each other and one dies, he (the other) shall give one person.[29]

Hebrew Laws

12   ¶He that smiteth a man, so that he die, shall be surely put to death.

---

23. Presumably the husband receives this compensation for his loss of offspring. The assault on the woman personally and her possible death are not considered.

24. I.e., the abductors.

25. There is no compensation here, because the pursuit and fight took place in the exercise of a legal right; the victims were in the act of committing a crime. The opposite case, where the pursuer or some of his helpers are killed, does not require mention; it is self-evident that compensation must be paid.

26. Since in this case the rescuer is interfering with the course of justice, there is no compensation for his death.

27. It is impossible to tell here who takes the guilty man—the family of the victim or the authorities.

28. This shows an intermediary stage between a system of pecuniary compensation for a life and the principle of talion: the offender is not pushed into the fire.

29. The smallness of the penalty is due to the extenuating circumstance of the fight; the act of killing was unintentional.

13 And if a man lie not in wait, but God deliver him into his hand; then I will appoint thee a place whither he shall flee.[30]

14 But if a man come presumptuously upon his neighbor, to slay him with guile; thou shalt take him from mine altar, that he may die.[31]

15 ¶And he that smiteth his father, or his mother, shall be surely put to death.

20 ¶And if a man smite his servant, or his maid, with a rod, and he die under his hand; he shall be surely punished.

21 Notwithstanding, if he continue a day or two,[32] he shall not be punished: for he is his money.

22 ¶If men strive, and hurt a woman with child, so that her fruit depart from her, and yet no mischief follow: he shall be surely punished, according as the woman's husband will lay upon him; and he shall pay as the judges determine.

23 And if any mischief follow, then thou shalt give life for life,

24 Eye for eye, tooth for tooth, hand for hand, foot for foot,

25 Burning for burning, wound for wound, stripe for stripe.

28 ¶If an ox gore a man or a woman, that they die: then the ox shall be surely stoned, and his flesh shall not be eaten[33]; but the owner of the ox shall be quit.

29 But if the ox were wont to push with his horn in time past, and it hath been testified to his owner, and he hath not kept him in, but that he hath killed a man or a woman; the ox shall be stoned, and his owner also shall be put to death.[34]

30 If there be laid on him a sum of money,[35] then he shall give

30. This is evidently a case of unintentional homicide, in which the offender has the right of sanctuary.
31. For intentional homicide, the right of sanctuary is denied.
32. I.e., survives for a day or two.
33. The ox is treated as a murderer and his flesh is rendered unclean. Compare with Hammurabi's law no. 250, p. 157.
34. Compare Hammurabi's law no. 251, p. 157.
35. I.e., instead of the death penalty.

for the ransom of his life whatsoever is laid upon him.

31   Whether he have gored a son, or have gored a daughter, according to this judgment shall it be done unto him.

Exodus 21

9   ¶And the Lord spake unto Moses, saying,

10   Speak unto the children of Israel, and say unto them, When ye be come over Jordan into the land of Canaan:

11   Then ye shall appoint you cities to be cities of refuge for you; that the slayer may flee thither, which killeth any person at unawares.

12   And they shall be unto you cities for refuge from the avenger; that the manslayer die not, until he stand before the congregation in judgement.[36]

13   And of these cities which ye shall give six cities shall ye have for refuge.

14   Ye shall give three cities on this side Jordan, and three cities shall ye give in the land of Canaan, which shall be cities of refuge.

15   These six cities shall be a refuge, both for the children of Israel, and for the stranger, and for the sojourner among them: that every one that killeth any person unawares may flee thither.

16   And if he smite him with an instrument of iron, so that he die, he is a murderer: the murderer shall surely be put to death.

17   And if he smite him with throwing a stone, wherewith he may die, and he die, he is a murderer: the murderer shall surely be put to death.

18   Or if he smite him with an hand weapon of wood, wherewith he may die, and he die, he is a murderer: the murderer shall surely be put to death.

19   The revenger of blood himself shall slay the murderer: when he meeteth him, he shall slay him.

36. This represents an attempt to regulate the primitive custom of blood revenge. The law thus tacitly forbids the slaying of the offender's kinsmen to satisfy the feud. Compare Middle Assyrian law no. A 10, p. 157.

20 But if he thrust him of hatred, or hurl at him by laying of wait, that he die;

21 Or in enmity smite him with his hand, that he die: he that smote him shall surely be put to death; for he is a murderer: the revenger of blood shall slay the murderer, when he meeteth him.

22 But if he thrust him suddenly without enmity, or have cast upon him any thing without laying of wait,

23 Or with any stone, wherewith a man may die, seeing him not, and cast it upon him, that he die, and was not his enemy, neither sought his harm:

24 Then the congregation shall judge between the slayer and the revenger of blood according to these judgments:

25 And the congregation shall deliver the slayer out of the hand of the revenger of blood, and the congregation shall restore him to the city of his refuge, whither he was fled: and he shall abide in it unto the death of the high priest, which was anointed with the holy oil.

26 But if the slayer shall at any time come without the border of the city of his refuge, whither he was fled;

27 And the revenger of blood find him without the borders of the city of his refuge, and the revenger of blood kill the slayer; he shall not be guilty of blood:

28 Because he should have remained in the city of his refuge until the death of the high priest: but after the death of the high priest the slayer shall return into the land of his possession.

29 So these things shall be for a statute of judgment unto you throughout your generations in all your dwellings.

30 Whoso killeth any person, the murderer shall be put to death by the mouth of witnesses; but one witness shall not testify against any person to cause him to die.

31 Moreover ye shall take no satisfaction for the life of a murderer, which is guilty of death: but he shall be surely put to death.

32 And ye shall take no satisfaction for him that is fled to the city of his refuge, that he should come again to dwell in the land, until the death of the priest.

33   So ye shall not pollute the land wherein ye are: for blood it
        defileth the land: and the land cannot be cleansed of
        the blood that is shed therein, but by the blood of him
        that shed it.
34   Defile not therefore the land which ye shall inhabit,
        wherein I dwell: for I the Lord dwell among the chil-
        dren of Israel.

Numbers 35

SLAVERY AND SERVITUDE

Laws of Hammurabi[1]

15   If a man has let a slave of a palace or a slave-girl of a palace
        or the slave of a villein or the slave-girl of a villein es-
        cape by the great gate, he shall be put to death.[2]
16   If a man has harboured a lost slave or slave-girl of a palace
        or of a villein in his house and then has not brought
        (them) out at the proclamation of the herald, that
        owner of the house shall be put to death.
17   If a man has caught either a slave or a slave-girl[3] fugitive
        in the open country and hales him to his owner, the
        owner of the slave shall give him two shekels of silver.
18   If that slave does not then declare (the name of) his owner,
        he shall hale him to the palace; the facts of his case

1. Aiding the flight of a slave is analogous to kidnapping, which is a form
of theft. The flight of slaves seems to have been a common occurrence in
Babylonia; for contracts of sale are extant which provide safeguards against
this, and other documents deal with their return to their owners if taken in
flight.
   Modern concepts of slavery have been influenced by Roman law, in which
the master had the power of life and death over his slave; but in both Babylonia and Israel there was little difference between the hired workman and
the slave.
2. The law is especially strict in the case of a slave of the palace because
the offender is aiding in an offense against the king. Probably the villein's
slave is included in these provisions because the villein is closely connected
with the palace.
3. This law refers to slaves in general, rather than the special class of
slaves dealt with in nos. 15 and 16, above.

shall be found, and they shall restore him to his master.

19 If he detains that slave in his house (and) afterwards the slave is caught in his possession, that man shall be put to death.

117 If a man has become liable to arrest under a bond and has sold his wife, his son, or his daughter or gives (them) into servitude, for three years they shall do work in the house of him who has bought them or taken them in servitude; in the fourth year their release shall be granted.

118 If he gives a slave or a slave-girl into servitude, the merchant shall let (the period of redemption) expire (and) shall sell (him); he shall not be (re)claimed.

119 If a man has become liable to arrest under a bond and sells his slave-girl who has borne him sons, the owner of the slave-girl shall pay the money which the merchant has given (for her) and shall redeem his slave-girl.[4]

146 If a man has married a priestess[5] and she has given a slave-girl to her husband and she bears sons, (if) thereafter that slave-girl goes about making herself equal to her mistress, because she has borne sons her mistress shall not sell her; she may put the mark (of a slave) on her and may count her with the slave-girls.[6]

147 If she has not borne sons, her mistress may sell her.

175 If either a slave of a palace or a slave of a villein has mar-

---

4. I.e., a man has the right to buy back a slave-girl who has borne him sons, whether or not the new owner wishes to sell her.

5. There are several classes of priestesses mentioned in the laws. These probably have their origin in Sumerian civilization, as their titles are always written in the Sumerian language. Marriage with a priestess apparently had a special legal status: the wife was not allowed to bear children, but could present her husband with a slave-girl, whose sons were then considered the sons of the priestess.

The custom of regarding the sons of a slave or servant as the sons of the wife is also recorded in the Bible (Genesis 30), where the maids of Leah and Rachel bear sons to Jacob. Leah and Rachel, of course, were not priestesses.

6. Obviously the position of the slave-girl who has borne sons was normally higher than that of the ordinary slave-girl.

ried a lady[7] and she bears sons, the owner of the slave shall make no claim to the sons of the lady for slavery.

226 If a barber has excised a slave's mark[8] without (the knowledge of) his owner so that he cannot be traced, they shall cut off the fore-hand of that barber.

227 If a man has constrained the barber and he excises the slave's mark so that he cannot be traced, they shall put that man to death and shall hang him at his (own) door; the barber may swear "Surely I excised (it) unwittingly," and he then goes free.

278 If a man will buy a slave (or) a slave-girl and his month's warranty has not expired and the falling sickness smites him, he shall render (him) to his seller and the buyer shall take (back) the silver that he has paid.

279 If a man will buy a slave (or) a slave-girl and he or she becomes liable to a claim, he who has sold him shall meet the claims.

280 If a man buys a man's slave (or) slave-girl in a foreign country and then, whenever they come (back) into the country, the owner of the slave or of the slave-girl discovers either his slave or his slave-girl, if that slave and slave-girl are natives of the country, their release shall be then granted without (any payment of) money.[9]

281 If (they are) natives of another country, the buyer indeed shall state before a god (the amount of) the money

7. The marriage of a slave with a lady was obviously considered a valid marriage within the law.

8. This was a mark branded or incised into the flesh, generally on the forehead or hand. Its purpose was chiefly to identify the owner and enable a fugitive slave to be restored to him, not merely to show that the person thus marked was a slave rather than a free man. Defacement of the slave-mark thus injured the slave-owner's property rights, as it made restoration difficult.

9. This law (and no. 281) applies only where the Babylonian owner has lost the slave involuntarily through flight or theft.

Possibly it was forbidden by law to sell Babylonian slaves abroad, or perhaps Babylonian law did not recognize as lawful any dealings with a Babylonian slave in a foreign country. The dealer thus acquired no legal right by the purchase of the slave. Ordinarily the seller of the slave would be responsible for the loss; but in this case he is abroad and beyond the reach of Babylonian law.

which he has paid and the owner of the slave or the
slave-girl shall give the money which he has paid to
the merchant and shall redeem (?) his slave or his
slave-girl.[10]

282 If the slave states to his master "Thou art not my master,"[11]
his master shall convict him as his slave and cut off his
ear.

Middle Assyrian Laws

c2 [If a man has sold] to another man for (a sum of) money
[a man] or lady by birth who is dwelling [in his
house] as (security for) money or as [a pledge,[12] or]
has sold [any one else] who is dwelling in his house
(and) [charge has been brought against him], he shall
forfeit his money; he shall give his equivalent [accord-
ing to his price] to the owner of the (person who is
his) property, he shall be beaten [x blows with a rod]
and do labour for the king for twenty days.[13]

c3 [If a man] has sold into another country for (a sum of)
money [either a man] or lady by birth [who is dwelling in his house] as (security for) money or as a
pledge, (and) [charge] (and) proof have been brought
against him, he shall forfeit his money; he shall give
[his equivalent according to his price to] the owner of
the (person who is his) property; he shall be beaten
[x blows with a rod] and do labour for the king for
forty days.[14] [If the man whom he has sold] has died

10. Here the buyer is indemnified, since presumably he had no reason to
suspect that the seller did not have legal ownership of a foreign slave.
11. The application of this law is somewhat obscure. It can scarcely apply
to the case of law no. 280, since there is no reason why the Babylonian slave
should deny his master if he is to be set free upon identification, or why the
master should trouble to identify him.
12. A pledge is a man or woman taken by a creditor in repayment of a debt
who lives and works in the creditor's household until the debt is extinguished
by his services or until the debtor redeems him.
13. The persons covered by this law are not the creditor's absolute property,
and he has no right to sell them.
14. If the crime of selling a pledge is compounded by selling him in a
foreign country, the penalty increases in severity.

in the other country, [he shall pay (on the principle of) a life (for a life)]. An Assyrian man or an Assyrian woman [who] has been taken [at the full price][15] (in discharge of the debt) may be sold into another country.

Hittite Laws

22   If a slave escapes and anyone brings him back, if he[16] finds him in the vicinity, he (the owner) shall give him shoes; if (he is caught) on this side of the river, he shall give him[16] two shekels of silver; if on the other side of the river he shall give him three shekels of silver.[17]

23   If a slave escapes and goes to the country of Luiyaš, to him who brings him back he (the owner) shall give six shekels of silver. If a slave escapes and goes to an enemy country, he who brings him back shall himself take him.[18]

24   If a male-slave or a female-slave escapes, he in whose home his master finds him shall give as a man's wages [. . . shekels of silver] a year; but as a woman's wages he shall give fifty (?) shekels of silver [a year].[19]

173 . . . If a slave rises against his master, he shall go into the pot.[20]

---

15. In this case the pledge has been foreclosed and is therefore irredeemable. The owner has lost the right of redemption, and the pledge becomes the absolute property of the creditor, who may dispose of it as he pleases.

16. I.e., the finder.

17. The river is presumably a natural boundary of the country. The shoes were supplied to the captor to indemnify him for the use of his own shoes in chasing the slave. Punishment of the recaptured slave was apparently left to the master's discretion.

18. The principle here is that when a slave has escaped to a hostile country the proprietary rights of his original master automatically cease.

19. If the finder detains the slave in his house, the finder is not put to death as in the laws of Hammurabi (nos. 16 and 19), but merely has to pay compensation for the use of the slave's labor while in his possession.

20. Presumably this was an ignominious form of capital punishment, whereby the culprit was buried alive in a pot.

175 If a shepherd or an *agrig*[21] takes a free woman, she shall be a slave in the second or in the fourth year. Also her children shall be slave-born; they shall wear the girdle[22] (?) and no one shall take the girdle.

176B[23] If anyone buys a craftsman (and) buys either a potter, a smith, a carpenter, a leather-worker, a tailor, a weaver or a lace-maker, he shall give ten shekels of silver.

177 If anyone buys a . . . an augur, he shall give twenty-five shekels of silver. If anyone buys an unskilled man or woman, he shall give twenty shekels of silver.

Hebrew Laws

2 If thou buy an Hebrew servant, six years he shall serve: and in the seventh he shall go out free for nothing.

3 If he came in by himself, he shall go out by himself: if he were married, then his wife shall go out with him.

4 If his master have given him a wife, and she have borne him sons or daughters; the wife and her children shall be her master's, and he shall go out by himself.

5 And if the servant shall plainly say, I love my master, my wife, and my children; I will not go out free:

6 Then his master shall bring him unto the judges; he shall also bring him to the door, or unto the door post; and his master shall bore his ear through with an aul; and he shall serve him for ever.

7 ¶And if a man sell his daughter to be a maidservant, she shall not go out as the menservants do.

8 If she please not her master, who hath betrothed her to

---

21. The shepherd and the *agrig* were among the lowest-ranking slaves. The meaning of *agrig* is uncertain; but presumably it refers to an inferior official of the temple.

22. Translation uncertain. In ancient times girdles (belts) were employed to show a person's status.

23. These laws (nos. 176B and 177), as well as others from the Hittite collection not reproduced here, attempt to fix the price of the sale, rather than the hire, of certain types of workmen and artisans, and to establish a uniform price system in town and village.

himself, then shall he let her be redeemed: to sell her unto a strange nation he shall have no power, seeing he hath dealt deceitfully with her.

9   And if he have betrothed her unto his son, he shall deal with her after the manner of daughters.

10   If he take him another wife: her food, her raiment, and her duty of marriage, shall he not diminish.

11   And if he do not these three unto her, then shall she go out free without money.

Exodus 21

39   ¶And if thy brother[24] that dwelleth by thee be waxen poor, and be sold unto thee; thou shalt not compel him to serve as a bondservant:

40   But as an hired servant, and as a sojourner, he shall be with thee, and shall serve thee unto the year of jubile.[25]

41   And then shall he depart from thee, both he and his children with him, and shall return unto his own family, and unto the possession of his fathers shall he return.

42   For they are my servants, which I brought forth out of the land of Egypt: they shall not be sold as bondmen.

43   Thou shalt not rule over him with rigour; but shalt fear thy God.

44   Both thy bondmen, and thy bondmaids, which thou shalt have, shall be of the heathen that are round about you; of them shall ye buy bondmen and bondmaids.

45   Moreover of the children of the strangers that do sojourn among you, of them shall ye buy, and of their families that are with you, which they begat in your land: and they shall be your possession.

46   And ye shall take them as an inheritance for your children after you, to inherit them for a possession; they shall be your bondmen for ever: but over your brethren the children of Israel ye shall not rule one over another with rigour.

24. I.e., another Hebrew.
25. (Jubilee): Every fiftieth year, i.e. in the year following seven sabbatical years, all property was to return to its original owners.

47 ¶And if a sojourner or stranger wax rich by thee, and thy
brother that dwelleth by him wax poor, and sell himself unto the stranger or sojourner by thee, or to the
stock of the stranger's family:

48 After that he is sold he may be redeemed again; one of his
brethren may redeem him:

49 Either his uncle, or his uncle's son, may redeem him, or
any that is nigh of kin unto him of his family may
redeem him; or if he be able, he may redeem himself.

50 And he shall reckon with him that bought him from the
year that he was sold to him unto the year of jubile:
and the price of his sale shall be according unto the
number of years, according to the time of an hired
servant shall it be with him.

51 If there be yet many years behind, according unto them
he shall give again the price of his redemption out of
the money that he was bought for.

52 And if there remain but few years unto the year of jubile,
then he shall count with him, and according unto his
years shall he give him again the price of his redemption.

53 And as a yearly hired servant shall he be with him: and the
other shall not rule with rigour over him in thy sight.

54 And if he be not redeemed in these years, then he shall go
out in the year of jubile, both he, and his children
with him.

55 For unto me the children of Israel are servants; they are
my servants whom I brought forth out of the land of
Egypt: I am the Lord your God.

Leviticus 25

12 ¶And if thy brother, an Hebrew man, or an Hebrew woman,
be sold unto thee, and serve thee six years; then in the
seventh year thou shalt let him go free from thee.

13 And when thou sendest him out free from thee, thou shalt
not let him go away empty:

14 Thou shalt furnish him liberally out of thy flock, and out
of thy floor, and out of thy winepress; of that where-

with the Lord thy God hath blessed thee thou shalt give unto him.

15   And thou shalt remember that thou wast a bondman in the land of Egypt, and the Lord thy God redeemed thee: therefore I command thee this thing to day.

Deuteronomy 15

15   ¶Thou shall not deliver unto his master the servant which is escaped from his master unto thee:

16   He shall dwell with thee, even among you, in that place which he shall choose in one of thy gates, where it liketh him best: thou shalt not oppress him.

Deuteronomy 23

FAMILY LAW

Laws of Hammurabi

128 If a man has taken a (woman to) wife and has not drawn up a contract for her, that woman is not a wife.[1]

137 If a man sets his face to divorce a lay-sister who has borne him sons or a priestess who has provided him with sons, they shall render her dowry[2] to her and shall give her a half-portion of field plantation or chattels and she shall bring up her sons; after she has then brought up her sons, they shall give her a share like (that of) a single heir in anything that has been given (to her)

---

1. The Babylonians recognized at least two types of marriage: that by written contract, and the less formal type whereby a man cohabits with a woman and treats her as his wife, but has no contract. This law says not that a marriage is null and void if no contract is drawn up, but that a woman married without contract does not acquire the rights and liabilities of a wife with a contract.

2. At the completion of the marriage, the bride's father makes her a gift of property by sealed deed called her "dowry." The same gift is made if the daughter becomes a priestess. A woman has at most a life-interest in her dowry, as at her death it passes to her sons or returns to her father. The husband has the management of the dowry, since he must replace it if he divorces her.

for her sons, and a husband after her heart may marry her.[3]

138 If a man wishes to divorce his first wife who has not borne him sons, he shall give her money to the value of her bridal gift[4] and shall make good to her the dowry which she has brought from her father's house and (so) divorce her.

139 If there is no bridal gift, he shall give her one maneh of silver for divorce-money.

140 If (he is) a villein, he shall give her one-third of a maneh of silver.

144 If a man has married a priestess and that priestess has given a slave-girl to her husband[5] and she has then brought sons into the world, (if) that man sets his face to marry a lay-sister, they shall not allow that man (to do this); he shall not marry a lay-sister.

145 If the man has married a priestess and she has not provided him with sons and so he sets his face to marry a lay-sister,[6] that man may marry a lay-sister (and) take her into his house; that lay-sister shall not then make herself equal to the priestess.

159 If a man, who has had a gift brought to his father-in-law's house (and) given a bridal gift,[7] has then looked upon another woman and states to his father-in-law "I will

---

3. The woman may be divorced at the will of her husband, even though she has committed no fault and has borne him sons. But the fact that a man has to give up so large a proportion of his property to his divorced wife protects her from capricious divorce.

This law deals with an inferior type of marriage, since a "lady" cannot be divorced unless she has committed some fault.

4. This is distinct from the dowry, and is given before marriage. As soon as the gift has been brought, an inchoate marriage has been contracted. The marriage is completed only with the delivery of the bride to the bridegroom. If the wife dies without sons, the husband gets it back; but he has no claim to it in case of divorce.

5. The kind of priestess here referred to may not bear children.

6. The husband may marry an inferior kind of priestess (lay-sister) for the purpose of begetting sons.

7. As soon as the gift and the bridal gift have been given (the "gift" includes provisions for the wedding-feast), the bride is regarded as married, though still living with her father.

not take thy daughter to wife,"[8] the father of the girl shall take and keep anything that has been brought to him.

160 If a man has had a gift brought to his father-in-law's house (or) has given a bridal gift, and the father of the girl states "I will not give thee my daughter (in marriage,)"[9] he must double everything that has been brought to him and restore (it).

161 If a man has had a gift brought to his father-in-law's house (and) has given a bridal gift, and his friend has then slandered him, (if) his father-in-law states to the (prospective) husband of the wife "Thou shalt not take my daughter (in marriage)," he must double and restore everything that has been brought to him; and his friend shall not marry his wife.

185 If a man has taken an infant[10] in adoption (to be called) by his name and brings him up, that adopted child shall not be (re)claimed.

186 If the man has taken the infant in adoption (and) when he has taken it, it persists in searching for its father and its mother, that adopted child shall return to its father's house.

188 If a craftsman has taken a son for bringing up (in his craft) and teaches him his handicraft, he shall not be (re)claimed.

189 If he does not teach him his handicraft, that adopted child may return to its father's house.

190 If a man does not count the infant that he has taken in adoption and has brought up with his (other) sons, that adopted child shall return to its father's house.

191 If the man, who has taken the infant in adoption to himself and has brought him up, has built him a house (and) afterwards gets sons and sets his face to expel the

8. The groom has refused to complete the marriage by taking the bride to his house.

9. I.e., will not allow the marriage to be completed.

10. This need not be an infant in the usual sense, merely a child below the age of puberty, though children were in fact often adopted in infancy.

adopted child, that son shall not then go destitute; the father who has brought him up shall give him one-third of his inheritance out of his property when he goes; (but) he shall not give him any (portion) of field plantation or house.

Middle Assyrian Laws

A24 If a married woman has run away from her husband[11] (and) has entered an Assyrian('s) [12] house, whether it is within that city (where her husband lives) or (in one) of the neighbouring cities where he has appointed (?) a house for her, (and) she has stayed with the mistress of the house (and) has passed the night (there) three (or) four times, (and) the master of the house did not know that a married woman was staying in his house, (then, if) afterwards that woman is caught, the master of the house whose wife has run away [from] him [shall mutilate his wife and] take her (back).[13] The married woman with whom his wife stayed shall have her ears cut off; if he pleases, her husband shall pay three talents thirty manehs of lead as the price for her or, if he pleases, she shall be taken (away).[14] But if the owner of the house [knew] that the married woman was staying in his house with [his] wife, he shall pay the "third" . . . Or, if the man whose wife has run away from him has not mutilated his wife but takes (back) his wife, there is not any punishment (inflicted on either party).

11. There is no allegation of adultery here, merely that the wife has run away.
12. The use of this word in other passages suggests that it is not merely a local designation (citizen of the city of Ashur or the country of Assyria), but a person of lower social standing than the seignior. Perhaps the woman would be better able to conceal herself with such a person than with someone of her own station in life; and it eliminates the defense that the fugitive woman was merely paying a friendly visit.
13. The husband of the fugitive punishes his wife, because her offense is against him.
14. The other woman has not injured her own husband; thus her penalty is set by law rather than by her husband.

A30 If a father has conveyed (or) brought the (customary) gift to the house of his son's father-in-law (and) the woman has not been given to his son,[15] and another of his sons, whose wife is dwelling in her father's house, has died, he shall give his dead son's wife to be a spouse to his other son to whose father-in-law's house he has brought (the gift).[16] If the owner of the girl, who has accepted the present, is not willing to give his daughter, the father who has brought the present, if he pleases, may take his daughter-in-law (and) give her to his son[17]; or, if he pleases, he may surely take (back) so much as he has brought, lead, silver, gold, (or other things) not being edible, in full amount; he shall not claim the things which are edible.

A34 If a man cohabits with a widow[18] without having drawn up a marriage-contract (and) she dwells two years in his house, she (becomes) a wife; she shall not go forth.[19]

A35 If a widow enters a man's house[20] (to live with him), everything she brings (with her becomes) all her husband's; or, if the man enters into (the house of) the woman[21] (to live with her), everything which he brings (with him becomes) all the woman's.

15. I.e., the marriage has not been completed.
16. This is the custom of the levirate, whereby when a son died his brother had an obligation to marry the widow.
17. Evidently a third son, since it is difficult to believe that the law would insist on the enforcement of the contract if the girl would be merely a second wife instead of the first wife of the son for whom she was intended. The meaning apparently is that when a father has acquired another man's daughter as a bride for a specific son, he may decide to give her to another of his sons even against the wishes of the girl's father.
18. Widow in Assyrian usage refers to a woman who not only has lost her husband through death but also has neither adult sons nor father-in-law.
19. This rule is applicable only to widows, who have no natural protectors. It is not known whether the widow would have the right to return to her father's house and claim support. But presumably her dowry represented her share in her father's estate, so that she was unlikely to have any additional claim to it.
20. A technical term for the marriage of a woman.
21. This refers to a temporary arrangement, where no marriage is intended.

A36 If a woman is still dwelling in her father's house or if her husband has made her to dwell apart and her husband has gone to the field(s)[22] (and) has left her neither oil nor wool nor clothing nor food nor anything else and has had no provision (?) brought to her from the field(s), that woman shall remain faithful to her husband for five years (and) not go to dwell with an-(other) husband. If she has sons (and) they hire themselves out and earn their own living, the woman shall respect her husband (and) shall not go to dwell with an(other) husband. If she has no sons, she shall respect her husband for five years; at the beginning of the sixth year she may go to dwell with the husband of her choice. Her husband on coming (back) shall not claim her; she is free for her later husband. If he has delayed beyond the term of five years (and) has not kept himself away of his own accord, (inasmuch as) either a brigand (?) has seized him and he has disappeared, or he has been seized as (if he were) a robber (?) and been delayed (in returning), on coming (back) he shall make a (formal) claim (and) give a woman equivalent to his wife; and (then) he shall take back his wife. Or, if the king has sent him to any other country (and) he has been delayed beyond the term of five years, his wife shall respect him and shall not go to dwell with an(other) husband. But, if she has gone to dwell with an(other) husband before the end of five years and has borne children, her husband on coming (back) shall take her herself and also her children, because she has not respected the marriage-contract but has been married.[23]

A37 If a man divorces his wife, if (it is) his will, he shall give

---

22. This law probably is concerned with civilians: the husband's absence is due to his having gone to work in the fields or into royal service.
23. I.e., if the woman has not respected the stipulation to be faithful for five years, the first husband may take her back without giving any compensation to the second.

her something; if (it is) not his will, he shall not give her anything; she shall go forth empty.[24]

A38 If a woman is still dwelling in her father's house and her husband divorces her, he may take the ornaments which he himself has bestowed on her; he shall not claim the bridal gift which he has brought; he (then) is quit in respect to the woman.

A41 If a man will veil[25] his concubine (?), he shall summon five (or) six of his neighbours to be present (and) veil her before them (and) shall speak, saying: "She (is) my wife"; she (thus becomes) his wife.[26] A concubine (?) who has not been veiled before the men (and) whose husband has not spoken, saying: "She (is) my wife," (is) not a wife but (still) a concubine (?). If a man has died (and) his veiled wife has no sons, the sons of concubines (?) (become his) sons; they shall take a share (of his property).

A45 If a woman has been given (in marriage) and the enemy has taken her husband (prisoner and) she has no father-in-law or son, she shall remain faithful to her husband for two years.[27] During these two years, if she has nothing to eat, she shall come forward and make a declaration, (and) she becomes a dependent (?) of the residency. . . . She shall wait for two full years (and) she may (then) go to live with the husband of her choice, (and) they shall write her a tablet as (for) a widow. If afterwards her missing husband returns to

24. It is probable that in Babylonian and Assyrian law, the husband can always divorce his wife regardless of her guilt. Only special circumstances limit his power to divorce his wife at will and send her away with nothing.
25. Veiling was a privilege granted only to married women and to ladies of the upper classes. A captive maid or concubine was forbidden to veil herself except on the street in the company of the chief wife.
26. This evidently describes an unusual type of marriage, carried out by the persons themselves. The woman is already the man's property. The right of her sons to inherit may depend upon her status as a wife.
27. It is not clear why the waiting period here is only two years: perhaps when a man is taken captive and transported to a foreign country, the chances are that unless he returns soon he will not return at all. Or perhaps since the state is obliged to maintain his wife, it is not averse to shortening the waiting period.

the country, he shall take back his wife who has been married away (from him)[28]; he shall not claim the sons whom she has borne to her latter husband, but her latter husband shall take (them). . . .

A59 Apart from the penalties for [a married woman] which [are prescribed] on the tablet, a man [may scourge] his wife, pluck (her hair), may bruise and destroy [her] ears. There is no liability therefor.

Hittite Laws

28 If a maiden has been promised to a man and someone else elopes with her,[29] whatever the first man paid as a bride-price, he who elopes with her shall make restitution to him; the father and mother shall make no restitution. If the father and mother give her to another man, the father and mother shall make restitution. But if the father and mother do not do so, they shall take her away from him.

29 If a maiden is affianced to a man and he has given her the bride-price,[30] and subsequently the father and mother object to it and take her away from the man, they shall give him back double the bride-price.

30 If that man has not yet taken the maiden and refuses her, he shall forfeit the bride-price which he has given.

31 If a free man and a female-slave are in love and live together and he takes her as his wife and they set up a house and have children,[31] and subsequently dissen-

28. The certificate of widowhood and the provision that she must return to her first husband if he returns may perhaps be a special privilege granted him as an officer.

29. This is elopement with the woman's consent—a form of 'free" marriage. Capture may result in the establishment of power over a woman but not in marriage. For the latter, a second act is necessary which makes the woman a wife.

30. Evidently the bride has not yet been handed over to the husband; for if she had been, the marriage would have been complete and the power of the parents over the daughter extinguished.

31. This law, as well as laws 32, 33, and 35, deals with a less formal type of marriage, a form of contract which is more appropriate to "mixed marriages" than the formal contracts employed where both parties are free persons.

sion arises between them and they agree (to separate)[32] and they divide the house, the man shall take the children and one child the woman shall take.

32 If a slave takes a woman as his wife, it shall be the same.

33 If a male-slave takes a female-slave, it shall be the same.[33]

34 If a slave gives the bride-price to a woman and takes her as his wife, no-one shall surrender her.[34]

35 If an *agrig* or a shepherd elopes with a free woman (and) does not give the bride-price for her, she shall become a slave in the third year.[35]

192 If the wife of a man dies, (and) [he takes her] sist[er] (there shall be) no punishment.[36]

193 If a man has a wife and the man dies, his brother shall take his wife, then his father shall take her. If also his father dies, his brother shall take his wife [and also] the son of his brother shall [take her].[37] (There shall be) no punishment.

---

32. Unlike the Babylonians and Assyrians, the Hittites did not treat divorce as a formal act. "Agree" is certainly not a technical term for divorce. The verb implies that, as far as the right to bring about divorce is concerned, the legal position of the wife is the same as that of the husband.

33. Divorce must also have been possible between free persons, though no provision for it appears in these laws. It appears that in marriages between free persons the power of granting divorce was the privilege of the husband, since the woman was legally an object in marriage.

34. This provision shows that originally a free woman was penalized for contracting marriage with a slave. This law indicates a change in attitude in favor of the slave.

35. The *agrig* (probably an inferior temple official) and the shepherd were in the lowest class of slaves. The elopement was probably owing to the opposition of the girl's parents.

36. The levirate—the obligation of the relatives of the deceased to provide another partner for the widowed spouse—here applies to the case of the wife's death as well as the husband's. This law appears incomplete: perhaps it supplements some other law now unknown. We may conclude from the wording that relations with the wife's sister are forbidden during the lifetime of the first wife.

37. These laws lay down the order of obligation in levirate marriage: (1) brother of the deceased; (2) father of the deceased; (3) paternal uncle; (4) paternal nephew. As between brothers, it may be supposed that the duty fell first upon the eldest. As long as the widow's age permitted her to give birth to children, all the above persons were under an obligation to marry her.

Hebrew Laws

16 ¶And if a man entice a maid that is not betrothed, and lie
with her, he shall surely endow her to be his wife.

17 If her father utterly refuse to give her unto him, he shall
pay money according to the dowry of virgins.

Exodus 22

28 ¶If a man find a damsel that is a virgin, which is not betrothed, and lay hold on her, and lie with her, and
they be found;

29 Then the man that lay with her shall give unto the damsel's father fifty shekels of silver, and she shall be his
wife; because he hath humbled her, he may not put
her away all his days.

Deuteronomy 22

1 When a man hath taken a wife, and married her, and it
come to pass that she find no favour in his eyes, because he hath found some uncleanness in her: then
let him write her a bill of divorcement, and give it in
her hand, and send her out of his house.

2 And when she is departed out of his house, she may go and
be another man's wife.[38]

3 And if the latter husband hate her, and write her a bill of
divorcement, and giveth it in her hand, and sendeth
her out of his house; or if the latter husband die, which
took her to be his wife;

4 Her former husband, which sent her away, may not take
her again to be his wife, after that she is defiled; for
that is abomination before the Lord; and thou shalt

---

38. Compare Matthew 5:31-2: "It hath been said, Whosoever shall put
away his wife, let him give her a writing of divorcement: But I say unto
you, That whosoever shall put away his wife, saving for the cause of fornica-
tion, causeth her to commit adultery: and whosoever shall marry her that
is divorced committeth adultery."

not cause the land to sin, which the Lord thy God giveth thee for an inheritance.

Deuteronomy 24

5   ¶If brethren dwell together, and one of them die, and have no child, the wife of the dead shall not marry without unto a stranger: her husband's brother shall go in unto her, and take her to him to wife, and perform the duty of an husband's brother unto her.

6   And it shall be, that the firstborn which she beareth shall succeed in the name of his brother which is dead, that his name be not put out of Israel.[39]

7   And if the man like not to take his brother's wife, then let his brother's wife go up to the gate unto the elders, and say, My husband's brother refuseth to raise up unto his brother a name in Israel, he will not perform the duty of my husband's brother.

8   Then the elders of his city shall call him, and speak unto him: and if he stand to it, and say, I like not to take her;

9   Then shall his brother's wife come unto him in the presence of the elders, and loose his shoe from off his foot, and spit in his face, and shall answer and say, So shall it be done unto that man that will not build up his brother's house.[40]

Deuteronomy 25

39. I.e., the purpose of this provision was to prevent the extinction of the family.
40. I.e., the brother must suffer public humiliation.

THEFT[1]

Laws of Hammurabi

6   If a man has stolen property belonging to a god or a palace,[2] that man shall be put to death, and he who has received the stolen property from his hand shall be put to death.

8   If a man has stolen an ox or a sheep or an ass or swine or a boat, if (it is the property) of a god (or) if (it is the property) of a palace,[3] he shall pay thirtyfold; if (it is the property) of a villein, he shall replace (it) tenfold. If the thief has not the means of payment, he shall be put to death.

14   If a man kidnaps[4] the infant (son)[5] of a (free) man, he shall be put to death.

19   If (a man) detains (a fugitive) slave in his house (and) afterwards the slave is caught in his possession, that man shall be put to death.

21   If a man has broken into a house, they shall put him to death and hang him before the breach which he has made.[6]

1. The Laws contain no general statement of the law of theft. It can be inferred from the text that the usual penalty for theft was death and restitution of the stolen property. If the thief was dead, compensation was payable by his heirs.

2. This offense is a violation of the sanctity of the temple as the house of the god or of the palace as the king's house. Although the old theory of the divinity of the king had ceased to have much meaning in Hammurabi's day, it may still have retained enough force to cause the god's and the king's property to be placed in the same category.

3. This law evidently refers to moveable property kept within the precincts of the temple or palace, but not regarded as sacred; therefore the difference in the punishments prescribed here from those in law 6.

4. Kidnapping is regarded as a form of theft; thus it is included within the section of laws on theft.

5. "Infant" is not exactly defined in Babylonian law, but probably it refers to a son too young to perform his father's feudal service or to marry. In the Assyrian laws, the term indicates a child ten years old or under.

6. Probably a stake is driven through his corpse, which is left exposed at the breach he has made in the wall of the house. The punishment thus reflects the crime: as he has made a hole in the wall of the house, so a hole is made in his body.

22   If a man has committed robbery and is caught, that man
     shall be put to death.

25   If a fire has broken out in a man's house and a man who
     has gone to extinguish (it) has coveted an article of
     the owner of the house and takes the article of the
     owner of the house, that man shall be cast into that
     fire.

253 If a man has hired a man to look after his field and has
     entrusted him with meal (and) given cattle into his
     charge and has engaged him by contract [to] cultivate
     his field, if that man has stolen seed or fodder and it
     is seized in his hand(s), they shall cut off his fore-
     hand.

254 If he has taken the meal and so has weakened the cattle,
     he shall replace twofold (?) the corn which he has
     received.

255 If he has then hired out the man's cattle or has stolen the
     seed and so has not sown (it) on the field, they shall
     convict that man and he shall pay sixty gur[7] of corn
     for every bur[8] of land at the harvest.[9]

256 If he cannot discharge his liability, they shall have that
     man drawn to and fro on the field by the oxen.

259 If a man has stolen a water-wheel on the water-land, he
     shall give five shekels of silver to the owner of the
     water-wheel.[10]

260 If he has stolen a plough or a harrow, he shall give (him)
     three shekels of silver.[10]

264 If a herdsman to whom cattle or sheep have been given to
     tend, having received his full wages and been satisfied,
     reduces the cattle (or) reduces the sheep (or) dimin-
     ishes the offspring, he shall give offspring and prod-

7. *Gur* (or *kur*): a solid measure of a little over seven bushels, divided
into 300 *qu* (or *qa*).

8. (Or *iku*): a land measure equal to about seven-eighths of an acre.

9. The penalty may be regarded as a multiplication of the crop which the
stolen seed-corn would have produced.

10. Perhaps these laws (nos. 259 and 260) are aimed not at the theft, but at
the illegal borrowing of agricultural implements. Babylonian law evidently
distinguishes between theft and misappropriation.

ucts (to their owner) according to the terms of his contract.

265 If a herdsman to whom cattle or sheep have been given to tend feloniously alters the brand (on them) and sells (them), they shall convict him and he shall replace what he has stolen tenfold (in) cattle or sheep to their owner.

Middle Assyrian Laws

A1 If a woman, [whether] a married woman or a lady by birth, has entered a temple and has stolen [from] the temple anything [belonging to] the sanctuary[11] (and) it has been found (in her hand),[12] whether charge or proof has been brought against [her], the stolen proof [shall be taken and] enquiry shall be made of the god; as he orders [the woman to be treated], she shall be treated.[13]

A3 If a man either is ill or has died (and) his wife has stolen anything from his house (and) delivered it either to a man or to a woman or to any other (free) person, the man's wife and also the receivers shall be put to death. And, if a married woman, whose husband is alive and well, has stolen anything from her husband's house (and) delivered (it) either to a man or to a woman or to any other (free) person, the man shall

11. Probably this was not a casual entry to commit theft. It is likely that the woman has come to reside in the temple either as a pledge for a debt owed to the god, or possibly to fulfill a period of sacred prostitution. It may be that in Assyria a married woman performed the latter duty before the completion of her marriage, which would explain why there is no mention in the law of any husband.

This case is very different from the sections of the Babylonian laws treating of a man who comes in from outside to rob the temple—a far more serious crime. Here the woman's entry into the temple was not unlawful. This may be the reason for the law, if it was felt that her case did not come under any provisions of the existing laws.

12. Assyrian law attached some importance to finding the stolen article in the criminal's hand.

13. The priests normally have jurisdiction to deal with crimes committed within the sanctuary. However, if the woman was not a regular member of the temple staff, a special law may have been required to cover her case.

charge his wife and shall inflict a punishment, and the receiver who has received the stolen property from the hand of the man's wife shall give up the stolen property, and the same punishment as the man has inflicted on his wife shall be inflicted on the receiver.[14]

A4   If either a slave or a slave-girl[15] has received anything from the hand of a married woman, the nose and the ears of the slave or slave-girl shall be cut off, (and thereby) (the theft of) the stolen property shall be requited;[16] the man shall cut off his wife's ears. Or, if the man has let his wife go free (and) has not cut off her ears, (the nose and ears) of the slave or the slave-girl shall not be cut off and (the theft of) the stolen property shall not be requited.

B4   [If] brothers (are) in (joint occupation of) a field which has not been divided[17] [(and) one brother] amongst them has . . . sown seed (and) . . . tilled the field, (but) [another brother] has come forward (and) [taken the corn] of his brother's tillage[18] [for] the second time[19] (and) charge (and) proof have been brought against him,[20] [on the day (when) the former]

14. It was a principle of Assyrian law that when a wife has committed against her husband a wrongful act in which a third party is involved, both wrongdoers must suffer a similar penalty. If the husband forgives his wife, the third party must also go unpunished.

It may be noted that neither this law nor the following (A 4) has any parallel in the Babylonian laws, supporting the suggestion that the Assyrian laws are supplementary.

15. The slaves must belong to someone other than the injured husband; for it is unlikely that the law would restrict a man's right to punish his own slaves.

16. Presumably the monetary compensation customarily paid in cases of theft cannot be paid by slaves, who have no money. Thus the compensation is payable in their own persons in the form of mutilation.

17. It appears that in Assyria only males inherit.

18. Although interpretation is difficult owing to the mutilated state of this text, it would seem that one brother has worked the land and another has taken the produce. Presumably both brothers ought to have shared in the work.

19. Evidently if the second brother offends in this way once, he is excused; but if he repeats the offense and is formally convicted, he is liable to some penalty.

20. I.e., formal charge and proof are required.

comes forward, [the brother who] has tilled [the field] shall take [his share].

C8   [If a man has stolen either] a beast or anything else[21] (and) charge (and) proof have been brought against him, he shall pay [x manehs] of lead; [he] shall be beaten fifty blows with a rod (and) shall do [labour for the king for x days]. The judges of the land (?) [shall give] this judgement. But (if) he goes before [the king],[22] [he shall restore] the stolen thing, so much as he has stolen, [to the whole value], small or great indeed, [and (shall bear) the punishment which] the king as he will shall inflict on [him].

C10   [If a man] has overstated [(the amount of) a trust][23] from his neighbour (and) [written (this in a deed) (and) charge] (and) proof have been brought against him, that (man is) a thief and (shall bear) the punishment which the king [as he will] shall inflict on him.

Hittite Laws

20   If any man of Hatti steals a Hittite slave from the land of Luiyaš and brings him to the country of Hatti, and his master finds him, then he shall give twelve shekels of silver, and his estate shall be liable.[24]

21   If anyone steals a slave of a man from Luiyaš from the country of Luiyaš and brings him to the country of Hatti, and his master finds him, he shall take his slave (and there is) no compensation.[25]

21. Probably domestic animals of any sort.

22. Two courts seem to be mentioned here: the first of the judges and the second of the king. The court of the judges can apparently only order a penalty; but the king's court may order restitution together with an additional penalty.

23. Though this law is not entirely clear, it seems that the man has committed some sort of fraud in connection with property.

24. It is remarkable that the restitution in this case exceeds that for murder and homicide. Compensation in such cases is unknown in Semitic legislation, where abduction was a capital offense.

25. The reason no compensation is paid must remain unknown until the constitutional relationship between the land of Hatti and the town of Luiyaš has been elucidated.

49   If a *hipparaš*[26] steals, there shall be no compensation. [If
     there] is [a gu]ild,[27] the guild shall compensate. I[f]
     they do [not] give [back] the theft, they shall all be
     guilty and are all thieves. He shall seize him, and he
     shall be put in the king's cell.

57   If anyone steals a bull . . . hitherto they used to give
     thirty oxen, (but) now he shall give fifteen oxen: five
     two years old, five oxen one year old, and five oxen half
     a year old he shall give and his estate shall be liable.

58   If anyone steals a stallion . . . hitherto they used to give
     thirty horses, (but) now he shall give fifteen horses:
     five horses two years old, five horses one year old, and
     five horses half a year old he shall give, and his estate
     shall be liable.

60   If anyone finds a bull and removes its mark, and its owner
     finds it, he shall give seven oxen: two oxen two years
     old, three oxen one year old, and two oxen half a year
     old shall he give, and his estate shall be liable.

71   If anyone finds an ox or a horse or a mule, he shall bring
     it to the royal gate. But if he finds it in the country, it
     shall be brought before the elders and he may continue
     to harness it. But if its owner finds it and receives it as
     it was, he shall not hold him as a thief. If he does not
     bring it before the elders, he is a thief.

94   If a free man steals (in) a house, he shall compensate in
     full. Hitherto the thieves used to give one maneh of
     silver, but now he shall give twelve shekels of silver.
     If he steals much, they shall impose much on him,
     and if he steals little, they shall impose little on him,
     and his estate shall be liable.[28]

26. The exact meaning of this word is unknown, but undoubtedly it dealt
with a person of the lower classes. The *hipparaš* was incapable of holding
property in private ownership or of enjoying certain other rights, and was
not personally liable for delicts he committed.
27. The *hipparaš* evidently belonged to some sort of corporate body (guild)
which was capable of acquiring rights and incurring liabilities, and was answerable for the debts of its individual members. It had its own property,
which was not the property of the indiidual members. The *hipparaš* does
not seem to have had a master in the legal sense of the word.
28. Anyone who steals in a house must, in addition to giving full compensation, pay a fine comparable to the value of the stolen goods.

95 If a slave steals (in) a house, he shall compensate in full. The thief shall (also) give six shekels of silver; they shall cut off the nose and ears of the slave[29] and they shall return him to his master. If he steals much, they shall impose much on him; if he steals little, they shall impose little on him. If his master says "I will compensate for him," he shall compensate.[30] If he refuses he shall surrender the slave.

149 If anyone . . . sells (another man's) ox and he says "he is dead" and the owner finds it, he shall take it, and in addition he shall give two persons, and his estate shall be liable.[31]

Hebrew Laws

1 If a man shall steal an ox, or a sheep, and kill it, or sell it; he shall restore five oxen for an ox, and four sheep for a sheep.

2 ¶If a thief be found breaking up,[32] and be smitten that he die, there shall no blood be shed for him.

3 If the sun be risen upon him,[33] there shall be blood shed for him; for he should make full restitution; if he have nothing, then he shall be sold for his theft.

4 If the theft be certainly found in his hand alive, whether it be ox, or ass, or sheep; he shall restore double.

7 ¶If a man shall deliver unto his neighbour money or stuff to keep, and it be stolen out of the man's house; if the thief be found, let him pay double.

8 If the thief be not found, then the master of the house shall be brought unto the judges, to see whether he have put his hand unto his neighbour's goods.

9 For all manner of trespass, whether it be for ox, for ass,

29. Again, in addition to restoring the stolen object the thief must pay compensation and suffer punishment by mutilation.

30. It is clear that the master is liable for the wrongs of his slave; but he has the alternative of taking the consequences or surrendering the slave to the injured party. Presumably the slave's work will indemnify the victim against the theft.

31. It is impossible to say why the punishment in this case is so severe.

32. I.e., breaking in.

33. I.e., if he is not killed in the act of committing the theft.

for sheep, for raiment, or for any manner of lost thing, which another challengeth to be his, the cause of both parties shall come before the judges; and whom the judges shall condemn, he shall pay double unto his neighbour.

Exodus 22

11   ¶Ye shall not steal, neither deal falsely, neither lie to one another.
13   ¶Thou shalt not defraud thy neighbour, neither rob him; the wages of him that is hired shall not abide with thee all night until the morning.

Leviticus 19

24   ¶When thou comest into thy neighbour's vineyard, then thou mayest eat grapes thy fill at thine own pleasure; but thou shalt not put any in thy vessel.
25   When thou comest into the standing corn of thy neighbour, then thou mayest pluck the ears with thine hand; but thou shalt not move a sickle unto thy neighbour's standing corn.

Deuteronomy 23

16   ¶And he that stealeth a man, and selleth him, or if he be found in his hand, he shall surely be put to death.

Exodus 21

7   ¶If a man be found stealing any of his brethren of the children of Israel, and maketh merchandise of him, or selleth him; then that thief shall die; and thou shalt put evil away from among you.

Deuteronomy 24

COMMERCE AND DEBT

Laws of Hammurabi

7   If a man buys silver or gold or slave or slave-girl or ox or
      sheep or ass or anything else whatsoever from a (free)
      man's son[1] or a (free) man's slave or has received
      (them) for safe custody without witnesses or contract,
      that man is a thief; he shall be put to death.

48   If a man incurs a debt and Adad[2] inundates his field or a
      flood has carried away (the soil) or else (if) corn is
      not raised on the field through lack of water, in that
      year he shall not render (any) corn to (his) creditor;
      he shall blot out (the terms inscribed on) his tablet
      and shall not pay interest for that year.

L   If a merchant has given corn on loan, he may take 100
      sila of corn as interest on 1 *gur*;[3] if he has given silver
      on loan, he may take 1/6 shekel 6 grains as interest on
      one shekel of silver.[4]

M   If a man who has raised a loan has no silver to repay (it)
      but has corn, [the merchant] may then take corn for
      his interest (at a rate) in accordance with the ordi-
      nances of the king; but, if the merchant has increased
      his interest above [100 *sila* of corn] on 1 *gur* [or]
      over 1/6 shekel 6 grains [on 1 shekel of silver] and
      has taken (it), he forfeits whatever he has given (on
      loan).[5]

1. The son must be a minor.
2. The god of storm and rain.
3. *Sila* (or *qu*): one three-hundredth of a *gur*, the *gur* measuring a little
over seven bushels. The interest on a loan of grain was thus 33-1/3 per cent.
4. A shekel was divided into 180 grains. The interest on a loan of money
was thus 20 per cent—probably not excessive in view of the high value of
money. There is nothing in any of these laws to show whether the interest
is payable by month, by year, or for some other period. The duration of the
loan is generally expressed vaguely in the surviving documents, i.e., repayment is fixed "at harvest time," "in such-and-such a month," etc.
5. I.e., he has exceeded the legal rate of interest. Taken literally, the law
states that the lender loses the original sum but retains the illegal interest,
which is illogical.
Note that there is no attempt to prohibit the charging of interest. In con-

R   If a man has received corn or silver from a merchant and
     has no corn or silver to give back but has goods, he
     may give anything that may be in his possession to
     his merchant before witnesses as and when he may
     bring (it); the merchant shall not refuse (?), he
     shall accept (it).[6]

U   If a man has given silver to a man for a partnership,[7] they
     shall divide the profit or the loss which there may be
     in proportion before a god.

100 If a merchant has given silver to an agent for trading and
     sent him on a journey, (and) the agent has then laid
     out (?) the silver which he has entrusted to him on the
     journey, if he perceives [a profit where] he has gone,
     he shall enter up so much increments on the money as
     he has taken and they shall reckon his days (of travel-
     ling) and he shall pay his merchant.

101 If he perceives no profit where he has gone, the agent then
     must double the silver which he has taken and give
     (it) to the merchant.[8]

102 If the merchant gives the silver to the agent for (mutual)
     advantage and he perceives a loss where he has gone,
     he shall repay the total amount of silver to the mer-
     chant.[9]

103 If an enemy causes him to jettison anything that he is car-

---

trast to the Hebrews and (later) Moslems, the Babylonians did not regard
taking interest on a commercial loan as immoral.

6. Witnesses are required partly for the purpose of identifying the goods
and partly because the contract will not be discharged in the manner agreed
upon in the original document, i.e., the law substitutes a new contract.

7. Partnership in Babylonia is not a long-term arrangement, but a joint
enterprise for carrying out some specific piece of business.

8. The implication is that the lack of profit is caused by the dishonesty or
negligence of the agent. The provision for "doubling the money" assures to
the merchant at least 100 per cent profit.

9. Evidently the money is lent to the agent, who uses it to trade for his own
benefit. There is no mention of profit, only of loss. Whereas in law no. 101
he had to "double the money," here he has to pay only the amount advanced.
Whether the loss is due to the normal perils of the journey or to the
agent's incompetence in trade, the assumption is that it was avoidable.

rying whilst he is going on the journey, the agent may take an oath by the life of the god and he then goes free.[10]

104 If a merchant has given corn (or) wool (or) oil or any goods to an agent for retail, the agent shall enter up the silver (obtained for them) and render (it) to the merchant; the agent shall take a sealed tablet for the silver which he shall give to the merchant.[11]

105 If the agent is careless and does not take a sealed tablet for the silver which he has given to the merchant, the silver not (entered) on a sealed tablet shall not be put in the account.

106 If an agent has taken silver from a merchant and contests (its receipt to) his merchant, that merchant shall convict the agent before a god and witnesses of having taken the silver and the agent shall give threefold so much as he has taken to the merchant.

112 If a man is engaged on a trading journey and has delivered silver (or) gold or (precious) stone(s) or any chattels in his possession to a man and has consigned them (to him) for consignment (to their destination), (if) that man has not delivered whatever was consigned (to him) where it was to be consigned but takes and keeps (it),[12] the owner of the consignment shall convict that man of not having delivered what was consigned (to him) and that man shall give fivefold anything that was delivered to him to the owner of the consignment.

114 If a man has not (a claim to) corn or silver against a man

10. In contrast to law no. 102, here the loss is caused by the king's enemies, and the agent cannot be held responsible for it.

11. Here as in no. 105, the merchant advances goods instead of money. It seems that the sales are to be made in the agent's own city, for no hazards of the road are contemplated.

12. Here it is not said that the carrier has stolen, but only "taken away." He has not taken the goods in theft, but received them lawfully through the voluntary act of the consignor and only subsequently converts them to his own use. Thus he is technically not a thief and the penalty is not death but monetary compensation.

and takes (a person as) a distress from him, for each distress[13] he shall pay one-third maneh of silver.

122 If a man wishes to give silver (or) gold or anything whatsoever to a man for safe custody, he shall show anything whatsoever that he gives to witnesses, he shall draw up a contract and (thus) give (them) for safe custody.[14]

123 If he has given (them) for safe custody without witnesses or a contract and those with whom he gave them contest (them), that case affords no cause of action.

151 If a woman who is dwelling in a man's house (as his wife) causes her husband to enter into a contract (ensuring) that no creditor of her husband shall seize her (and) causes a tablet to be executed (to that effect), (then,) if that man had incurred a debt before marrying that woman, his creditor shall surely not seize his wife. Or, if that woman incurs a debt before entering the man's house, her creditor shall surely not seize her husband.

152 If the debt is incurred by them after that woman has entered the man's house, both of them shall satisfy the creditor.

Middle Assyrian Laws

A32 If a woman is still dwelling in her father's house and (?) her settled property[15] has been given (to her), whether she is taken or is not taken to her father-in-law's house,

---

13. A pledge. The creditor has seized the property or a dependent of the debtor in order to compel him to pay his debts. If the debtor has defaulted on a debt, the creditor apparently is entitled to take as a pledge the wife, child, or slave of the debtor, without recourse to a court. The pledge is presumably retained and put to work by the creditor until either the debt is satisfied through his work or the loan is otherwise repaid.

14. These verbs are in the present and future tense: i.e., they show how a man who intends to leave valuables or goods with another person ought to proceed.

15. A settlement on the wife by the husband. The husband grants it by written deed, and seems to have retained possession or administration of it, as the wife obtains possession only at his death and is not entitled to enjoy it except during her widowhood. If the husband does not make such a settlement, the wife is entitled to a share of his estate equal to that of a son.

she shall bear (any) debts or liability or punishment
of her husband.[16]

A44 If an Assyrian man, or if an Assyrian woman, who is
dwelling in a man's house as a pledge for his value,
has been taken (in discharge of the debt) up to the
full value,[17] he may flog (him), he may pluck out
(his hair), he may bruise (and) bore his ears.[18]

Hittite Laws

146 If anyone is going to sell a house or a hamlet or a garden
or a pasture field, and another comes [and] stops it
and sells his own, the wrongdoer shall give one maneh
of silver [and he] shall buy (in accordance with) the
[fir]st transactions.[19]

178 The price of a plough-ox (shall be) twelve shekels of silver;
the price of a bull, ten shekels of silver; the price of a
big cow, seven shekels of silver; the price of a plough-
ox (and) a cow one year old, five shekels of silver. . . .[20]

183 The price of three measures of emmer (shall be) one shekel
of silver; . . . the price of one measure of wine—one
half-shekel of silver . . . the price of one *iku*[21] of ur-
ban (?) land—three [shekels of silver]; the price of
one *iku* of partitioned land—two shekels of silver; if
the field is further away (its price shall be) one shekel
of silver.

184 This (is) the tariff, in the town (and in) the country (it
shall be the same).

16. Receipt of the property proves the state of full marriage and makes the
wife responsible for her husband's debt and other liabilities, regardless of
where she is living.
17. I.e., the man or woman has become the property of the creditor, and is
no longer redeemable by the debtor.
18. The object of this law is to restrict the penalties which a person may
inflict at his own discretion on another who has become subject to his power.
19. The offense here is the encroachment upon someone else's livelihood by
depriving him of a customer.
20. These are prices for the sale, not the hire, of various kinds of animals.
21. A land-measure equal to about 7/8 of an acre.

Hebrew Laws

13 In the year of this jubile[22] ye shall return every man unto his possession.

14 And if thou sell ought unto thy neighbour, or buyest ought of thy neighbour's hand, ye shall not oppress one another:

15 According to the number of years after the jubile thou shalt buy of thy neighbour, and according unto the number of years of the fruits he shall sell unto thee.

16 According to the multitude of years thou shalt increase the price thereof, and according to the fewness of years thou shalt diminish the price of it: for according to the number of the years of the fruits doth he sell unto thee.

25 ¶If thy brother be waxen poor, and hath sold away some of his possession, and if any of his kin come to redeem it, then shall he redeem that which his brother sold.

29 And if a man sell a dwelling house in a walled city, then he may redeem it within a whole year after it is sold; within a full year may he redeem it.

30 And if it be not redeemed within the space of a full year, then the house that is in the walled city shall be established for ever to him that bought it throughout his generations: it shall not go out[23] in the jubile.

31 But the houses of the villages which have no wall round about them shall be counted as the fields of the country: they may be redeemed, and they shall go out in the jubile.

Leviticus 25

1 At the end of every seven years thou shalt make a release.

2 And this is the manner of the release: Every creditor that

22. Jubile(e): every fiftieth year.
23. Return to its original owner. Houses in walled cities were thus an exception to the general rule.

lendeth ought unto his neighbour shall release it; he shall not exact it of his neighbour, or of his brother; because it is called the Lord's release.

3 Of a foreigner thou mayest exact it again: but that which is thine with thy brother thine hand shall release.

6 For the Lord thy God blesseth thee, as he promised thee: and thou shalt lend unto many nations, but thou shalt not borrow; and thou shalt reign over many nations, but they shall not reign over thee.

Deuteronomy 15

19 ¶Thou shalt not lend upon usury to thy brother; usury of money, usury of victuals, usury of any thing that is lent upon usury;

20 Unto a stranger thou mayest lend upon usury; but unto thy brother thou shalt not lend upon usury; that the Lord thy God may bless thee in all that thou settest thine hand to in the land whither thou goest to possess it.

Deuteronomy 23

13 ¶Thou shalt not have in thy bag divers weights, a great and a small.

14 Thou shalt not have in thine house divers measures, a great and a small.

15 But thou shalt have a perfect and just weight, a perfect and just measure shalt thou have: that thy days may be lengthened in the land which the Lord thy God giveth thee.

Deuteronomy 25

MILITARY SERVICE

Laws of Hammurabi

26   If a runner[1] or a fisher[2] who is commanded to go on a mission of the king has not gone or has hired a hireling and sends (him as) his substitute, that runner or fisher shall be put to death; his hired (substitute) shall take and keep his house.

32   If either a runner or a fisher, who is taken captive on a mission of the king (and) a merchant[3] has ransomed him and so has enabled him to regain his city, has the means for ransoming (himself) in his house, he shall himself ransom himself; if there are not the means of ransoming him in his house, he shall be ransomed out of (the resources of) the temple of his city; if there are not the means of ransoming him in the temple of his city; the palace shall ransom him. His field, his plantation, and his house shall not be given for his ransom.

33   If a recruiting officer or adjutant levies men exempt from service or has accepted and dispatches a hired man as a substitute for a mission of the king, that recruiting officer or adjutant shall be put to death.

Hittite Laws

42   If anyone hires a person and he goes into battle and he dies, if the wages have been given, he shall not give compensation. If his wages have not been given, he

---

1. The runner seems to have performed certain military duties as well as others of a police nature, i.e., seeing that an order of the king is carried out, or bringing back fugitive slaves.

2. The fisher is evidently inferior in status to the runner. Since most Babylonian cities were built on the banks of rivers or canals, fishing was one of the principal industries. Perhaps fishing was a royal monopoly, and the fishers were employees of the king.

3. Here evidently a private trader, though in other passages he seems to be in some respects a public servant.

shall surrender one person.[4] And as wages he shall give twelve shekels of silver, and as the wages of a woman he shall give six shekels of silver.[5]

54 Hitherto the Manda warriors, the Šala warriors,[6] the warriors of the town of Tamalkiya,[7] the warriors of the town of Hatra,[7] the warriors of the town of Zalpa,[7] the warriors of the town of Tashiniya,[7] the warriors of the town of Himuwa,[7] the archers, the carpenters, the pages and the . . . did not render feudal dues and did not perform feudal duties.

55 When Hittite liegemen came and bowed down before the father of the king and said "No one gives us wages for they refuse, saying, 'You are liegemen,'"[8] then the father of the king [came] into the assembly and declared "Begone! As your comrades, so you too shall be."[9]

Hebrew Laws

1 When thou goest out to battle against thine enemies, and seest horses, and chariots, and a people more than thou, be not afraid of them: for the Lord thy God is with thee, which brought thee up out of the land of Egypt.

2 And it shall be, when ye are come nigh unto the battle, that the priest shall approach and speak unto the people.

3 And shall say unto them, Hear, O Israel, ye approach this

4. The law thus fixes a penalty for not paying in advance, i.e., before the person is obliged to risk his life.

5. It seems that the legislator sought to advance the situation of the working class by fixing a scale of wages. In general, the Hittite laws pay little attention to the rights of the laborer.

The nature of the women's work in the army is unknown.

6. Manda and Šala: probably ethnic groups of a particular social character.

7. Tamalkiya, Hatra, Zalpa, Tashiniya, Himuwa: the first two were located in southern Asia Minor, Zalpa apparently in the Hittite homelands in the Halys basin, the others uncertain.

8. The Hittite liegemen are protesting against excluding from feudal dues the warriors of certain cities and groups (see law no. 54, above).

9. This law seems to be an extract from the records of the Assembly in which judgment was pronounced. It contains a decision in a single case applicable to a group of people of the same status.

day unto battle against your enemies: let not your hearts faint, fear not, and do not tremble, neither be ye terrified because of them:

4   For the Lord your God is he that goeth with you, to fight for you against your enemies, to save you.

5   ¶And the officers shall speak unto the people, saying, What man is there that hath built a new house, and hath not dedicated it? let him go and return to his house, lest he die in the battle, and another man dedicate it.

6   And what man is he that hath planted a vineyard, and hath not yet eaten of it? let him also go and return unto his house, lest he die in the battle, and another man eat of it.

7   And what man is there that hath betrothed a wife, and hath not taken her? let him go and return unto his house, lest he die in the battle, and another man take her.

8   And the officers shall speak further unto the people, and they shall say, What man is there that is fearful and fainthearted? let him go and return unto his house, lest his brethren's heart faint as well as his heart.

9   And it shall be, when the officers have made an end of speaking unto the people, that they shall make captains of the armies to lead the people.

Deuteronomy 20

LAW OF WAR

Hebrew Laws

10   ¶When thou comest nigh unto a city to fight against it, then proclaim peace unto it.

11   And it shall be, if it make thee answer of peace, and open unto thee, then it shall be, that all the people that is found therein shall be tributaries unto thee, and they shall serve thee.

12   And if it will make no peace with thee, but will make war against thee, then thou shalt besiege it:

13   And when the Lord thy God hath delivered it into thine
        hands, thou shalt smite every male thereof with the
        edge of the sword:

14   But the women, and the little ones, and the cattle, and all
        that is in the city, even all the spoil thereof, shalt thou
        take unto thyself; and thou shalt eat the spoil of thine
        enemies, which the Lord thy God hath given thee.[1]

15   Thus shalt thou do unto all the cities which are very far
        off from thee, which are not of the cities of these
        nations.

16   But of the cities of these people, which the Lord thy God
        doth give thee for an inheritance, thou shalt save alive
        nothing that breatheth:

17   But thou shalt utterly destroy them; namely, the Hittites,
        and the Amorites, the Canaanites, and the Periz-
        zites, the Hivites, and the Jebusites;[2] as the Lord thy
        God hath commanded thee:

18   That they teach you not to do after all their abominations,
        which they have done unto their gods; so should ye
        sin against the Lord your God.

19   ¶When thou shalt besiege a city a long time, in making war
        against it to take it, thou shalt not destroy the trees
        thereof by forcing an ax against them: for thou mayest
        eat of them, and thou shalt not cut them down (for
        the tree of the field is man's life) to employ them in
        the siege:

20   Only the trees which thou knowest that they be not trees
        for meat,[3] thou shalt destroy and cut them down; and
        thou shalt build bulwarks against the city that maketh
        war with thee, until it be subdued.

Deuteronomy 20

---

1. The object of this section is to prescribe a degree of moderation in the
conduct of war.
2. Canaanites, Perizzites, Hivites, Jebusites: various of the early non-Israel-
ite inhabitants of Palestine, which the Israelites were expected to displace.
3. Edible fruit or nuts.

III
Monotheism

THE EGYPTIANS

Monotheism

THE EGYPTIANS

Introduction to A Hymn to Amon-Re

It would certainly be incorrect to describe the traditional faith of Egypt as monotheistic, for the Egyptians revered a vast pantheon of deities. Many of these were the patrons of a particular region, temple, or function; their powers were limited to a special geographical area or to the practitioners of certain trades. Other deities, e.g., the celestial gods of the sun, sky, moon, and stars, embraced the entire world.

The evolution of Egyptian religious ideas tended toward the identification of minor gods with one of the heavenly powers and the subjugation of local or provincial deities by the god of the capital city. When in pre-dynastic times Egypt was consolidated into the two states of Upper and Lower Egypt, Horus and Seth, the gods of the two religious capitals, became the patron deities of their respective kingdoms. After the unification of the whole country under the kings of Upper Egypt, Horus became the national god, a position he retained throughout Egyptian history. He acquired the characteristics of the sun-god to become Re-Harakhti (Harakhti meaning "Horus-of-the-Horizon"); and the Pharaohs were regarded as his incarnation.

In a similar way, the god Amun (Amon), patron of Thebes, became a national god when under the Eighteenth Dynasty (1552-1304 B.C.) his city became the capital of Egypt. He, too, became identified with the sun-god to become Amun-Re. In essence, he was nothing more than an amalgamation of the old sun-gods: Khepri, the morning sun; Atum, the sun at evening; and Re-Harakhti. Like them, Amun-Re sailed over the celestial ocean and fought the Apophis-dragon; all of Re's sanctuaries, names, and attributes became his. Like Re, he was regarded as the creator and preserver of life. Because Egypt under the New Kingdom was an imperial power, the supremacy of Amun-Re, unlike that of his predecessors, extended over foreigners as well as Egyptians.

The following well-known hymn, while devoted to the praise of one god, does not reject the others. Rather, it exalts Amun-Re by ascribing to him the other gods' functions and powers.

A HYMN TO AMON-RE

Adoration of Amon-Re, the Bull[1] Residing in Heliopolis,[2] chief of all gods, the good god, the beloved, who gives life to all that is warm[3] and to all good cattle.

1   Hail to thee, Amon-Re,
     Lord of the Thrones of the Two Lands, Presiding over
          Karnak,[4]
     Bull of His Mother,[5] Presiding over His Fields![6]
     Far-reaching of stride, presiding over Upper Egypt,
     Lord of the Madjoi[7] and ruler of Punt,[8]
     Eldest of heaven, first-born of earth,
     Lord of what is, enduring in all things, enduring in all
          things.
     UNIQUE IN HIS NATURE LIKE THE FLUID of the gods,
     The goodly bull of the Ennead,[9] chief of all gods,
     The lord of truth and father of the gods.
     Who made mankind and created the beasts,
     Lord of what is, who created the fruit tree,
     Made herbage, and gave life to cattle.
     The goodly daemon whom Ptah made,[10]

From *Ancient Near Eastern Texts Relating to the Old Testament*, J. B. Pritchard, ed., John A. Wilson, trans., Princeton University Press, 1950, 1955, pp. 365-7. Reprinted by permission.

1. Designation for the king and certain gods.
2. Sacred city of the sun-god, near modern Cairo.
3. Probably, all that lives.
4. District of the city of Thebes where the temple of Amun was located.
5. The sun-god is the son of the sky-goddess, re-creating himself each day.
6. As the bull rules over the pasture, so the sun rules over the sky.
7. A people of Nubia (northern Sudan) which furnished Egypt with sol-diers and police.
8. The spice-bearing region south of the Red Sea.
9. I.e., leader of the nine great gods.
10. Ptah, the craftsman-god, has given form to Amun.

2   The goodly beloved youth to whom the gods give praise,
Who made what is below and what is above,[11]
Who illuminates the Two Lands
And crosses the heavens in peace:
The King of Upper and Lower Egypt: Re, the triumphant,[12]
Chief of the Two Lands,
Great of strength, lord of reverence,
The chief one, who made the entire earth.
MORE DISTINGUISHED IN NATURE THAN any (other) god,
In whose beauty the gods rejoice,
To whom is given jubilation in the Per-wer,[13]
Who is given ceremonial appearance in the Per-nezer.[14]
Whose fragrance the gods love, when he comes from Punt,
Rich in perfume, when he comes down (from) Madjoi,
The Beautiful of Face who comes (from) God's Land.[15]
The gods FAWN (at) his feet,
According as they recognize his majesty as their lord,
The lord of fear, great of dread,
Rich in might, terrible of appearances,
Flourishing in offerings and making provisions.
Jubilation to thee who made the gods,
Raised the heavens and laid down the ground!

3   THE END.

He who awakes in health,[16] Min-Amon,[17]
Lord of eternity, who made everlastingness,
Lord of praise, presiding over [the Ennead],
Firm of horns,[18] beautiful of face,
Lord of the uraeus[19] serpent, lofty of plumes,

11. I.e., men and stars.
12. The hieroglyphic is written as though Re were a former Pharaoh.
13. "Great House": the religious center of Upper Egypt at el-Kab.
14. Religious center for Lower Egypt at Buto.
15. The east, where the sun rises.
16. This phrase is generally applied to the resuscitated god Osiris.
17. Amon was originally regarded as merely a form of the fertility god, Min.
18. The god's crown was adorned with horns, feathers, and serpents.
19. The royal serpent worn by both the sun-god and the Pharaoh.

Beautiful of diadem, and lofty of White Crown.[20]
The serpent-coil and the Double Crown,[21] *these are before him,*
The aromatic gum which is in the palace,
The Double Crown, the head-cloth, and the Blue Crown.[22]
Beautiful of face, when he receives the *atef*-crown,[22]
He whom the crowns of Upper and Lower Egypt love,
Lord of the Double Crown, when he receives the *ames*-staff,[22]
Lord of the *mekes*-scepter,[22] holding the flail.[22]
THE GOODLY ruler, CROWNED WITH THE WHITE CROWN,
The lord of rays, who makes brilliance,
To whom the gods give thanksgiving,
Who extends his arms to him whom he loves,
(But) his enemy is consumed by a flame.
It is his Eye that overthrows the rebels,[23]
That sends its spear into him that sucks up Nun,[24]

4.   And makes the fiend disgorge what he has swallowed.[25]
HAIL TO THEE, O Re, lord of truth!
Whose shrine is hidden,[26] the lord of the gods,
Khepri[27] in the midst of his barque,
Who gave commands, and the gods came into being.[28]
Atum,[29] who made the people,
Distinguished their nature, made their life,
And separated colors, one from another.[30]
Who hears the prayer of him who is in captivity,
Gracious of heart in the face of an appeal to him.

20. The crown of Upper Egypt.
21. The joint crowns of Upper and Lower Egypt.
22. Various other symbols of royalty.
23. Reference to the legend in which the Eye of the sun repulsed the Apophis-dragon which tried to halt the sun's journey across the sky.
24. The primeval waters from which life arose; also the sky-goddess.
25. The Apophis-dragon drank up the celestial ocean so that the sun's ship could not voyage upon it.
26. Word play on Amon and *amen* (meaning "hidden").
27. The morning sun.
28. A play on Khepri and *kheper* ("come into being").
29. The sun at night.
30. I.e., even the barbarians are god's children.

SAVING THE FEARFUL FROM THE TERRIBLE OF HEART,
Judging the weak and the injured.
Lord of Perception, in whose mouth Command is placed,[31]
For love of whom the Nile has come,
Possessor of sweetness, greatly beloved;
When he comes, the people live.
He who gives scope to every eye that may be made in
      Nun,[32]
Whose loveliness has created the light,

5   In whose beauty the gods rejoice;
Their hearts live when they see him.
THE END.

O RE, ADORED IN KARNAK,
Great of appearances in the House of the *Benben*,[33]
The Heliopolitan, lord of the New Moon Feast,
For whom the Sixth-Day and Quarter Month feasts are
      celebrated.[34]
The Sovereign—life, prosperity, health!—lord of all gods;
[They] behold him in the midst of the horizon,
The overlord of men *of the silent land*,[35]
Whose name is hidden from his children,
In this his name of Amon.[36]
HAIL TO THEE, WHO ART IN PEACE!
Lord of joy, terrible of appearances,
Lord of the uraeus-serpent, lofty of plumes,
Beautiful of diadem, and lofty of White Crown.
The gods love to see thee
With the Double Crown fixed upon thy brow.
The love of thee is spread throughout the Two Lands,
When thy rays shine forth in the eyes.

31. Perception and Command (or mind and speech) are creative forces. See
"The Theology of Memphis" in Vol. I of this series.
32. See note 24 above. "Every eye" is figurative for "everybody."
33. A sacred stone at Heliopolis.
34. These are festivals of the moon. Their relation to the sun-god is not clear.
35. Probably the burial ground.
36. "Hidden." See note 26 above.

The good of the people is thy arising;
The cattle grow languid when thou shinest.[37]
The love of thee is in the southern sky,[38]

6   The sweetness of thee is in the northern sky.[38]
The beauty of thee carries away hearts;
The love of thee makes arms languid;
Thy beautiful form relaxes the hands;
And hearts are forgetful at the sight of thee.
THOU ART the sole one, WHO MADE [ALL] THAT IS,
[The] solitary sole [one], who made what exists,
From whose eyes mankind came forth,
And upon whose mouth the gods came into being.[39]
He who made herbage [for] the cattle,
And the fruit tree for mankind,
Who made that (on which) the fish in the river may live,
And the birds *soaring in* the sky.
He who gives breath to that which is in the egg,
Gives life to the son of the slug,
And makes that on which gnats may live,
And worms and flies in like manner;
Who supplies the needs of the mice in their holes,
And gives life to flying things in every tree.
HAIL TO THEE, WHO DID ALL THIS!
Solitary sole one, with many hands,[40]

7   Who spends the night wakeful, while all men are asleep,
Seeking benefit for his creatures.
Amon, enduring in all things, Atum and Har-akhti[41]—
Praises are thine, when they all say:
"Jubilation to thee, because thou weariest thyself with us!
Salaams to thee, because thou didst create us!"

37. Growing languid is apparently regarded as a pleasant thing.
38. Possible reference to the gods dwelling in these skies.
39. From whose eyes and upon whose mouth: reference to the myth by
which mortals were created as the tears of the god, the other gods as his
spittle.
40. Hands which the god must possess to have created so much.
41. Atum and Har-akhti: forms of the sun-god.

HAIL TO THEE FOR ALL BEASTS!
Jubilation to thee for every foreign country—
To the height of heaven, to the width of earth,
To the depth of the Great Green Sea!
The gods are bowing down to thy majesty
And exalting the might of him who created them,
Rejoicing at the approach of him who begot them.
They say to thee: "Welcome in peace!
Father of the fathers of all the gods,
Who raised the heavens and laid down the ground,
WHO MADE WHAT IS AND CREATED WHAT EXISTS;
Sovereign—life, prosperity, health!—and chief of the gods!

8   We praise thy might, according as thou didst make us.
Let (us) act for thee, because thou brought us forth.
We give thee thanksgiving because thou hast wearied thy-
        self with us!"
HAIL TO THEE, WHO MADE ALL THAT IS!
Lord of truth[42] and father of the gods,
Who made mortals and created beasts,
Lord of the grain,
Who made (also) the living of the beasts of the desert.
Amon, the bull beautiful of countenance,
The beloved in Karnak,
Great of appearances in the House of the *Benben*,
Taking again the diadem in Heliopolis,
Who judges the Two[43] in the great broad hall,
The chief of the Great Ennead.
THE SOLITARY SOLE ONE, WITHOUT HIS PEER,
Presiding over Karnak,
The Heliopolitan, presiding over his Ennead,
And living on truth every day.[44]
The horizon-dweller, Horus of the east,[45]

---

42. Often a designation for Ptah, the craftsman-god, who fashioned everything.
43. The gods Horus and Seth, who contended for the rule of Egypt.
44. I.e., truth is his life-principle.
45. I.e., king of the eastern countries.

From whom the desert creates silver and gold,
Genuine lapis lazuli for love of him,

9   *Benzoin*[46] and various incenses from Madjoi,
And fresh myrrh for thy nostrils—
Beautiful of face when coming (from) Madjoi!
Amon-Re, Lord of the Thrones of the Two Lands,
Presiding over Karnak,
The Heliopolitan, presiding over his harem!
THE END.

The sole king, like the *fluid* of the gods,
With many names, unknown in number,[47]
Rising in the eastern horizon,
And going to rest in the western horizon;
Who overthrows his enemies,
(RE)BORN EARLY EVERY DAY.
Thoth lifts up his two eyes,[48]
And satisfies him with his effective deeds.
The gods rejoice in his beauty,
He whom his apes exalt.[49]
Lord of the evening barque and the morning barque;[50]
They cross Nun in peace for thee.
Thy CREW IS IN JOY,
When they see the overthrow of the rebel,[51]
His body licked up by the knife.

10   Fire has devoured him;
His soul is more consumed than his body.
That dragon, his (power of) motion is taken away.

46. Perhaps myrrh?
47. The name was an element of personality and power. Having a hidden name was considered a source of supremacy.
48. Thoth was the god of wisdom and scribe of the gods. His two eyes were the sun and the moon.
49. At dawn the apes warm themselves in the sun's rays.
50. The sun god's two ships.
51. The Apophis-dragon. See note 25 above.

The gods are in joy,
The crew of Re is in satisfaction,
Heliopolis is in joy,
For the enemies of Atum are overthrown.
Karnak is in satisfaction, Heliopolis is in joy,
The heart of the Lady of Life[52] is glad,
For the enemy of her lord is overthrown.
The gods of Babylon[53] are in jubilation,
They who are in the shrines are salaaming,
WHEN THEY SEE HIM RICH IN HIS MIGHT.
The daemon[54] of the gods,
The righteous one, Lord of Karnak,
In this thy name of Maker of Righteousness;[55]
The lord of provisions, bull of *offerings*,
In this thy name of Amon, Bull of His Mother;
Maker of all mankind,[56]
Creator and maker of all that is,

11   In this thy name of Atum-Khepri.[57]
Great falcon, festive of bosom,
Beautiful of face, festive of breast,
Pleasing of form, lofty of plume,
On whose brow the two uraei *flutter*.
To whom the hearts of mankind make approach,
To whom the people turn about;
Who makes festive the Two Lands with his comings forth.[58]
Hail to thee, Amon-Re, Lord of the Thrones of the Two
     Lands,
Whose city loves his rising!
IT HAS COME (TO ITS END) . . .

---

52. Epithet of a goddess, here probably the Eye of the sun.
53. Egyptian Babylon was a city close to the site of modern Cairo.
54. Perhaps: the most mighty?
55. "Righteousness" can also mean "truth."
56. "All mankind," *ta-tem*, is a pun on the name Atum.
57. *Sekheper*, "creator," is a pun on Khepri.
58. This hymn was evidently intended for one of the festivals in which an image of the god was taken in procession out of his temple.

Introduction to The Hymn to the Aton

The Pharaoh Amenhotep IV, or Akh-en-Aton (reigned 1362-1345 B.C.), has often been described as a monotheist. Not only did he worship but one God—the sun-disk Aton—but he also rejected all other gods and persecuted their adherents. However, in contrast to the Hebrew Yahweh, the Aton never became a truly national deity. It was never accepted by the Egyptian people, who continued to worship their various local gods, but only by the family and immediate followers of the Pharaoh. When Akh-en-Aton died, the new faith died with him.

Quite probably Akh-en-Aton's religious development was influenced by the priesthood of Heliopolis, the sacred city of the old sun-god, Re-Harakhti. It was then only a century since Amun had been elevated from the position of obscure patron deity of Thebes to chief god of the Egyptian empire. The priests of Re at Heliopolis naturally resented the power and riches which devolved upon the priests and temples of Amun; and perhaps Akh-en-Aton absorbed some of their hostility. The doctrine that the purest form of the sun-god was the physical sun-disk, or Aton, seems also to have been developed at Heliopolis.

Immediately upon his accession as co-ruler with his father, Akh-en-Aton began to promote respect for the Aton and to stress its identification with the old god Re-Harakhti. Several new temples were built in honor of the Aton, who is depicted on the reliefs in exactly the same form as Re-Harakhti: a figure with the head of a falcon crowned by a sun-disk and encircled by the uraeus-serpent. Akh-en-Aton felt that the Aton, like other gods, should have a city of his own; thus was founded Akhetaton ("Horizon of Aton"), now known as Tell el-Amarna, halfway between Thebes and Memphis.

From merely favoring the new god, Akh-en-Aton proceeded to make Aton-worship the state religion, and to persecute the followers of other gods, particularly the god Amun. Statues of the old gods were destroyed, their images in temple reliefs erased, their names blotted out. The name of Amun was banned wherever it appeared— in temples, private tombs, or personal names. Thus Amenhotep IV (meaning "Amun Is Satisfied") became Akh-en-Aton ("He Who Is Beneficial to Aton").

No doubt this persecution represented an attempt to do away with polytheistic concepts of the Deity. The Aton's title was altered to eliminate any association with the traditional religion. Images of the Aton were strictly forbidden, though it had been the practice in Egypt to portray gods in human or animal form. Unlike the old gods also, the Aton was worshipped not in dimly lighted temples, but in open courtyards exposed to the full force of the sun's rays. But at the same time, Akh-en-Aton maintained the traditional doctrine of Pharaoh's identity with the sun-god, except that now the god was the Aton.

Perhaps the new faith might have outlived its founder if Akh-en-Aton had been granted a long life. But the king was frail, and he died young. Though we have no record of any overt opposition to his reforms, such drastic changes must have aroused much resentment. Akh-en-Aton's associates lacked their chief's religious conviction; and when he died, they preferred to make peace with the old gods. As a result, the Aton doctrines remained without serious effect upon the subsequent religious development of the world; while the old deities were worshipped in Egypt far into the days of her decline.

The following hymn comes from the tomb of Akh-en-Aton's courtier, Ai (or Eye) at Tell el-Amarna. Ai was a comparatively minor official, who apparently gained favor with the Pharaoh by his ardent profession of the new faith. Akh-en-Aton died without a male heir; one of his successors on the throne was Ai, who as Pharaoh upheld the restored worship of the god Amun.

THE HYMN TO THE ATON

Praise of Re Har-akhti,[1] Rejoicing on the Horizon, in His Name as Shu[2] Who Is in the Aton-disc,[3] living forever and ever; the living great Aton who is in jubilee, lord of all that the Aton

From *Ancient Near Eastern Texts Relating to the Old Testament*, J. B. Pritchard, ed., John A. Wilson, trans., Princeton: Princeton University Press, 1950, 1955, pp. 370-71. Reprinted by permission.
    1. The name of the sun-god worshipped at Heliopolis.
    2. God of the atmosphere, son of Re, and ancient sun-god.
    3. The name of the Aton was written within an oval-shaped cartouche including the three ancient solar deities, Re, Horus-of-the-Horizon, and Shu.

encircles, lord of heaven, lord of earth, lord of the House of
Aton in Akhet-Aton[4]; (and praise of) the King of Upper and
Lower Egypt, who lives on truth, the Lord of the Two Lands:
Nefer-kheperu-Re Wa-en-Re;[5] the Son of Re, who lives on truth,
the Lord of Diadems: Akh-en-Aton, long in his lifetime; (and
praise of) the Chief Wife of the King, his beloved, the Lady of
the Two Lands: Nefer-neferu-Aton Nefert-iti, living, healthy,
and youthful forever and ever; (by) the Fan-Bearer on the Right
Hand of the King . . . Eye. He says:

Thou appearest beautifully on the horizon of heaven,
Thou living Aton, the beginning of life!
When thou art risen on the eastern horizon,
Thou hast filled every land with thy beauty.
Thou art gracious, great, glistening, and high over every land;
Thy rays encompass the lands to the limit of all that thou hast
     made:
As thou art Re, thou reachest to the end of them,[6]
(Thou) subduest them (for) thy beloved son.[7]
Though thou art far away, thy rays are on earth;
Though thou art in *their* faces, *no one knows thy* going.

When thou settest in the western horizon,
The land is in darkness, in the manner of death.
They sleep in a room, with heads wrapped up,[8]
Nor sees one eye the other.
All their goods which are under their heads might be stolen,
(But) they would not perceive (it).
Every lion is come forth from his den;
All creeping things, they sting.
Darkness *is a shroud*, and the earth is in stillness,
For he who made them rests in his horizon.

4. The name of Akh-en-Aton's new capital at Tell el-Amarna.
5. Official name of Akh-en-Aton.
6. Pun on *Ra* "Re," and *er-ra* "to the end."
7. Akh-en-Aton.
8. I.e. to protect them from the cold.

At daybreak, when thou arisest on the horizon,
When thou shinest as the Aton by day,
Thou drivest away the darkness and givest thy rays.
The Two Lands are in festivity *every day*,
Awake and standing upon (their) feet,
For thou hast raised them up.
Washing their bodies, taking (their) clothing,
Their arms are (raised) in praise at thy appearance.[9]
All the world, they do their work.

All beasts are content with their pasturage;
Trees and plants are flourishing.
The birds which fly from their nests,
Their wings are (stretched out) in praise to thy *ka*.[10]
All beasts spring upon (their) feet.
Whatever flies and alights,
They live when thou hast risen (for) them.
The ships are sailing north and south as well,
For every way is open at thy appearance.
The fish in the river dart before thy face[11];
Thy rays are in the midst of the great green sea.

Creator of seed in women,
Thou who makest fluid into man,
Who maintainest the son in the womb of his mother,
Who soothest him with that which stills his weeping,[12]
Thou nurse (even) in the womb,
Who givest breath to sustain all that he has made!
When he descends from the womb to *breathe*
On the day when he is born,
Thou openest his mouth completely,
Thou suppliest his necessities.
When the chick in the egg speaks within the shell,

9. I.e., in the morning prayer to the sun.
10. Here, a poetic expression for "thee." The birds raise their wings in praise just as men raise their arms.
11. I.e., to greet the sun also.
12. The Aton prevents the babe in the womb from weeping.

Thou givest him breath within it to maintain him.
When thou hast made him his fulfillment within the egg, to
    break it,
He comes forth from the egg to speak at his completed (time);
He walks upon his legs when he comes forth from it.

How manifold it is, what thou hast made!
They are hidden from the face (of man).[13]
O sole god, like whom there is no other!
Thou didst create the world according to thy desire,
Whilst thou wert alone:
All men, cattle, and wild beasts,
Whatever is on earth, going upon (its) feet,
And what is on high, flying with its wings.

The countries of Syria and Nubia, the *land* of Egypt,[14]
Thou settest every man in his place,
Thou suppliest their necessities:
Everyone has his food, and his time of life is reckoned.
Their tongues are separate in speech,
And their natures as well;
Their skins are distinguished,
As thou distinguishest the foreign peoples.
Thou makest a Nile in the underworld,[15]
Thou bringest it forth as thou desirest
To maintain the people (of Egypt)
According as thou madest them for thyself,
The lord of all of them, wearying (himself) with them,
The lord of every land, rising for them,
The Aton of the day, great of majesty.
All distant foreign countries, thou makest their life (also),
For thou hast set a Nile in heaven,
That it may descend for them and make waves upon the moun-
    tains,

13. I.e., they are too numerous to be counted.
14. Placing foreign countries on the same level with Egypt represents a
sharp break with tradition.
15. According to Egyptian belief, the Nile comes from the waters under the
earth.

Like the great green sea,
To water their fields in their towns.[16]
How effective they are, thy plans, O lord of eternity!
The Nile in heaven, it is for the foreign peoples
And for the beasts of every desert that go upon (their) feet;
(While the true) Nile comes from the underworld for Egypt.

The rays suckle every meadow.
When thou risest, they live, they grow for thee.
Thou makest the seasons in order to rear all that thou hast made,
The winter to cool them,
And the heat that *they* may taste thee.
Thou hast made the distant sky in order to rise therein,
In order to see all that thou dost make.
Whilst thou wert alone,
Rising in thy form as the living Aton,
Appearing, shining, *withdrawing or approaching,*
Thou madest millions of forms of thyself alone.
Cities, towns, fields, road, and river—
Every eye beholds thee over against them,[17]
For thou art the Aton of the day over *the earth*. . . .

Thou art in my heart,
And there is no other that knows thee
Save thy son Nefer-kheperu-Re Wa-en-Re,[18]
For thou hast made him well-versed in thy plans and in thy
    strength.[19]

The world came into being by thy hand,
According as thou hast made them.[20]
When thou hast risen they live,
When thou settest they die.

16. The rain of foreign countries is like the Nile of rainless Egypt.
17. I.e., wherever one is, the sun appears in the same place.
18. Akh-en-Aton. Though the hymn is recited by the official (later king)
Ai (Eye), he states that only Akh-en-Aton knows the Aton.
19. In the new as well as the old religion, Pharaoh was the intermediary
between the god(s) and the people.
20. Namely, its inhabitants.

Thou art lifetime thy own self,
For one lives (only) through thee.
Eyes are (fixed) on beauty until thou settest.
All work is laid aside when thou settest in the west.
(But) when (thou) risest (again),
[*Everything is*] made to flourish for the king, . . .
Since thou didst found the earth
And raise them up for thy son,
Who came forth from thy body:
the King of Upper and Lower Egypt, . . . Akh-en-Aton, . . .
    and the Chief Wife of the King . . . Nefert-iti, living
    and youthful forever and ever.

[The hymn concludes with various epithets of praise.]

Introduction to The Restoration Inscription of Tutankhamun

With the death of the Pharaoh Akh-en-Aton in 1345 B.C., the religion
he had established lost its principal supporter. Akh-en-Aton's successor, Tutankhamun (reigned 1345-1336 B.C.), a boy of eight or nine at
his accession, had no firm hereditary claim to the throne, and was in
no position to enforce submission to the religion of the Aton. The new
king's advisers evidently realized that an accommodation with the
powerful adherents of the old gods was necessary in order to
strengthen Tutankhamun's shaky throne. Akh-en-Aton's new capital
at Tell el-Amarna was abandoned; the court returned to Thebes,
city of the god Amun. All possible traces of the worship of Aton
were destroyed.

    The following inscription, after some conventionally phrased flat-
tery of Pharaoh (omitted here), alludes briefly to the internal confusion and foreign disasters suffered by Egypt under the weak government of Akh-en-Aton. Such misfortunes, it implies, must be at-
tributable to godly anger. Thus the chief work of Tutankhamun was
to restore Egypt to favor with the traditional gods.

THE RESTORATION INSCRIPTION OF
TUTANKHAMUN

Now when His Majesty arose as king,
the temples of the gods and goddesses, beginning from Elephantine [down] to the marshes of the Delta,
[their? . . . had] fallen into neglect,
their shrines had fallen into desolation and become tracts overgrown with K—— plants,
their sanctuaries were as if they had never been,
their halls were a trodden path.
The land was in confusion, the gods forsook this land.
If an [army ? was] sent to Djahy[1] to widen the frontiers of Egypt, it met with no success at all.
If one prayed to a god to ask things of him, [in no wise] did he come.
If one made supplication to a goddess in like manner, in no wise did she come.
Their hearts were weak of themselves (with anger); they destroyed what had been done.

After some days had passed by this, [His Majesty app]eared on the throne of his father;
he ruled the countries of Horus,
the Black Land and the Red Land were under his dominion,
and every land was in obeisance to his might.

Behold His Majesty was in his palace, which is in the estate of Akheperkare,[2] like Re in the heavens,
and His Majesty was administering this land, and making daily governance of the Two River-banks.

From "The Restoration Inscription of Tutankhamun," John Bennett, *Journal of Egyptian Archaeology*, XXV (1939), 9-11. Reprinted by permission.
1. General term for Syria.
2. King Thutmose I (reigned 1506-1495 B.C.). The "estate of Akheperkare" was at Memphis, near modern Cairo.

Then His Majesty took counsel with his heart,

searching out every excellent occasion, seeking what was beneficial to his father Amun,

for fashioning his august image of real fine-gold.

He has added to what was done in former time,

he has fashioned (an image of) his father Amun upon thirteen
carrying-poles,[3]

his holy image being of fine-gold, lapis-lazuli, [turquoise], and
every rare costly stone,

whereas formerly the majesty of this august god had been upon
eleven carrying-poles.

He has fashioned (an image of) Ptah, South of his Wall, lord
of Ankhtawe,[4]

his august image being of fine-gold, [upon eleven carryi]ng-
poles,

his holy image being of fine-gold, lapis-lazuli, turquoise, and
every rare costly stone,

whereas formerly the majesty of this august god had been upon
[six?] carrying-poles.

And His Majesty has made monuments for the gods,

[fashioning] their statues of real fine-gold, the best of foreign
lands,

building anew their sanctuaries as monuments of eternal age,
they being endowed with property for ever,

establishing for them divine gifts as a lasting daily sacrifice,

and supplying them with food-offerings upon earth.

He has added to what was in former time,

he has surp[assed that] done since the time of the ancestors,

he has inducted priests and prophets, children of the notables
of their towns, each the son of a noted man, and one whose
name is known;[5]

he has multiplied their [wealth?] with gold, silver, bronze and
copper, without limit of [all things?],

3. This refers to the poles used for carrying a portable shrine. Thirteen
would seem to be an unusually large number of poles.

4. A district of Memphis.

5. I.e., he has installed these people (who were evidently out of favor
under Akhnaton) in official positions.

he has filled their storehouses with slaves, men and women, the
    fruit of His Majesty's plundering.

All the [possessions?] of the temples are doubled, trebled and
quadrupled with silver, gold, lapis-lazuli, turquoise, all rare
costly stones, royal linen, white cloth, fine linen, olive oil, gum,
fat, [. . .] incense, *ihmt* incense and myrrh, without limit of
all good things.

His Majesty (may he live, prosper and be in health!) has
hewn their barques which are on the river of fresh cedar, the best
of the hill-slope, the pick of Negau,[6] worked with gold, the best of
foreign lands; and they illumine the river.

His Majesty (may he live, prosper and be in health!) has
consecrated men and women slaves, singers and dancers, who
are servants in the house of the King; and their wages are
charged to the [. . .] palace of the Lord of the Two Lands.

"I cause them to be protected and preserved for my fathers,
all the gods, in the desire to placate them by doing that which
their *kas*[7] love, so that they may protect [Ta-mery]."

The gods and goddesses who are in this land, their hearts are
    joyful,
the possessors of shrines are glad,
lands are in a state of jubilation and merry-making,
exaltation is throughout [the whole land];
a goodly [state?] has come to pass.

The ennead of the gods who are in the temple,[8]
their arms are (raised) in adoration,
their hands are full of jubilees [of] eternity and everlastingness,

6. A place somewhat south of Byblos, the chief port from which cedars
were shipped.
7. *Ka:* the vital force, or personality of a man, sometimes translated as
"soul" or "double." "Their *kas*" in this context is merely a poetic expression
for "they."
8. Probably the temple of Atum, the sun-god, at Heliopolis.

all life and prosperity with them (are placed) to the nose of
    Horus who is born again,

beloved son [of his father Amun-Re, lord of the Thrones of the
    Two Lands?—]

he (Amun) has fashioned him that he (himself) may be fash-
    ioned;

king of Upper and Lower Egypt, Nebkheprure,[9] beloved of
    Amun,

his beloved, real eldest son,

who protects the father who fashioned him

that he may exercise the kingship over ki[ngs in all lands];

son of Re, Tutankhamun, ruler of Hermonthis,[10]

a son who is profitable to him who fashioned him,

wealthy in monuments, rich in wonders,

who makes monuments in righteousness of heart for his father
    Amun;

beautiful of birth, sovereign [who assumed the crowns in Chem-
    mis].[11]

On this day One was in the goodly palace, which is in the estate
    of Akheperkare, justified;

behold, [His Majesty (may he live, prosper and be in health!)]
    was rejuvenated,

he who seizes (?) hastened of himself.[12]

Khnumu[13] has moulded him [as a mighty one (?) . . .],

he is mighty of arm,

great of strength, one distinguished more than the mighty,

vast of strength like the son [of Nut[14] . . .],

mighty of arm like Horus,

there exists no equal to him among the mighty ones of all lands
    together;

he who knows like Re,

9. Tutankhamun.
10. City of the god Mont, south of Thebes.
11. This phrase emphasizes the king's hereditary right to the throne, liken-
ing him to Horus, who was said to have been destined from birth for the
kingship.
12. Meaning unclear.
13. The ram-headed creator god.
14. The sky-goddess, mother of Seth, the war-god.

who [. . .s like] Ptah,
who understands like Thoth,[15]
who ordains excellent laws,
who commands [. . .],
excellent of utterance;

King of Upper and Lower Egypt, lord of the Two Lands, lord of rites, lord of the strong arm, Nebkheprure, he who placates the gods, beloved son of Re of his body, lord of every foreign land, lord of crowns, Tutankhamun, ruler of Hermonthis, given life, stability and prosperity like Re [for ever and ever].

15. God of wisdom.

THE HEBREWS

THE HEBREWS

Introduction to the Book of Exodus

The Hebrews were one of the many semi-nomadic groups of herdsmen who occupied the fringe areas of the great civilizations of the
ancient Near East. Probably they were somehow related to the Habiru, a people whose name appears frequently in Mesopotamian
sources from about the eighteenth century B.C. onward, and in Egyptian sources from the time of the Eighteenth Dynasty (1552-1304
B.C.). Their settlement in the Nile Delta ("the land of Goshen"),
narrated in the Biblical story of Joseph and his brothers, probably
occurred around 1650 B.C. According to the Bible, the Hebrews spent
four hundred years in Egypt, which would make Ramses II (reigned
1290-1224 B.C.) the Pharaoh of the Exodus. Many scholars, however,
regard the Hebrews' migration into Egypt as a part of the Hyksos
invasion (*ca.* 1650 B.C.) and connect the events of the Exodus with
the expulsion of the Hyksos by Ahmose I in 1542 B.C. The ascertain-
able historical facts of the matter are slight. The only actual mention of the term "Israel" in Egyptian sources is in the so-called
Israel Stele of Pharaoh Merneptah,* which records that in the fifth
year of Merneptah's reign (1220 B.C.) a people called Israel occupied
the region which today is northwest Transjordan. The Habiru, however, are mentioned as living in Palestine in the fourteenth century B.C.

In any event, at a time when the Hebrews were adopting a more
settled mode of existence, they required both a code of law and a
re-affirmation of their ancient religion. A prime element of that religion was the conviction that the Jews were God's chosen people,
bound to him through a special Covenant. Therefore they were commanded to worship him only; the idols favored by neighboring nations were forbidden. Perhaps most significantly, God's demands
upon his people were ethical. In comparison with the all-too-human
deities of pagan nations, the Yahweh of the Hebrews demanded from
his worshippers a high standard of moral behavior.

* See above, "Hymn on the Victory over the Libyans," p. 20.

FROM THE BOOK OF EXODUS

Chapter 20

1   And God spake all these words, saying,

2   I am the Lord thy God, which have brought thee out of the
land of Egypt, out of the house of bondage.

3   Thou shalt have no other gods before me.

4   Thou shalt not make unto thee any graven image, or any
likeness of any thing that is in heaven above, or that
is in the earth beneath, or that is in the water under
the earth:[1]

5   Thou shalt not bow down thyself to them, nor serve them:
for I the Lord thy God am a jealous God, visiting the
iniquity of the fathers upon the children unto the
third and fourth generation of them that hate me;

6   And shewing mercy unto thousands of them that love me,
and keep my commandments.

7   Thou shalt not take the name of the Lord thy God in vain;
for the Lord will not hold him guiltless that taketh his
name in vain.[2]

8   Remember the sabbath day, to keep it holy.

9   Six days shalt thou labour, and do all thy work:

10 But the seventh day is the sabbath of the Lord thy God:
in it thou shalt not do any work, thou, nor thy son,
nor thy daughter, thy manservant, nor thy maidservant, nor thy cattle, nor thy stranger that is within thy
gates;

11 For in six days the Lord made heaven and earth, the sea,
and all that in them is, and rested the seventh day:
wherefore the Lord blessed the sabbath day and hallowed it.

12 ¶Honour thy father and thy mother: that thy days may be

Exodus 20:1-24, King James Bible.

1. This prohibition was significant in a day when idol-worship was very
common.

2. I.e., God's name must be treated with reverence and not used lightly.

long upon the land which the Lord thy God giveth thee.

13 Thou shalt not kill.

14 Thou shalt not commit adultery.

15 Thou shalt not steal.

16 Thou shalt not bear false witness against thy neighbour.

17 Thou shalt not covet thy neighbour's house, thou shalt not covet thy neighbour's wife, nor his manservant, nor his maidservant, nor his ox, nor his ass, nor any thing that is thy neighbour's.

18 ¶And all the people saw the thunderings, and the lightnings, and the noise of the trumpet, and the mountain smoking: and when the people saw it, they removed, and stood afar off.

19 And they said unto Moses, Speak thou with us, and we will hear: but let not God speak with us, lest we die.

20 And Moses said unto the people, Fear not: for God is come to prove you, and that his fear may be before your faces, that ye sin not.

21 And the people stood afar off, and Moses drew near unto the thick darkness where God was.

22 ¶And the Lord said unto Moses, Thus thou shalt say unto the children of Israel, Ye have seen that I have talked with you from heaven.

23 Ye shall not make with me gods of silver, neither shall ye make unto you gods of gold.

24 ¶An altar of earth thou shalt make unto me,[3] and shalt sacrifice thereon thy burnt offerings, and thy peace offerings, thy sheep, and thine oxen: in all places where I record my name I will come unto thee, and I will bless thee.

3. I.e., Yahweh was to be worshipped upon the simplest kind of altar at whatever place He chose to reveal himself.

Introduction to the Book of Deuteronomy

The Book of Deuteronomy, meaning "second law," concludes the first section of the Old Testament, called the Pentateuch ("Five Books of the Law"). It consists of a series of addresses believed to have been delivered by Moses on the plains beyond the Jordan River, shortly before the Hebrews entered the Promised Land. The laws of Deuteronomy are a revised and expanded version of the Laws of the Book of Exodus. The core of the book is ancient, but was enlarged and edited in the seventh century B.C. by men under the influence of the great eighth-century prophets.

In later times, the Jews selected chapter 6, verses 4-9, of this book for recitation twice daily. Jesus called verse 5, "Thou shalt love the Lord thy God with all thine heart, and with all thy soul, and with all thy might," the greatest of all the Commandments.*

* In Matthew 22:37; Mark 12:29-30; Luke 10:27.

FROM THE BOOK OF DEUTERONOMY

Chapter 6

4   Hear, O Israel: the Lord our God is one Lord:

5   And thou shalt love the Lord thy God with all thine heart, and with all thy soul, and with all thy might.

6   And these words, which I command thee this day, shall be in thine heart:

7   And thou shalt teach them diligently unto thy children, and shalt talk of them when thou sittest in thine house, and when thou walkest by the way, and when thou liest down, and when thou risest up.

8   And thou shalt bind them for a sign upon thine hand, and they shall be as frontlets between thine eyes.

9   And thou shalt write them upon the posts of thy house, and on thy gates.

Deuteronomy 6:4-15; 13:1-11, King James Bible.

10   And it shall be, when the Lord thy God shall have brought
        thee into the land which he sware unto thy fathers,
        to Abraham, to Isaac, and to Jacob, to give thee great
        and goodly cities, which thou buildest not,

11   And houses full of all good things, which thou filledst not,
        and wells digged, which thou diggedst not, vineyards
        and olive trees, which thou plantedst not; when thou
        shalt have eaten and be full;

12   Then beware lest thou forget the Lord, which brought thee
        forth out of the land of Egypt, from the house of
        bondage.

13   Thou shalt fear the Lord thy God, and serve him, and shalt
        swear by his name.

14   Ye shall not go after other gods, of the gods of the people
        which are round about you;

15   (For the Lord thy God is a jealous God among you) lest the
        anger of the Lord thy God be kindled against thee,
        and destroy thee from off the face of the earth.

Chapter 13

1   If there arise among you a prophet, or a dreamer of dreams,
        and giveth thee a sign or a wonder,

2   And the sign or the wonder come to pass, whereof he spake
        unto thee, saying, Let us go after other gods, which
        thou hast not known, and let us serve them;

3   Thou shalt not hearken unto the words of that prophet, or
        that dreamer of dreams: for the Lord your God prov-
        eth you, to know whether ye love the Lord your God
        with all your heart and with all your soul.

4   Ye shall walk after the Lord your God, and fear him, and
        keep his commandments, and obey his voice, and ye
        shall serve him, and cleave unto him.

5   And that prophet, or that dreamer of dreams, shall be put
        to death; because he hath spoken to turn you away
        from the Lord your God, which brought you out of the
        land of Egypt, and redeemed you out of the house of
        bondage, to thrust thee out of the way which the Lord

thy God commanded thee to walk in. So shalt thou put the evil away from the midst of thee.

6   ¶If thy brother, the son of thy mother, or thy son, or thy daughter, or the wife of thy bosom, or thy friend, which is as thine own soul, entice thee secretly, saying, Let us go and serve other gods, which thou hast not known, thou, nor thy fathers;

7   Namely, of the gods of the people which are round about you, nigh unto thee, or far off from thee, from the one end of the earth even unto the other end of the earth;

8   Thou shalt not consent unto him, nor hearken unto him; neither shall thine eye pity him, neither shalt thou spare, neither shalt thou conceal him:

9   But thou shalt surely kill him; thine hand shall be first upon him to put him to death, and afterwards the hand of all the people.

10   And thou shalt stone him with stones, that he die; because he hath sought to thrust thee away from the Lord thy God, which brought thee out of the land of Egypt, from the house of bondage.

11   And all Israel shall hear, and fear, and shall do no more any such wickedness as this is among you.

Introduction to the Book of Isaiah

When the prophet Isaiah first heard the call to become God's spokesman (*ca.* 740 B.C.), a period of peace and affluence in the Kingdom of Judah was about to end. Isaiah inveighed against the dissoluteness, oppression, bribery, sensuality, and idol worship which he saw around him, and prophesied that Assyria would serve as God's instrument to punish the Jews for their disobedience to His commands. Indeed, by 734 B.C. Assyria had conquered the northern kingdom of Israel and deported large numbers of Jews to Mesopotamia. But while predicting imminent doom, Isaiah also foresaw a day when all nations would accept the rule of Yahweh and war would cease forever.

FROM THE BOOK OF ISAIAH

Chapter 1

11   To what purpose is the multitude of your sacrifices unto me? saith the Lord: I am full of the burnt offerings of rams, and the fat of fed beasts; and I delight not in the blood of bullocks, or of lambs, or of he goats.

12   When ye come to appear before me, who hath required this at your hand, to tread my courts?

13   Bring no more vain oblations; incense is an abomination unto me; the new moons and sabbaths, the calling of assemblies, I cannot away with; it is iniquity, even the solemn meeting.

14   Your new moons and your appointed feasts my soul hateth: they are a trouble unto me; I am weary to bear them.

15   And when ye spread forth your hands, I will hide mine eyes from you: yea, when ye make many prayers, I will not hear: your hands are full of blood.

16   ¶Wash you, make you clean; put away the evil of your doings from before mine eyes: cease to do evil;

17   Learn to do well; seek judgment, relieve the oppressed, judge the fatherless, plead for the widow.

18   Come now, and let us reason together, saith the Lord: though your sins be as scarlet, they shall be as white as snow; though they be red like crimson, they shall be as wool.

Chapter 2

1   The word that Isaiah the son of Amoz saw concerning Judah and Jerusalem.

2   And it shall come to pass in the last days, that the mountain of the Lord's house shall be established in the top

Isaiah 1:11-17; 2:1-22; 11:1-6, King James Bible.

of the mountains, and shall be exalted above the hills; and all nations shall flow unto it.

3   And many people shall go and say, Come ye, and let us go up to the mountain of the Lord, to the house of the God of Jacob; and he will teach us of his ways, and we will walk in his paths: for out of Zion shall go forth the law, and the word of the Lord from Jerusalem.

4   And he shall judge among the nations, and shall rebuke many people: and they shall beat their swords into plowshares, and their spears into pruninghooks: nation shall not lift up sword against nation, neither shall they learn war any more.

5   O house of Jacob, come ye, and let us walk in the light of the Lord.

6   ¶Therefore thou hast forsaken thy people the house of Jacob, because they be replenished from the east,[1] and are soothsayers like the Philistines, and they please themselves in the children of strangers.

7   Their land also is full of silver and gold, neither is there any end of their treasures; their land is also full of horses, neither is there any end of their chariots:

8   Their land also is full of idols; they worship the work of their own hands, that which their own fingers have made:

9   And the mean man boweth down, and the great man humbleth himself:[2] therefore forgive them not.

10   ¶Enter into the rock, and hide thee in the dust, for fear of the Lord, and for the glory of his majesty.

11   The lofty looks of man shall be humbled, and the haughtiness of men shall be bowed down, and the Lord alone shall be exalted in that day.

12   For the day of the Lord of hosts shall be upon every one that is proud and lofty, and upon every one that is lifted up; and he shall be brought low:

1. I.e., close contacts with foreign peoples have caused the Hebrews to depart from the sole worship of Yahweh.
2. I.e., humbleth himself before idols.

13 And upon all the cedars of Lebanon, that are high and lifted up, and upon all the oaks of Bashan,[3]

14 And upon all the high mountains, and upon all the hills that are lifted up,

15 And upon every high tower, and upon every fenced wall,

16 And upon all the ships of Tarshish,[4] and upon all pleasant pictures.

17 And the loftiness of man shall be bowed down, and the haughtiness of men shall be made low: and the Lord alone shall be exalted in that day.

18 And the idols he shall utterly abolish.

19 And they shall go into the holes of the rocks, and into the caves of the earth, for fear of the Lord, and for the glory of his majesty, when he ariseth to shake terribly the earth.

20 In that day a man shall cast his idols of silver, and his idols of gold, which they made each one for himself to worship, to the moles and to the bats;

21 To go into the clefts of the rocks and into the tops of the ragged rocks, for fear of the Lord, and for the glory of his majesty, when he ariseth to shake terribly the earth.[5]

22 Cease ye from man, whose breath is in his nostrils: for wherein is he to be accounted of?[6]

Chapter 11

1 And there shall come forth a rod out of the stem of Jesse,[7] and a Branch shall grow out of his roots:

2 And the spirit of the Lord shall rest upon him, the spirit of wisdom and understanding, the spirit of counsel and

3. A region in Palestine east of the Sea of Tiberias.

4. A Phoenician colony, probably Tartessus in southern Spain. Large commercial ships, regardless of where they operated, were often called "ships of Tarshish."

5. Verses 12 to 21 describe the Day of the Lord, when the worldly things in which men trust will be proved useless, the idols will be destroyed, and all people will be terrified at the Lord's coming.

6. This verse does not appear in the Greek translation of the Bible. Evidently it was added by a later writer to emphasize the weakness of mankind.

7. The father of King David.

might, the spirit of knowledge and of the fear of the
Lord;

3   And shall make him of quick understanding in the fear of
the Lord; and he shall not judge after the sight of his
eyes, neither reprove after the hearing of his ears:

4   But with righteousness shall he judge the poor, and reprove
with equity for the meek of the earth: and he shall
smite the earth with the rod of his mouth, and with the
breath of his lips shall he slay the wicked.

5   And righteousness shall be the girdle of his loins, and faith-
fulness the girdle of his reins.

6   The wolf also shall dwell with the lamb, and the leopard
shall lie down with the kid; and the calf and the young
lion and the fatling together; and a little child shall
lead them.

7   And the cow and the bear shall feed; their young ones
shall lie down together: and the lion shall eat straw
like the ox.

8   And the sucking child shall play on the hole of the asp, and
the weaned child shall put his hand on the cockatrice'
den.

9   They shall not hurt nor destroy in all my holy mountain:
for the earth shall be full of the knowledge of the Lord,
as the waters cover the sea.

10   ¶And in that day there shall be a root of Jesse, which shall
stand for an ensign of the people; to it shall the Gen-
tiles seek: and his rest shall be glorious.

11   And it shall come to pass in that day, that the Lord shall
set his hand again the second time to recover the
remnant of his people, which shall be left, from Assyria, and from Egypt, and from Pathros,[8] and from
Cush,[9] and from Elam,[10] and from Shinar,[11] and from
Hamath,[12] and from the islands of the sea.[13]

8. A name for Upper Egypt from south of Memphis to the First Cataract.
9. Ethiopia, sometimes including parts of the modern Sudan.
10. Susiana (southwestern Iran).
11. Babylonia.
12. A kingdom in Syria which bordered Israel in King Solomon's time.
13. This generally means the Mediterranean coastlands, or sometimes dry
land as opposed to water.

12   And he shall set up an ensign for the nations, and shall
      assemble the outcasts of Israel, and gather together
      the dispersed of Judah from the four corners of the
      earth.

13   The envy also of Ephraim[14] shall depart, and the adver-
      saries of Judah shall be cut off: Ephraim shall not
      envy Judah, and Judah shall not vex Ephraim.[15]

14   But they shall fly upon the shoulders of the Philistines to-
      ward the west; they shall spoil them of the east to-
      gether: they shall lay their hand upon Edom[16] and
      Moab;[17] and the children of Ammon[18] shall obey them.

15   And the Lord shall utterly destroy the tongue of the Egyp-
      tian sea; and with his mighty wind shall he shake
      his hand over the river, and shall smite it in the seven
      streams, and make men go over dryshod.[19]

16   And there shall be an highway for the remnant of his peo-
      ple, which shall be left, from Assyria; like as it was
      to Israel in the day that he came up out of the land
      of Egypt.

14. Region of north central Palestine. The term is often used as a synonym
for the northern kingdom of Israel, as opposed to the southern kingdom of
Judah.
15. I.e., the long enmity between the two Hebrew kingdoms of Israel and
Judah will cease.
16. Region of Palestine between the Dead Sea and the Sinai Peninsula.
17. The tableland east of the Dead Sea.
18. Transjordan.
19. I.e., a second Exodus.

THE PERSIANS

THE PERSIANS

Introduction to The Gathas of Zarathustra

The prophet Zarathustra, or Zoroaster, as he is usually called in the West, probably flourished in the first half of the sixth century B.C., though his exact dates have not been established with certainty. He may have been a native of Media in northwestern Iran, but his prophetic activity occurred in Chorasmia, the region of the lower Oxus south of the Aral Sea. Here he found refuge with King Vishtaspa, who was perhaps the chief of a Chorasmian confederation later overthrown by Cyrus. The message of Zarathustra is inseparable from this milieu—that of a peaceful herding population subject to the harassment of nomadic marauders. The Zoroastrian moral dualism between the followers of the Truth (Asha) and the Lie (Druj) had its counterpart in the opposition of herdsmen and cattle-breeders to the fierce nomadic warriors.

The religion into which Zarathustra was born—and of which he was probably a priest—was undoubtedly a polytheistic faith similar to that of the Indians of the Rig Veda. Indeed, at one time Indians and Iranians had formed a single group, as is proven by, among other things, the similarity between the Sanskrit and Old Persian languages and by the many deities which the two peoples held in common. The chief of the Iranian gods prior to the Zoroastrian reform was probably a deity closely akin to the Indian sky-god Varuna, who was in Iran usually called simply Ahura, or Lord. Zarathustra immensely exalted the status of Ahura from merely the first of his peers to the all-powerful, all-knowing creator and preserver of the entire universe. Probably it was he also who gave to Ahura the appellation Mazda ("wise"); for in his day the name was imperfectly established: its two components were written separately and their order was interchangeable.

The sacred book of the Zoroastrians is the Avesta. Its language is an eastern Iranian dialect very similar to the Sanskrit of the Indian Vedas. The oldest part of the Avesta consists of Gathas, which are hymns or songs written in an earlier form of Iranian than the rest of the Avesta, and generally considered to be the work of Zarathustra himself. Only a fraction of the original Avesta survives. Originally it was transmitted by word of mouth, and only much later committed to writing.

The religious reform of Zarathustra was itself radically transformed by later generations. Almost immediately, elements of the old polytheism crept into it. The abstractions used by Zarathustra to describe the attributes or characteristics of the Wise Lord—attributes in which man can share—soon became personified, appearing in later Zoroastrianism almost as separate deities. The six most important of these, together with Ahura Mazda himself, became a heptad known as the Bounteous Immortals (Amesha Spentas), though it is probable that the prophet himself did not intend them to have a separate existence. Zarathustra had indeed believed in the close connection between the spiritual and material worlds; but after his death each of the Immortals came to be identified with a specific element: earth, fire, metals, etc. Probably he meant to reform existence here on earth: but subsequently his followers transferred the coming of the Kingdom into another world; and the figure of the Saoshyans, or saviour, assumed much greater importance.

Until the defeat of the last Achaemenian king by Alexander of Macedon in 330 B.C., Zoroastrianism in some form was the official religion of the Persian empire. Darius and Xerxes seem to have accepted its basic doctrines; Artaxerxes I adopted a Zoroastrian calendar. But the original vision of Zarathustra had already become enmeshed in innumerable beliefs and practices alien to his way of thought. The Achaemenians, with their policy of religious tolerance, consciously or unconsciously favored this process; and they were aided by the Magi, the priestly caste which served as guardian of the national religion.

When Iran came under Macedonian rule, Zoroastrianism lost its official status; and the Parthian dynasty that followed (250 B.C.—A.D. 226) showed little interest in that faith. With the advent of the Sassanian kings in A.D. 226, Zoroastrianism came back into royal favor. But much of its original tradition had already been lost irretrievably. Every form of Iranian religion, whatever its character, now bore the name of the prophet. The Sassanian priests who attempted to restore the pure doctrine of Zarathustra were unable to understand the language of the ancient texts; and their interpretations were often fanciful. Ultimately, Zoroastrianism proved unable to withstand the strict monotheism of Islam. It survives today only among the descendants of a small group of believers who preferred exile to Islam—the Parsees of India, who still practice the ancient Iranian rituals.

FROM THE GATHAS OF ZARATHUSTRA

Yasna 29

1   To you[1] did the soul of the ox complain:
"For whom did you create me? Who made me?
Fury[2] and violence oppress me, and cruelty and tyranny.
I have no shepherd other than you: then obtain good pastures for me."

2   Then the creator of the ox[3] asked the Right[4]: "Hast thou a judge for the ox,
That you may give him, with the pasture, the care for the raising of the cattle?
Whom did you appoint his master who shall put to flight Fury together with the wicked?"[5]

3   As Righteousness, reply was made:[6] "No companion is there for the ox
That is free from hatred. Men do not understand
How the great[7] deal with the lowly.
Of all beings he is the strongest
To whose aid I come at his call.

From *The Hymns of Zarathustra*, Jacques Duchesne-Guillemin, ed.; trans. from the French by Mrs. M. Henning (Wisdom of the East ser.), London: John Murray Ltd., 1952. Reprinted by permission.
  1. Ahura Mazda and the other Bounteous Immortals (Amesha Spentas).
  2. (Aeshma): a half-personified supernatural force, like the Amesha Spentas, but in the service of the Lie.
  3. The Ox-creator appears to be an aspect of, but not identical to, Ahura Mazda.
  4. Asha, translated as Right or Righteousness, one of the Amesha Spentas.
  5. I.e., the followers of the Lie (Druj).
  6. Or: Asha replied . . .
  7. I.e., the followers of the Right.

4   The Wise One[8] it is who best remembers
       The plans carried out of yore by false gods[9] and men
       Or that will be carried out in the future.
       He, the Lord,[10] will decide, it shall be according to his will."

5   —"With hands outstretched we[11] pray to the Lord,
       We two, my soul and the soul of the mother-cow,
       Urging the Wise One to command that no harm shall come
              to the honest man,[12]
       To the herdsman, in the midst of the wicked who surround
              him."

6   Then spoke the Wise Lord himself, he who understands the
              prayers in his soul:[13]
       "No master has been found, no judge according to Right-
              eousness:
       For the breeder and the herdsman has the creator fashioned
              thee.[14]

7   The ordinance of sprinkling the water[15] of the cattle, for
              the welfare of the ox,
       And the milk for the welfare of men desiring food,
       This has the Wise Lord, the Holy One,
       Fashioned by his decree, in accord with Righteousness."[16]
       (The Ox-soul:)

8. I.e., Ahura Mazda.
9. Or daevas: originally a class of gods common to both the Iranians and the Indians of Rig-Vedic times. In Iran the word gradually acquired the meaning of "demon." Zoroaster refers in this way to the gods worshipped by his opponents.
10. Ahura was a generic term for "lord" or "god." Zoroaster also spoke of "lords" in the plural, indicating that he did not entirely deny the existence of other gods besides his own Ahura Mazda (see Yasna 30.9). Here the word undoubtedly refers to Ahura Mazda.
11. The souls of the ox and of the mother-cow.
12. I.e., the follower of the Right.
13. Perhaps meaning: "he who understands the order of things, the laws of creation."
14. I.e., cattle were created in order to be useful to mankind.
15. Elsewhere translated as "the oblation of fat," meaning that the ox was created to serve both as food for man and as a sacrificial animal.
16. I.e., Righteousness is an aspect of the Lord.

—"Whom hast thou, as Good Mind,[17] who may take care of us two for men?"[18]

8 (The Good Mind:)
"I know but this one: Zarathustra Spitama, the only one who has heard our teaching;
He will make known our purpose, O Wise One, and that of Righteousness.
Sweetness of speech shall be given to him."[19]

9 And then moaned the Ox-soul: "That I should have to be content
With the powerless word of a man without strength for a guardian,
I who wish for a strong master!
Will he ever be, he who shall help him[20] with his hands?"

10 Do you, O Lord,[21] with the Right and the Good Mind,
Grant them that he[22] should have Dominion enough
To obtain good dwellings for them and peace.
I, O Lord, have recognized thee as the first provider of these.

11 Where are Righteousness, Good Mind, Dominion?[23] (? O immortal ones?),
Admit me to the great sacrament,[24] O Wise One, that I may achieve knowledge;
To our aid now, O Lord! May we have part in the bounty of such as you!

17. Here the Lord acts as Good Mind or Good Thought (Vohu Manah). Cattle were considered the special province of Vohu Manah.
18. I.e., Whom among men hast thou to take care of us?
19. Through the eloquence which will be given him, Zarathustra will protect the cattle.
20. The ox.
21. This is Zarathustra addressing Ahura Mazda.
22. I.e., the promised protector.
23. Dominion (Kshathra), meaning power on earth, one of the Amesha Spentas.
24. Perhaps the sacrament which will unite Zarathustra with the three entities mentioned; or possibly a term for the community of followers of Ahura Mazda.

Yasna 30

1   Now will I[1] speak to those who will hear
Of the things which the initiate should remember:
The praises and prayer of the Good Mind[2] to the Lord
And the joy which he shall see in the light who has re-
      membered them well.

2   Hear with your ears that which is the sovereign good;
With a clear mind look upon the two sides
Between which each man must choose for himself,[3]
Watchful beforehand that the great test may be accom-
      plished in our favour.

3   Now at the beginning[4] the twin spirits have declared their
      nature,
The better and the evil,[5]
In thought and word and deed. And between the two
The wise ones[6] choose well, not so the foolish.

4   And when these two spirits came together,
In the beginning they established life and non-life,[7]
And that at the last the worst existence should be for the
      wicked,
But for the righteous one the Best Mind.[8]

1. Zarathustra speaking.
2. Vohu Manah.
3. I.e., man enjoys complete freedom to choose between good and evil.
4. I.e., the beginning of creation.
5. Spenta Mainyu (Holy Spirit) and Angra Mainyu (Evil Spirit) are the Ormazd and Ahriman of later Zoroastrianism, when Spenta Mainyu came to be identified with Ahura Mazda. Here, however, both spirits are merely aspects of the Wise Lord. Note that they were not good or evil from eternity, but as the result of a primeval choice.
6. I.e., wise men.
7. I.e., good and evil existence.
8. "Manah," the term translated as "Mind" or "Thought," actually is virtually synonymous with "principle of life." Thus "worst existence" is the opposite of "Best Mind," i.e., "best existence."

5 Of these two spirits, the evil one chose to do the worst
        things;
   But the Most Holy Spirit, clothed in the most steadfast
        heavens,
   Joined himself unto Righteousness;
   And thus did all those who delight to please the Wise Lord
        by honest deeds.

6 Between the two, the false gods[9] also did not choose rightly,
   For while they pondered they were beset by error,
   So that they chose the Worst Mind.
   Then did they hasten to join themselves unto Fury,[10]
   That they might by it deprave the existence of man.

7 And to him[11] came Devotion,[12] together with Dominion,
        Good Mind and Righteousness:
   She[13] gave endurance of body and the breath of life,
   That he may be thine apart from them,
   As the first by the retributions through the metal.[14]

8 And when their punishment shall come to these sinners,[15]
   Then, O Wise One,[16] shall thy Dominion, with the Good
        Mind,
   Be granted to those who have delivered Evil into the hands
        of Righteousness,[17] O Lord!

9. See Yasna 29, note 9.
10. See Yasna 29, note 2.
11. I.e., mankind.
12. Armaiti, one of the Bounteous Immortals (Amesha Spentas).
13. Devotion, giving man strength to endure until the final reward.
14. This refers to the ordeal of the last day, when a molten flood of metal
will be poured out, through which all men must pass. To the righteous, it
will seem like warm milk, while to the wicked it will feel like what it is. In
this burning flood the sins of the wicked will be purged away.
15. This is one of the earliest, if not the earliest, statements of the relation
between man's moral conduct and his reward or punishment after death.
16. Ahura Mazda.
17. I.e., power on earth will be given to the righteous.

9   And may we be those that renew this existence![18]
     O Wise One, and you other Lords,[19] and Righteousness,
          bring your alliance,
     That thoughts may gather where wisdom is faint.

10   Then shall Evil cease to flourish,[20]
     While those who have acquired good fame
     Shall reap the promised reward
     In the blessed dwelling of the Good Mind, of the Wise One,
          and of Righteousness.[21]

11   If you, O men, understand the commandments which the
          Wise One has given,
     Well-being and suffering—long torment for the wicked and
          salvation for the righteous—
     All shall hereafter be for the best.

18. This phrase indicates that the existence to be renewed is on earth, not in
the afterlife.
19. Evidently Zarathustra did not deny the existence of deities other than
Ahura Mazda, although he seldom mentioned them.
20. I.e., a kind of Golden Age will ensue.
21. These three—the most important of the Amesha Spentas—are frequently
mentioned together.

From Yasna 31

7   He who first through the mind[1] filled the blessed spaces
          with light,
     He it is who by his will created Righteousness,[2]
     Whereby he upholds the Best Mind.[3]
     This[4] thou hast increased, O Wise One, by thy Spirit
     Which is even now one with thee, O Lord!

1. Note the spiritual nature of creation: the Lord creates by his mind and
will. Compare John 1:1—"In the beginning was the Word, and the Word
was with God, and the Word was God."
2. I.e., Righteousness is not an independent entity, but a product (and aspect) of the Lord. Compare line 2 of verse 8, below.
3. Here the interpretation of Manah (Mind) as "existence" or "life principle" would apply. See note 8 of Yasna 30.
4. I.e., "Best Mind."

8   Through the mind,[5] O Wise One, have I known thee as the
first and the last,[6]
As the father of the Good Mind,
When I perceived thee with mine eyes[7] as the true creator
of Righteousness,
As the Lord in the deeds of existence;

9   Thine was Devotion, thine the creator of the ox,[8]
Thine the force of the spirit, O Wise Lord,
When thou didst give a free path[9] to the ox
Towards the herdsman or one who is not a herdsman;

10   Then of the two did it choose for itself the cattle-tending
herdsman,
As a just master, as an advancer of the Good Mind.
He who is no herdsman, despite his striving,
O Wise One, he shall have no share in the Good Message.

11   Since thou, O Wise One, at the first didst create for us by
thy mind[10]
Beings and consciences and wills,
Since thou didst give a body to the soul of life,
Since thou didst create deeds and words, that man may
decide freely,

12   Since then does the man of false words lift up his voice as
well as the man of true words,
The initiate as well as the non-initiate, each according to
his heart and his mind.
May Devotion put to the proof, one after the other, the
spirits where there is bewilderment!

5. Not only does the Lord create through the mind, but mankind through
mind knows Him.
6. I.e., as the beginning and the end of existence.
7. Zarathustra had experienced a direct revelation or vision of the Lord.
8. Perhaps because of Devotion's close relationship to the earth it is mentioned together with the Ox-creator.
9. The ox, like man, is permitted to exercise free choice.
10. Compare verse 8, line 1, above.

From Yasna 33

1   Towards the wicked man and the righteous one
     And him in whom right and wrong meet[1]
     Shall the judge act in upright manner,
     According to the laws of the present existence.

2   He who by word or thought or hands
     Works evil to the wicked one,[2]
     Or he who converts his clansman to the good,
     They please the Lord and fulfil his will.

3   He who, belonging to family or village or tribe, O Lord,
     Is most good to the righteous man, or labours for the care
         of the herd,[3]
     He shall be in the pasture of Righteousness and of Good
         Mind.

4   I who by my prayer will keep from thee, O Wise One,
         disobedience and Bad Mind,
     Discord[4] from the family, from the village the evil that is
         very near,
     The oppressors from the tribe, and from the herd's pasture
         the worst steward,

5   I who will invoke thy Discipline as the mightiest of all,
     At the outcome, when I shall attain the long life,
     The Dominion of the Good Mind and the straight paths of
         Right
     Wherein dwells the Wise Lord,

6   I who, a priest,[5] would learn through Righteousness,

---

1. I.e., in whom good and evil balance.
2. Zarathustra's God is just, rather than merciful.
3. Proper care of the herd is here placed on an equal plane with righteous behavior.
4. Discord is the opposite of Devotion. The word might be taken to mean "heresy."
5. Zarathustra himself was perhaps born into the priestly caste serving the ancient Iranian religion which he would later denounce.

Would learn from the Best Mind the straight paths,
Henceforth to practise husbandry in the sense in which it
 has been ordained,
I strive therefore to see thee and take counsel with thee,
 O Wise Lord!

. . . .

From Yasna 46

1 To what land shall I flee? Where bend my steps?
I am thrust out from family and tribe;
I have no favour from the village to which I would belong,
Nor from the wicked rulers of the country:[1]
How then, O Lord, shall I obtain thy favour?

2 I know, O Wise One, why I am powerless:
My cattle are few, and I have few men.
To thee I address my lament: attend unto it, O Lord,
And grant me the support which friend would give to
 friend.[2]
As Righteousness teach the possession of the Good Mind.

3 When, O Wise One, shall the wills of the future saviours[3]
 come forth,
The dawns of the days when, through powerful judgment,
The world shall uphold Righteousness?[4]
To whom will help come through the Good Mind?

1. This is the lament of Zarathustra before he had acquired the royal patronage of King Vishtaspa.
2. Note that Zarathustra speaks of the Lord as a "friend" rather than as a remote, awesome, incomprehensible Being.
3. Later Zoroastrians believed that a Saviour (*Saoshyans*) would appear at the end of time to raise the bodies of the dead and unite them with their souls. Some traces of this belief, though not yet systematically worked out, are already present in the *Gathas*, i.e., the reference to a great conflagration at the end of the world when all men must wade through a stream of molten metal (see Yasna 30, note 14). But Zarathustra himself seems to have thought primarily of reforming existence here on earth; the saviours are righteous men like himself.
4. Reference to the future Golden Age on earth.

To me, for I am chosen for the revelation by thee, O Lord.

4   The wicked one, ill-famed and of repellent deeds,[5]
Prevents the furtherers of Righteousness from fostering
    the cattle
In the district and in the country.
Whoever robs him of Dominion or of life, O Wise One,
Shall walk foremost in the ways of the doctrine.[6]

5   (?) Whoever, holding power or the nobility of the Vow,[7]
Or living by the rules decreed for the covenants,
Should seize a stranger coming to him,
If he, a righteous man himself, can recognize an evil one,[8]
And if he proclaims his action before his family,
Mayest thou, O Lord, keep him from bloodshed!

6   (?) But he[9] who, being asked, does not side with him,
He shall return to the creatures of Evil,
Who in the sight of the evil one is the best.
It is righteous to love the righteous,
Since thou, Lord, didst create the first consciences.

7   Who, O Wise One, shall be sent as a protector to such as
    I am,
If the evil one seeks to do me harm?
Who but thy fire[10] and thy mind, O Lord,
Whose acts shall bring Righteousness to maturity?
Do thou proclaim this mystery to my conscience!

8   Whoever seeks to injure my living possessions,
May danger not come to me through his deeds!

5. The "wicked one" might be either a supernatural figure or simply an epithet for the marauding nomads who harassed peaceful herdsmen.
6. Note that this treatment of opponents is recommended as a religious duty.
7. Perhaps a vow binding the members of Zarathustra's religious community.
8. Perhaps: "convert an evil one." This passage is obscure.
9. The stranger.
10. Fire was closely associated with Ahura Mazda, though less so in the Gathas than in the later Avesta, where fire is called the son of Ahura Mazda. The reference here is perhaps to the fire employed in religious ritual.

May all his actions turn against him with hostility, O
    Wise One,
And take him from the good life, not the bad life!

9   (A listener):
      "Who is he, the zealous man who first
      Taught me to honour thee[11] as the most powerful,
      As the righteous Lord, holy in his action?"
      (Zarathustra:)
      What he said to thee,[12] to thee as Righteousness,
      What he said to Righteousness, the creator of the cattle,
      They ask it of me through thy Good Mind.

10   Whoever, man or woman, O Wise Lord,
      Shall give me what thou knowest is the best of this exist-
          ence,
      —To wit: reward for Righteousness and the Dominion
          (?)[13] with (?) the Good Mind—
      And all those whom I shall induce to worship such as you,
      With all those will I cross the Bridge of the Separator![14]

11   The sacrificers and the sorcerer princes[15]
      Have subdued mankind to the yoke of their Dominion,
      To destroy existence through evil deeds:
      They shall be tortured by their own soul and their own
          conscience,
      When they come to the Bridge of the Separator,
      For ever to be inmates of the house of Evil.[16]

. . . .

11. Ahura Mazda.
12. The Ox-creator to Ahura Mazda in the latter's character as Righteousness.
13. Zarathustra seems to be promising rewards in the afterlife to whoever
will favor him in this life.
14. Where after death men will be judged according to their good or evil
deeds on earth and receive the appropriate reward.
15. Sacrificers (*Karapans*): a priestly caste in the service of the old religion
which Zarathustra condemned. Sorcerer princes (*Kavis*): Zarathustra's political opponents, possibly the leaders of nomad tribes who still professed the
old Iranian religion.
16. House of the Lie (Druj)—a kind of Hell.

Yasna 47

1   The Wise Lord, as the Holy Spirit,[1] shall give us
     For Best Mind and deed and word true to Righteousness,
     Through Dominion and Devotion,[2] Salvation and Immortality.

2   (?) The sovereign good of this Most Holy Spirit,
     May he accomplish it, the Wise One, who is the father of
         Right,
     According to the words spoken by the tongue of Good
         Mind,
     According to the deed done by the hands of Devotion![3]

3   Thou art the holy father of this Spirit,[4]
     Which has, O Wise One, created for us the cattle, the
         source of good fortune,
     And, giving us peace, has created Devotion for the care of
         the cattle,
     If she takes counsel with the Good Mind.

4   From this Holy Spirit do the wicked turn away, O Wise
         One,
     But not so the Righteous!
     Whether a man be master of little or of much,
     Let him be good to the righteous, evil to the wicked.

5   As Holy Spirit, O Wise Lord,
     Thou hast promised to the righteous the sovereign good.

1. The Holy Spirit (Spenta Mainyu) is here merely the attribute of Ahura
Mazda, though in later Zoroastrianism the two were considered identical.
2. There appears to be a hierarchy among the Bounteous Immortals
(Amesha Spentas)—Righteousness being mentioned first (see also verse 2).
Righteousness (Asha) and Good Mind (Vohu Manah) undoubtedly stand
closer to Ahura Mazda than do the other Immortals.
3. Note the personification of Good Mind and Devotion, here described as
having tongue and hands!
4. Since Ahura Mazda is called the father (i.e., creator) of the Holy Spirit,
it is evident that some distinction between the two is maintained—perhaps
analogous to that between the Father and the Holy Ghost in Christianity.

Shall the wicked one share in it without thy will,
Who by his deeds belongs to Evil Mind?

6   O Wise Lord, as this Holy Spirit,
Through the fire[5] thou shalt accomplish, supported by
Devotion and Right,
The apportioning of the good between the two parties.
This will surely bring to the choice the many who desire it.

5. The ordeal of molten metal at the end of the world?

Yasna 48

1   When at the time of the rewards[1] he[2] shall conquer Evil
through the Right,
When the alternative[3] shall be fulfilled
Which was foretold[4] for immortality[5] to both false gods[6]
and mortals,
Then shall the salvation (of so many beings) increase thy
worship, O Lord!

2   Tell me the things which thou knowest, O Lord.
Shall the righteous man defeat the wicked one, O Wise
One,
Even before the coming of the punishments[7] which thou
hast conceived?
For this is known as the good renewal of existence.

3   For the initiate,[8] that is the best of the doctrines

1. I.e., the Last Judgment, which will occur at a point in time.
2. Ambiguous. Elsewhere this clause is rendered as: "When Right shall conquer Evil."
3. Of salvation or damnation.
4. I.e., the outcome of the Judgment Day is predestined.
5. Either in Heaven or in Hell (House of the Good Mind or House of the
Lie).
6. See Yasna 29, note 9.
7. Zarathustra is inquiring whether Right shall triumph here on earth even
before the final judgment.
8. Whoever has accepted the secret doctrines (line 4 below) which the Lord
has revealed to Zarathustra.

Which the beneficent Lord teaches, as Righteousness, the
    Holy One which thou art,
Thou who knowest also, O Wise One,
Through the strength of Good Mind the secret doctrines.

4   (?) He who makes his thought better and worse,[9] O Wise
      One,
Better and worse his conscience, by deed and by word,
He follows his leanings, his wishes, his likings.
In thy mind's force, at the end of times, he shall be set
    apart.

5   May good rulers, not bad ones, rule over us![10]
By the works of the good doctrine, O Devotion,
Prepare the greatest good for man: rebirth;
Through the labour of husbandry, let the ox grow fat for
    our nourishment.

6   She[11] has given us good shelter, strength and endurance,
She, the consecrated of the Good Mind.
For her has the Wise Lord as Righteousness[12] made the
    plants to grow
At the birth of the first existence.

7   Let Fury be suppressed! Put down violence,
You who would ensure yourselves, through Righteousness,
The reward of the Good Mind, whose companion is the
    holy man.
He shall have his abode in thy house, O Lord!

8   (?) How shall the possession of thy good Dominion,[13] O
      Wise One,

---

9. This evidently refers to the person who vacillates between good and evil.
10. Zarathustra here expresses the wish that the followers of the Right may
dominate the earth.
11. Armaiti (Devotion), who is closely associated with the earth.
12. Righteousness (Asha, the equivalent of the Indian *rta*) is here meant in
the sense of "natural order," i.e., the law of the universe.
13. (Kshathra): power on earth.

How that of thy reward be mine, O Lord?

How will thy manifestation, as Righteousness,[14] of the actions

Be welcomed (?) by the faithful?

9   When I shall know whether you have power, O Wise One, and Righteousness,

Over all those who threaten me with destruction,

Let the prayer of the Good Mind be rightly spoken by me!

May the future Saviour[15] know what his destiny will be!

10 When, O Wise One, will the warriors[16] understand the message?

When wilt thou smite this filth of drink[17]

Through which the sacrificers wickedly

And the evil masters of the countries of their own will

Commit their deeds of malice?

11 When, O Wise One, shall Devotion come with Righteousness?

When with the Dominion the good dwelling rich in pastures?

Who are they that will give safety from the bloodthirsty wicked?

Who they to whom the doctrine of Good Mind will come?

12 Those are the future saviours of the peoples

Who through Good Mind strive in their deeds

To carry out the judgment which thou hast decreed, O Wise One, as Righteousness.

For they were created the foes of Fury.

---

14. I.e., the Lord reveals himself in his character as Righteousness.
15. Though in the later Avesta the Saviour (*Saoshyant*) became an eschatological figure, here he appears to be Zarathustra himself, who will establish the good Dominion on earth.
16. The nomad raiders, Zarathustra's opponents.
17. Haoma (the Indian Soma) was an intoxicating drink made from a plant. The drink was employed in the ritual of sacrifice by the worshippers of the old Iranian gods, and was believed to grant immortality.

From Yasna 51

.   .   .   .

8   Then will I speak, O Wise One—for one must speak of it
        to the initiate—
     Both of the evil which threatens the wicked one
     And of the bliss of him who upholds Righteousness.
     For with joy does the prophet speak of this to the initiate.

9   What reward thou hast appointed to the two parties, O
        Wise One,
     Through thy bright fire and through the molten metal,[1]
     Give a sign of it to the souls of men,
     To bring hurt to the wicked, benefit to the righteous.

10   He who seeks to destroy me for whatever other cause than
        this,[2]
     He, O Wise One, is the son of the creation of Evil,
     And evil-doing therefore to mankind.
     Righteousness do I call to me to bring good reward.

11   What man is Zarathustra's sworn friend, O Wise One?[3]
     Who has taken counsel with Righteousness?
     Who was he, through Holy Devotion?
     Who has been mindful in uprightness of the sacrament of
        Good Mind?

12   The minion of the sorcerer prince, at the Bridge of the
        Winter,[4]
     Offended Zarathustra Spitama by refusing him shelter,

1. See Yasna 30, note 14.
2. I.e., any cause other than unrighteousness: Zarathustra is willing to submit to destruction by ordeal if he should deserve it.
3. Zarathustra asks the Lord for help in recognizing his true friends.
4. Perhaps a narrow mountain gorge or other troublesome passage: contrast
with Bridge of the Separator in the following stanza.

Him and his beasts of burden who came to him shivering
    with cold.[5]

13   Thus does the evil one's conscience forfeit the assurance of
    the straight (path);
    His soul (?) stripped naked (?) shall be afraid at the
    Bridge of the Separator,[6]
    Having strayed from the path of Righteousness
    By its deeds and those of his tongue.

14   The sacrificers do not submit to rule and ordinance of
    husbandry.
    For the suffering which they cause to the ox
    Reveal the judgment which shall at the end
    Consign them to the house of Evil for their deeds and
    judgments!

15   The house of Song which Zarathustra promised to the men
    of the sacrament as their gain,
    The Wise Lord was the first that entered it.
    It was promised to you[7] with all its blessings
    For your Good Mind and your Righteousness.

5. This evidently refers to an actual incident in the biography of Zarathustra, in which an adherent of the old religion refused his hospitality to the
Prophet.
6. See Yasna 46, note 14.
7. I.e., to the men of the sacrament, those who had accepted Zarathustra's
teaching.